A FOOTBALL FAN'S STORY

The Royal Navy Manchester City and Me

DON PRICE

authorHOUSE®

AuthorHouse™ UK
1663 Liberty Drive
Bloomington, IN 47403 USA
www.authorhouse.co.uk
Phone: 0800.197.4150

© 2016 Don Price. All rights reserved.

No part of this book may be reproduced, stored in a retrieval system, or transmitted by any means without the written permission of the author.

Published by AuthorHouse 05/21/2016

ISBN: 978-1-5246-3257-1 (sc)
ISBN: 978-1-5246-3256-4 (e)

Print information available on the last page.

Any people depicted in stock imagery provided by Thinkstock are models, and such images are being used for illustrative purposes only. Certain stock imagery © Thinkstock.

This book is printed on acid-free paper.

Because of the dynamic nature of the Internet, any web addresses or links contained in this book may have changed since publication and may no longer be valid. The views expressed in this work are solely those of the author and do not necessarily reflect the views of the publisher, and the publisher hereby disclaims any responsibility for them.

To

Ödzden and Kader

'Casper's'

BEST WISHES AND A

HAPPY NEW YEAR FOR 2017

[signature: Don Price]

Contents

Dedication vii
Acknowledgements ix
Introduction xi

Chapter 1   Prestwich 1
Chapter 2   Whitefield 23
Chapter 3   Joining the Royal Navy 34
Chapter 4   HMS Ganges 42
Chapter 5   HMS Dolphin 66
Chapter 6   Joining HMS Achilles 91
Chapter 7   HMS Osprey 137
Chapter 8   HMS Devonshire 153
Chapter 9   Civvy Street 168
Chapter 10 Prestwich and Whitefield
            Supporters Branch 184
Chapter 11 Royal British Legion 214
Chapter 12 Heaton Park Working Men's Club ... 263
Chapter 13 Pre-season Tour 286
Chapter 14 Charity Fundraising 305
Chapter 15 Feyenoord and Antwerp Blues 328
Chapter 16 Footballing Heroes 337

Chapter 17	Drinking Culture	377
Chapter 18	More Away Day Blues	387
Chapter 19	'Celebrities'	400
Chapter 20	Corporate Hospitality	413
Chapter 21	City v. Southampton	419
Chapter 22	The Final ever game at Maine Road	425
Chapter 23	Time to Call It a Day	432

Dedication

This book is dedicated to Debs who recently lost her brave fight against cancer, she was an inspiration to everyone who knew her, she loved her partner Ian, her family and she also loved watching football, she was great company to be with. Ian, Debs, Cath and myself had many great times together and those memories will never fade.

The book is also in loving memory of my mother Doris who passed away on March 12th 2014 and Cath's dad Tommy who passed away August 3rd 2013. They may no longer be with us but they will never be forgotten.

Acknowledgements

I am grateful for the help and advice my brother Bob gave me while putting the book together. Many thanks to Cath who spent ages typing and editing various bits and pieces of the book and gave me loads of advice and encouragement. Special mention for Debs who was always on at me to write a book.

A message from Bob.

'Thanks for a copy of the book. I found it a great read and very amusing and I was laughing out loud at times. I have lived abroad for nearly 40 years and can't remember you even writing a postcard then out of the blue you write a book. I don't know how you managed it but it is a fantastic effort well done'.

Introduction

As football supporters up and down the country and around the world know, following your favourite football team brings out the best and the worst in people. The most mild men and women can turn into a raving lunatic on a match day if their team is not living up to their expectations. The loudest of people can be at a loss for words if things are not going according to plan on the pitch. Six-foot blokes covered in tattoos can be reduced to tears when their team loses in the last minute of a game.

While at work or at home, the football fan is a picture of sanity and common sense; go to a football match though or meet your favourite player, and the most sensible of people can be left a gibbering wreck. That's what makes the game so exciting and appealing to young and old alike.

I have spent most of my life living, dreaming, and breathing football. I spent nearly eight years in the Royal Navy playing and watching football whenever and wherever I could. For ten years I was also the chairman of a massive supporters branch, organizing coach trips, sportsmen's dinners, charity events, and monthly meetings. During that time, I was introduced to many ex-players, first-team players, football chairmen, managers, and backroom staff from Manchester City and many other football clubs.

It was a time of ups and downs coupled with great excitement. Over the years as a supporters branch, we pulled out all the stops to get some of the greatest former and current players to come to our events. The list of people who attended reads like a who's who of the football world.

Many members of the branch and my mates have asked me to write a book about the times we had during those years. I thought they were having a laugh because I have not even written a letter in the last thirty years, so writing a book would be completely out of my comfort zone. At the time, it was not worth thinking about because although I can tell a good tale or to on the stage or in a pub, especially after a couple of beers. I thought who would want to listen to my ramblings? However, the more people mentioned it, the more I gave it some consideration. I was reluctant because I didn't want to be seen as someone on an ego trip, but what my mates pointed out was that what we achieved as a group of ordinary supporters at that time was a bit unreal considering how bad City were at the time.

My mates then convinced me that what we got up to at the time, and the people we met, was a story worth telling because it would appeal to football fans of all persuasions, who could certainly relate to what we did and the laughs we had over the years. Over a pint or two, I have told them many a story from my navy days, and some of these tales are incorporated into the book.

What finally made my mind up to put pen to paper is that there are many football hooligan books doing the rounds, but not many are written about ordinary supporters of a football club, especially about the stuff going on behind the scenes.

This book is entirely from memory, and so my recollection of events might differ from others. All I can say is that I have tried to make the book humorous and light-hearted while sticking to the facts. I have also not set out to embarrass or upset anyone.

So put your feet up, grab a Bovril or a cup of tea and a biscuit, and I hope you enjoy reading the book as much as I have enjoyed writing it.

Chapter 1

Prestwich

Although I don't go to many games nowadays, my passion for football in general, and Manchester City in particular, is as strong as ever. The club now has an abundance of riches, great players, a fantastic stadium, and full houses at every home game, but that hasn't always been the case.

The day I was born, 6 March 1954, City were beat at home 2-0 by Preston North End, so that should have been an early warning for me in what would lay ahead while watching City. It was also the same year as rationing, which was in place during and after the Second World War had finally come to an end. Families in all walks of life found the years after the war challenging, and though Churchill might have won the war for Britain and the general public were extremely grateful for his efforts, they didn't trust him to rebuild the country. In the first general election after the war, he was booted out to make way for a Labour government that promised the earth – new houses, jobs, decent wages, and the National Health Service.

Troops getting demobbed still found it hard to find employment, and houses, factories, and the whole infrastructure of the United Kingdom had to be rebuilt.

Playing and watching football was something cheap, accessible, and enjoyable that the working-class man could afford. Crowds at all football clubs, even the lower-league clubs, got big gates. Even though the standards of some of the grounds were appalling, people were not bothered. Watching football on a Saturday was an escape from the everyday hardship that most people found themselves in after the war years.

As a kid, it was great living in the Prestwich area. My house backed onto St Mary's Park, where we could play football all day long. Though Prestwich has an area called the Village, it is quite large and borders places such as Salford, Cheetham Hill, Agecroft, Blackley, and Whitefield. Not far from my house is a massive area called Heaton Park, and in years to come, this was where the Prestwich and Whitefield Manchester City Supporters Branch had their headquarters.

At one time, Heaton Park was one of the largest council-run parks in the country. It was over six hundred acres; if you are not into acres, let's just say it is frigin massive. As kids, one of the biggest attractions was the boating lake; it was like manna from heaven, a place where you could hire rowing boats, skiffs, and motorboats. You could also go on the launch, which set off round the lake once it was full. If you were pretty fit with a bit of muscle power (which I obviously wasn't) you could go dead fast on the skiffs. I stuck to the rowing boats. If anyone had any spare money as a treat, we would go to the café by the lake.

As kids, we used to muck about, much to the annoyance of authorities and adults alike. It was not unusual us for us to ram other boats, splash everyone we passed, or throw some poor unfortunate person in the lake. Inevitably, we would end up in a row and would have fights with people from other areas. It was never anything too serious; we saw it as part of growing up at that time.

In the 1970s, there were sometimes fights between different gangs of skinheads, especially on a Sunday. Once the pubs shut after the lunchtime trade, people used to gather in the park. If there were any rockers in the park, the skinheads would get together to fight them. I was at the boating lake once when it kicked off big style between the skinheads and the rockers. Even though there were many more skinheads, the fighting did not last long; the rockers had crash helmets on and were carrying chains; they were always going to come out on top. Fortunately these incidents did not happen that regularly.

The fun fair was another massive attraction when it came to the park. Kids came from all over Manchester to go on the rides and the other attractions. Even though fights broke out at the fair with gangs from different areas, I don't think anything too serious ever happened. It was usually more huffing and puffing and people acting hard rather than anyone having a pitched battle or anything like that.

To this day, the fair still comes to the park. They also have a huge fireworks display on bonfire night, and thousands of people attend. More often than not, it rains cats and dogs, and people get pissed wet through.

We also went to the park to play football. Sometimes there were marked-out football pitches, and even proper goal posts. We were dead chuffed then and thought we were big time. However, no one ever wanted to play in goals as we were only short arses at the time. If you ended up letting in a shed full of goals, your mates would end up taking the piss out of you. Everyone wanted to be a centre forward in the hope of scoring loads of goals and be the superstar. Anyone and everyone could join in, even if we didn't know who the kids were. All we wanted to do was have a kick about, and we used to play till we were knackered.

Nearby in the park, there is a magnificent building called Heaton Hall, a grade-one listed building. It is open to the public and has a museum and an events venue. Some of the hall is in a pretty bad state, but there is hope that a grant from the National Lottery or the Heritage Fund will bring it back up to standard. There is also an eighteen-hole golf course, a pitch-and-putt, and an animal farm. Nowadays there have been many pop concerts and festivals in the park; just a few years ago, Oasis was centre stage. It just so happens that Noel and Liam are fanatical City fans, but I didn't have to go to the park to listen to them. I could hear them from my house.

In the nineteenth century, they had horse racing where the boating lake now is. The horseracing was moved to Aintree, just outside Liverpool, where the Grand National is now held. Also in the nineteenth century, when they were in the process of laying a railway from Bury to Manchester, the project ran into trouble at Heaton Park. Lord Wilton, the landowner at the time, was not happy about a railway running through his land. In the end, as a compromise, he let a tunnel be built underneath his estate to accommodate the railway.

The park played a part in both World Wars. In the first, some battalions of the Manchester Regiment were trained and billeted there; they were known as the Manchester Pals. Sadly, about half of them were killed. Altogether, about thirteen thousand troops from the Manchester regiments tragically lost their lives in the First World War. There is now a memorial plaque in the park in recognition of these fallen heroes.

In the Second World War, the park was used as a depot for the Royal Air Force. In the south of the park, two housing estates were built. The area was short of houses, and it was decided that prefabricated buildings were much quicker to build. They also built a school. Even though they were only supposed to be temporary buildings, the houses stood the test of time and were not demolished till the 1960s. The school lasted till about 2012.

The park also hosted the lawn bowling event for the 2002 Commonwealth Games in Manchester. The park has a terrific history, and thousands come each year to visit and try to soak up the sunshine – but as any visitor to Manchester will know, that is a rare event.

When Pope John Paul II made a visit to the park in 1982, he was a bit too old to have a kick-about with the youngsters who were playing football there at the time. Thousands of people from all over the country came to have an audience with the pope.

The park is still going strong to this day. It is great that even though children now a days, have all the modern gadgets, they still enjoy doing the same things we did when we were kids. They like to go the park, go to the lake, and play football too.

My house backed onto St Mary's Park, and we had access to Bury New Road, where we could get the bus direct to Manchester or Bury. Prestwich is roughly slap-bang in the middle, give or take a couple of hundred yards it is roughly four miles to either destination. Before my time, it had a stream running through. Thankfully it wasn't there when we used to play football, otherwise we would have had to play in wellies. By Heaton Park standards, St Mary's was the size of a postage stamp, but to me and my mates, it was perfect. The only problem was the dog shit; it was a public park, and no one was daft enough in those days to collect the muck the dogs left behind. Inevitably, someone would get covered in it. Thank god for pooper scoopers nowadays. It's a pity they were not invented a bit earlier.

We didn't have any goalposts. Usually the first ones who turned up put their jackets or jumpers down. There were about six of us at first, but it sometimes ended up being twenty a side. Footballs were not always in plenty of supply, so whoever had a football was usually the captain and penalty taker. We had to keep the ball owner sweet because as soon as he went, that was the end of the game.

I loved playing football and would play all day, but I must admit I was pretty crap. That did not stop me from daydreaming that one day I would score Manchester City's winning goal at Wembley.

My claim to fame came and went when I was the unused substitute for my primary school, Park View, when we got to the final of the Compton Cup. I never got picked, but at least I was the sub. I don't think there was any intention of me playing unless someone broke a leg because they didn't even give me a football top to wear; instead I had the team photo in a City shirt. I like to say I was the lucky mascot because we went on to win.

I remember a lad from the local orphanage, Nazareth House, who used to come play with us when he was allowed out. I'm glad I never was in that place because it had a fearsome reputation which may or may not be justified. The lad was called Kev, and he was one of the few black lads in the area at that time. As kids in those days, it didn't matter who or what you were – black, brown, fat, skinny, good footballer, or a shit one – all we wanted to do was play football, and everyone was welcome.

There was a lad a bit older than me called Alfie who was head and shoulders above everyone else. We thought he might make it with a professional football team, but it wasn't meant to be. Unlike now, there were no organizations or groups to help young footballers and nurture or showcase their talents. In Prestwich, now there is a terrific organization called the Marauders; they also cover Whitefield and other areas in Manchester. Who knows – if they had been around at the time, one or two of the lads could have made it to the big time. The Marauders coach hundreds of kids from all ages, hold proper training sessions, play in leagues, and play football in the correct spirit. One season the supporters club sponsored the Marauders football kit, and players and officials from City came and presented the kids with the kit, which was a fantastic gesture. Everyone was pleased that they took the time and trouble to attend.

One person who lived in Prestwich for many years and did make it big was the late, great George Smith. George was born in Fleetwood, but he and his family moved to Salford when he was a youngster. George moved to City from Adelphi

Lads Club in the late 1930s shortly before the start of the Second World War. Because of the war, football was suspended, but that did not stop George playing for City against Stockport County late in 1939. He must not have taken his scoring boots, because the final score was 6-6 without George finding the target.

When George got called up for war service with the King's African Rifles in East Africa, in what is now called a blue-on-blue incident, George sustained a shocking injury when his unit was mistakenly fired on by the South African Air Force, He was so badly injured in the arm that it was left disfigured. He always kept his arm covered, plus his hand was partly paralyzed. If that happened nowadays, there would be a massive outcry by the public, the government would demand answers and at least an apology, and George would have received compensation. But for all intents and purposes, it was brushed under the carpet.

After George returned back to City, one would have thought the club would have welcomed him back as a returning hero, but he had to undergo trials before he could carry on earning his little over two pounds a week wages playing for the Blues. George played in a game against Tranmere Rovers and scored a hat trick, so that satisfied the head sheds at Maine Road.

It is hard to imagine the pain and trauma that George had to go through. The service and support the wounded would have received in those days during and after the war is not on par to the standards of the present time. It is a testimony to the great man that he just got on with it. He endeared himself to the City fans of the day when he scored all four goals against United in April 1946.

It was a 4-1 mauling of the reds in front of a mind-boggling 62,000 crowd at Maine Road. That was at the time we let them borrow our ground because Old Trafford had been bombed by the German air force. United fans of late are either ignorant or forgetful of that fact when they childishly make out we have no history. City sold George to Chesterfield for a measly five-thousand-pound transfer fee after scoring around 45 times in about 90 wartime games, and 80 goals in roughly 178 peacetime appearances. It was an amazing goal-scoring achievement for anyone, but with the injury George carried, it was truly out of this world. How much he would be worth in today's market is anyone's guess.

After finishing playing, George played part-time for Mossley AFC before returning back home to manage our local amateur club, Prestwich Heys, formerly known as Heys Old Boys in the 1950s.

Prestwich Heys was formed originally as Heys Old Boys after the school we used to go to on Heys Road, and the team has played in a variety of leagues. Three times they have been in second round qualifiers of the FA Cup, but in the 1973-74 season they narrowly lost 3-2 to Mosley, in the 1978-79 season they were soundly beaten 4-1 by Stalybridge Celtic, and in 1983-84 they got on the wrong end of a 1-0 score to Southport. For them to get to the second round qualifiers of the FA Cup was quite remarkable.

My brother Bob, always speaks fondly of the times when George was in St Mary's Park and joined in a kick about with us and our mates. When City got to the playoff finals in 1999, George's wife phoned me. I was then chairman of the Prestwich and Whitefield Manchester City

Supporters Club. She hoped I could get him a ticket for Wembley. I was unable to do so because tickets were extremely scarce. I hope he got sorted out by the club, but he was probably too proud to ask.

My footballing career went on hold again for a few weeks when I sprained my ankle and broke my wrist. This time it was self-inflicted. At the back of the park, there was some wasteland called Claremont. We used to play in there sometimes, and we had built a tree house, and our parents warned us about climbing the tree because it was high and dangerous. Did we listen? Hell, no. We were dead cocky and thought we were invincible. However, one day I slipped from the bottom branch and fell about fourteen feet. I was lucky not to be more seriously injured; in those days, mobile phones hadn't even been dreamed of, never mind invented. The public phone box nearby had been vandalized, and loads of houses in those days still did not have phones. Fortunately there was a phone in our house. The problem was how to get there.

My mate Jonny Ellis came up with a solution. He borrowed a workman's wheelbarrow, and he and a couple of other lads plonked me in it and wheeled me to my house for help. I must have looked a right sight, and I felt dead sorry for myself and felt a right pillock. I had to go to the hospital to get patched up. The nearest I got to football for the next few weeks was watching the lads playing in the park.

Not too long after that, I got arrested for the first time under the Theft and Larceny Act. Before you jump to any conclusions that I was a big-time gangster, nothing could be further from the truth. There were a couple of big sheds in the park which the groundsman used for storing stuff. Shortly after the annual carnival had finished, hundreds of bottles of Fanta were left in the largest shed, and someone had forgot to lock it. After a hard day of football, one of the lads helped himself to a crate and dished them out. Unfortunately for us, the local park keeper rode past on his push bike and reported us to the police. He knew where I lived, so I was the only one who was arrested. I had to go to a juvenile court and was charged with handling two bottles of stolen Fanta. I did not even think of getting legal advice or a solicitor, and I pleaded guilty. I had to pay 1s.6d. For the pop, and I got a conditional discharge, which meant 'Don't do it again'. For the crime of the week in Prestwich, I got a criminal record at the age of fourteen. Some of the others who also had the pop went on to have successful careers as bank managers, solicitors, nurses and a couple joined the police force. If they would have had a criminal record, they would have probably been prevented from joining their chosen professions. You live and learn, but unfortunately it wasn't my last brush with the law.

Another famous resident from the Prestwich and Whitefield area, but much before my time, was a gentleman called Jack Reynolds. Jack was born in Whitefield in 1888 and was on City's books, but he never played in the first team. The first time I heard of him was when I went to watch Ajax play Utrecht at the De Meer Stadium in Amsterdam about twenty-seven years ago. There was a stand called the

Jack Reynolds Stand, and I didn't think it sounded very Dutch. It transpired that after a pretty decent footballing career in England, he went overseas to manage Ajax of Amsterdam, where he introduced the philosophy and style which nowadays is called total football. He went on to become one of Ajax's most successful managers.

When Germany invaded Holland during the Second World War, Jack and other foreign nationals were interned in Poland, where I should imagine conditions were atrocious. All in all, Jack had a twenty-seven-year association with the club. Around twenty years ago, Ajax moved from the De Meer Stadium to the magnificent Ajax Arena, and even though Jack passed away in 1962, he was held in such high esteem that they named a reception area in his honour: the Jack Reynolds Lobby.

When I left Park View Primary School to join the big boy's school at Prestwich Heys, I hoped my footballing skills would improve. I still had dreams of getting that winner at Wembley, but though I might get ten out of ten for effort I was still crap, I had glandular fever in the first week of school and was off school for another six weeks. Then I was not fully fit and had to wait a few more weeks till I fully recovered, so there was no football for me for quite a while.

Sport was the main entertainment for the majority of the lads at the time. It was to be many years till the birth of all the electronic gadgets that are the norm nowadays. Besides football, I enjoyed swimming, and with the school we used to go to Blackfriars baths, not far from Manchester city centre. They were atrocious and filthy with flaking paint and horrible showers, and they used to put far too much chlorine in the water; our eyes stung for ages after. Worst of all, the place was infested by great big black beetles. The place is now long gone. How they were not condemned while we were going beggars belief. Someone somewhere must have made a fortune out of our misery because dozens of schools in the area used to send their pupils there.

As kids we also used to go to Radcliffe and Bury swimming baths, which were a lot cleaner. At Bury there were a couple of diving boards. Looking back now, we must have been barmy, but it seemed reasonably normal at the time as we launched ourselves off the top board and hoped to complete a somersault or two before we hit the water. After swimming at Bury, we went to the market, where we got the famous black puddings topped with mustard. It was only years later, when I discovered the main ingredients were blood and oatmeal, that I realised it was not the healthiest of foods, but they were delicious and cheap. Nowadays they are still popular.

One day my mum took me and a mate to the Galleon open-air pool at West Didsbury, which is in the posh part of Manchester. This place was a different class to anywhere I had been before. There was a restaurant and café, but what we had come for was the great big swimming pool. It looked magnificent, and there was not a water beetle in sight. How the other half lives, eh? Although I was only twelve at the time, I already had a total dislike of Manchester United, so I was a bit disappointed when George Best and David Sadler turned up. To make matters worse, my mate was a United fan, and he went over for some autographs. Apart from that, we had a great time. The only other downside was it took three busses each way to get there, so it was bit of a trek, but it was well worth the hassle.

One of our teachers at Heys Road was a great bloke called Brian Grundy. Besides being a teacher, he also played part-time football for Wigan Athletic. In those days Wigan was nothing like the team they are now. They played in the Cheshire League at a rundown stadium called Springfield Park. What a shithole that was. Generally speaking, most of the players would have been part-time.

While we were still at school, Wigan played Bury in the Lancashire Cup, and Brian played well and scored a goal. In fact he played so well that he impressed Les Shannon Bury's manager, who signed him for Bury the following week. Obviously the standard in the fourth division, which was the league Bury was in at the time, was of a much higher standard of the Cheshire League, and it was not long after signing that he left the school and went to play for Bury full-time.

The following year, 1968, he helped Bury win promotion from the old division four. He stayed at Bury for a couple more seasons before dropping out of the league, and he then played for a number of non-league teams. He went onto manage Glossop North End while also being the landlord of a local pub before emigrating to Spain.

While I was at Heys School, we went to watch many Bury games, especially if Brian was playing. We used to get vouchers, so it was very cheap to watch, plus they got decent crowds, which made for a great atmosphere. I remember watching them play Workington, Barrow, and Southport. All three teams subsequently got demoted from the football league, so they must have been pretty shit because in those days it was hard to get demoted from the fourth division; the bottom team usually got a reprieve instead of getting kicked out of the league.

Many lads my age who supported City at the time also watched Bury play, usually when Bury played at night or when City were playing away. Bury used to have some good young players, but the bigger clubs would come in and snatch them up. United fans we knew used to come as well, and we had a good laugh and enjoyed the matches, especially when we got in for next to nothing. There was no Sky or TV catch-up in them days; many houses by then had a TV, but most were black-and-white and only had three channels. Watching football live was a massive part of how we entertained ourselves. How would the kids of today cope without all the gadgets they have? I still have a soft spot for Bury, and I always look out for their results.

A lad from our school who went on to be a professional footballer was called Stuart Jump. He was two years older than me, and his mum and dad had a hardware shop in Prestwich Village. He joined Stoke City as an apprentice while still at school and progressed through the ranks till he signed as a full-time professional when he was eighteen. Obviously everyone at school and in Prestwich was chuffed for him because it was great when someone we knew achieved something as great as becoming a professional footballer. He stayed at Stoke before being transferred to Crystal Palace, and after a few years at Palace, he tried his luck in America, where he stayed for several years before he finished his career playing in the major indoor soccer league. Not bad for a Prestwich lad born in the early 1950s, eh? I did not know him as well as my brother Bob did. Bob went with a few other lads to Stoke for a midweek game against City, and they managed to meet up and have a quick chat with him after the game.

Prestwich has always had very strong support for City, and when we were young kids, some City fans really stood out. There was one of the groundsmen in St Mary's Park who always wore his blue and white City scarf to work. He used to chat with me and my brother about City, and if we hadn't been to the match, he would give us a kick-by-kick account of how the game went. If he was in a good mood and they were not busy, he would let us use the tennis courts. I was never really into tennis, but I couldn't look a gift horse in the mouth. It gave us something to do for an hour or so, and I could dream of being a Wimbledon champion. Plus, it was free. The courts were concrete, so we couldn't fling ourselves about like we would if it was grass. There was also a court that was shale, but we were never going to get an hour or two on there for free because that was the posh bit where the serious players went. There were also crown bowling greens and a putting area in the park, and if it weren't busy, we could have a go on them as well. It was quite nice, living in a house that backed on to the park and having a Blue as a groundsman.

Prestwich is mainly made up of different areas of council estates alongside many areas of private houses, plus the parks and the Village, which is made of pubs, shops, restaurants, and cafes, and which has always been a hotbed of support for City. There is also a massive Jewish area in Prestwich that straddles Broughton, and they have their own thriving community.

For years, one of the biggest employers in Prestwich was the hospital. The hospital has no accident or emergency unit because it cares for people with mental health issues. Prestwich Hospital was built as an asylum on the land owned by the Milne family in an area known as Prestwich Wood. For nearly 150 years, the hospital was the largest employer in the town. I later worked at the hospital for thirty years.

Back in the day it was the largest asylum in Europe, at one time catering to over two thousand patients. It was known as the Prestwich Lunatic Asylum. To us ignorant kids, it was known as the loony bin, and in later life the nuthouse. It has had a chequered history, with criticism and praise aimed at the hospital in equal measures. I imagine at the turn of the twentieth century, conditions for both patients and staff were less than desirable because it was a case of out of sight, out of mind.

I remember as a schoolkid going on an organized trip from school to certain parts of the hospital. I have recollections of it being a very grim place.

Nowadays it bears no resemblance to the run-down place I remember. It consists of specialist wards and secure units. I still have enormous respect for all who work at the hospital; they do a difficult job in difficult conditions, but unfortunately their efforts are not rewarded in terms of pay conditions and long-term job security.

Tesco took over some of the land about twenty years ago and have a giant store on part of the hospital site, employing hundreds of people. There is also a restaurant and hotel on the old site.

Chapter 2

Whitefield

Whitefield has three large council estates as well as private houses. It has always been a big Blue area, no more so than the newest of the estates, which is called Hillock. This estate was conceived back in the 1950s as a general overspill for the people – mainly from the Bradford, Beswick, and Miles Platting areas of Manchester, but other areas were also getting their old houses demolished and those people also moved to Hillock. Many of those houses which were getting demolished were run-down terraces which only had an outside toilet, so it was great for them to move into a brand-new house on a purpose-built estate.

The areas mentioned just happen to be where City's new ground now stands, and was a massive Blue area, the people who moved to Hillock obviously kept their loyalties with them when they relocated – as the saying goes, once a Blue, always a Blue. It was a huge building project and took many years to complete the estate, and although some people were sad to leave their old areas, most were happy with their new surroundings and were grateful they no longer had to go out in the cold when they wanted to go to the bogs.

Although there was never a big gang problem in our area, at times there were the normal rivalries between different areas, different schools, and different football supporters. While I was still at school, there were sometimes a few run-ins with some of the lads from Prestwich and the lads from Whitefield. It seemed to be the norm back then because everyone was pretty territorial, and that could lead to small confrontations. I never had a problem because I knew loads of the Whitefield lads from the matches, many still live on the estate and have kids and grandkids who are City fans. Some people, like Keith Roberts, Bri Livsey, Paul Holt, and Dave Mitch from the estate, played a massive part in making the supporters branch a huge success. Many a time even before the branch was formed, we would go together to the games both home and away. Besides the council estates, there are some really posh houses in Whitefield, especially the Ringley Road area. Needless to say, I don't know anyone from that neck of the woods.

There is no huge employer in Whitfield anymore because all the mills are long gone. Halls was the sweet factory which produced the famous Halls Mentholyptus (cough and throat lozenges), which were introduced in the 1930s and are still very popular to this day. Halls shut down in the 1980s, and the jobs went as well.

There must be a lot of fit living people in Whitefield nowadays because there are a couple of big gyms which are very popular. Although a lot of the popular pubs have closed, there are some fantastic restaurants still around, and if you are into chocolate, Whitefield is the place to be. The locals can be rightly proud of the award-winning Slattery's, which is a combined patisserie, chocolatier, and café. It is on the site of the old public house the Masons Arms, and it is slap bang on the main road from Bury to Manchester. It's always very popular and busy, and it is great to see a small, independent, local firm still doing so well and not being squeezed out by the large companies.

Sedgley Park Rugby Club is also based in Whitefield, and they play in the National League North. They are a thriving, community-based club with many junior teams. I have never been into rugby, but it is great that with limited finances, they are still going strong and play an important part in the local community. I confess to never watching them play, but I have been to their ground a few times, as I have been to some events at their fantastic function room.

Colin Bell, one of City's all-time greats, joined the Blues from Bury and even had his own restaurant in Whitefield. The local kids always tried to get his autograph. I don't think the customers were too pleased to see a load of grubby young kids hanging about while they went in for their meals, but bollocks to them. They just wanted an autograph. He opened the restaurant with his old teammate from Bury, Colin Waldron.

Colin Bell won every major honour with City and played many times for England. He was one of City's best ever players and was one of our favourite guests at the supporters club, recalling some of the great goals he scored during his career. He is still idolized by young and old alike.

If there was a better player in England in the late 1960s and the 1970s, I never saw him play. Don't get me wrong, there were some fantastic players about at that time, but Colin had absolutely everything to make him a world-class player. Colin also went on to play nearly fifty times for England. Many players of that era loved the limelight, but Colin was always happier in the background and did his talking on the football pitch.

He was only twenty-nine years old and still in his prime when he injured his knee after a challenge with Martin Buchan, when City played United in a League Cup game at Maine Road. It was a long, painful recovery before he went on to play again for City. Colin bravely fought back against all the odds, I was at the home game against Newcastle when Colin made his long-awaited return. Tony Book City's manager at the time once told us at a supporters meeting that it was his plan to bring Colin on for the last ten to twenty minutes of the game, but an injury to Paul Power before half-time forced him to change his plans. Rumours were sweeping round the Kippax Stand that Colin might be coming on. If I live to be one hundred, I will never again witness an ovation like I did that day. Grown men were shedding tears, handkerchiefs were out, fans were applauding and shouting and waving scarves, and the atmosphere was electric. The ovation got louder and went on and on. It was incredible, and whoever was there will never forget that moment. The king had returned.

City were inspired by his return and went on to win 4-0. Colin has always said coming on in that game is his number one memory in football. He never went on to reach the great heights of his heyday and did not play that many more games until he retired and hung up his boots for good.

After his retirement, Colin continued his service with the club, and being a youth team coach was one of his favourite roles. To City's eternal shame, he was sacked from that role, which was a shock and disappointment to all City fans.

One of the hardest things Colin ever did was take the club he'd served and idolized for so many years to an industrial tribunal. To the embarrassment of the football club but to the delight of Colin his family and the supporters, he won his claim. Looking back at the how City handled it, it was nothing short of disgraceful. Thankfully, Colin didn't hold it against the club, and he is now a club ambassador. He also has the honour of having a stand named after him, the Colin Bell Stand. The fans were asked to vote on the name of the stand, and naming it after Colin was a very popular decision. Colin can still be seen at the ground on match days, and fans young and old alike still want to have their photographs taken with him. Colin always gets a fantastic reception whenever he attends supporters' events.

Tony Towers was another City player and fan who was born and lived in Manchester. He supported the Blues as a kid, and he was a midfielder who played well over a hundred games for City and three games for England, till he was transferred to Sunderland as part of a deal that saw Denis Tueart and Micky Horswill come to City. Tony played for many clubs, including some in the North America soccer league, and he finished his playing career at Rochdale. Although Tony was never a superstar, as a Manchester lad he was welcomed with open arms when he attended our meetings.

The first time I met Tony was after a game. I went into a pub in called the Cleveland in Crumpsall, and a few of us were having a pint when we spotted a group of people wearing suits and ties. Usually the only time you would wear a suit in a pub like that was if you had just got out of court, or if you were in the CID. We soon recognized who it was and started talking to him, Tony and his group had been guests of the club and had been in one of the lounges – hence the suit and ties, Tony had a menu with him signed by a couple of players, and he very kindly gave it to me. He said he still enjoyed watching City play and went quite often to the games. That was when we invited him to a meeting, and he was only too willing to attend. Although it had been many years since he had been at the club, he got a great reception by all the members, and it was great listening to some of his stories.

Tony also ran a Joseph Holts Pub in Whitefield. It was called the Church Inn, and it was a brilliant pub full of characters. Sadly like Colin's restaurant, it is no longer there; the pub got knocked down to make way for a Morrison's Supermarket.

One thing all supporters from any club in the world love is when a player from their city, town, or area makes it at their club. It's even better when the players progress, and when they become an international.

Trevor Sinclair was born in London but was brought up on the Hillock Estate in Whitefield. He was a boyhood City fan, but unfortunately it took many years and a few clubs till he joined the Blues. He started with Blackpool and then went on to play for QPR and West Ham. Altogether Trevor played over eighty games for City and twelve games for the England team. He made history for the Blues by scoring the first competitive goal in the City of Manchester Stadium (now renamed the Etihad) against the Welsh side TNT. He also scored against United, and his famous quote after scoring was 'It's better than having sex', is immortalized in City fans history, whether he actually said it or if it is an urban myth is another matter.

The fans at City love Trevor because he is such a down-to-earth person. When he attended our branch meeting, he received a hero's welcome. The place was packed, but he didn't leave until all the people present, including dozens of kids, had their photos and autographs. After leaving City, Trevor went to Cardiff. He came on for the last few minutes at the cup final against Portsmouth.

Unfortunately for Trevor, Pompey went on to win 1-0. Trevor went on to become the assistant manager at Lancaster City, a club not too far from his first club, Blackpool. He is often a guest on TV as a football pundit, and his down-to-earth style is a treat for the fans. Recently on TV, he explained he became a City fan because everyone in Prestwich and Whitefield followed the Blues, and his mates were all City fans.

David Ball was also born in Manchester and brought up in Whitefield. He came up through the City youth team system, and he was a striker and a star player in both the youth and the reserve teams. In 2008, David scored in the final of the youth cup, which City went on to win. He was a guest a couple of times at our branch meetings, and even though he was young at the time, he handled himself well and came across as a smashing young lad. The fans took to him and always hoped he might break through into the first team; in fact, our branch sponsored his boots for him for a couple of seasons. Considering all the world-class players who were at City when David was there, it was always going to be hard for him to break into the first team, so it wasn't a great shock that he left City to play first-team football elsewhere. David went on to help Peterborough win promotion to Division One, and he also helped Fleetwood Town win promotion to Division One. Although David did not break through to the City first team, his training and development and learning from the first team players at City, certainly helped him in his future career. In November 2015 David was on the short list for the FIFA Puskas Award for the World Goal of the season, for his goal for Fleetwood against Preston North End. What a tremendous achievement! I am sure his mum and dad were so proud of him. The likes of Carlos Tevez and Lionel Messi were also in the top ten. I have met David's mum and dad a few times, and they are a great couple. All at the branch wish Trevor and David the very best for the future.

Sandwiched in the middle of Prestwich and Whitefield is a place called Besses o'th Barn. Don't worry – I have not made a spelling mistake. It might have a weird name, but they have a brilliant brass band, and in the early 1900s they did a couple of world tours, which would have been no mean feat. They also won many competitions and released some records to raise funds. There was a junior section called Besses Boys Band, which was formed just before the Second World War.

Peter Skelton, who had a hit record in the seventies with 'You're a Lady' and 'Love Is the Sweetest Thing', was a member of the Besses Brass

Band. Peter went on to have a successful career as a singer and songwriter. I never found out if he was Blue, though.

Just round the corner is the Bee Hive, a very popular local pub that serves both the locals and City fans very well. City fans meet in there before home and away games, and all the games are also shown on the telly. It is a smashing pub, and everyone in there is dead friendly. Both Prestwich and Whitefield have vibrant local communities, and this is one of the reasons why the supporters branch did so well over the years.

Chapter 3

Joining the Royal Navy

My footballing career was doomed before it had even started, and my academic studies were not fairing much better. To put it another way, wasn't really focused at school. I disliked most subjects apart from sports, but unfortunately I was not much good at them either. In those days you could leave school at fifteen, so as I was approaching that age it quickly dawned on me that I needed to get a job. I wasn't taking any exams at school, so unless I got some forged certificates, I wouldn't be able to show any prospective employer any CSEs or GSEs. Going to college for further studies did not appeal to me, and unfortunately being a professional footballer wasn't an option either. Joining the armed forces was another career option for me to consider.

My brother had been with the air cadets for a couple of years. I had only been to a couple of meetings with him, but it all seemed a bit too serious for me at the time. A mate of mine was in the navy sea cadets, and I once went with him to a meeting near Bury. I never figured out as to why Bury had a sea cadet school when it is nowhere near the bleeding sea, but never mind the small details – someone must have thought it was a good idea. I never went again because it burnt down soon after I visited and for some strange reason never got rebuilt.

I don't know where the idea came from, but I quite fancied the idea of being a chef. It was strange considering I had never cooked fuck all in my house or anywhere else. My expertise didn't even stretch to making toast. I think it must have been all the Fanny Cradock programs my mum used to watch on television.

My mate had applied to join the Royal Navy, so eventually I did the same. I thought I might as well take the plunge because I didn't have many other bright ideas. Whilst I also applied for the Royal Navy, I thought I would also apply to Radcliffe Catering College, which is between Whitefield and Bury. That went on the back-burner because in only a matter of weeks, I got invited to an interview at the Royal Navy Recruitment Centre in Manchester. When I got there, I was impressed by all the photographs on the walls showing really smart ships, different sized frigates, destroyers, and pictures of smart-looking sailors in uniform. They all looked like they were having fun, and they were very tanned and relaxed while abroad in exotic locations, usually with pretty girls by their side or drinks in their hands. I thought I would not mind a bit of that. At that time, it did not take much to impress me, and I was hooked in by the spiel the recruitment officer gave me. He talked about all the different opportunities, including catering, engineering, sports, and the different places around the world that the navy visited, and the free time I'd have when I was abroad. Add to the fact that I would get six weeks' paid leave a year, plus free train tickets as well that was enough to sway me. I thought, *'Yes, this is the life for me'*.

I must have done enough to impress because I got invited to the next stage of the recruitment process. So far, so good, but three obstacles stood in my way. First, I had to pass some written tests. Second, I had to pass a medical. Third, I had to get my parents to sign the paperwork so I could join up for twelve years.

When I went back, I must have done all right with the exams because I was invited back for a medical. Well, it was called a medical, but all I can remember was some old bloke asking me to drop my trolleys. It was embarrassing as fuck – I didn't even know the bloke or whether he was a doctor. Oh, well. In for a penny, in for a pound. He then pointed to my underpants next; he wanted them off as well. Next thing he had hold of my undercarriage and asked me to cough. Thank fuck I never got a hard-on – that would have been fucking embarrassing. Then it was time to bend over so he could look up my shit locker. What the fuck he expected to find up there was anyone's guess, but as a young lad of fifteen, it seemed very strange indeed. Anyway, he must have liked what he saw because I passed the medical. Two obstacles down; one more to go.

I knew my dad would sign the form, but I thought I might have to convince my mum. It might have helped my cause if I had previously told them I was applying. The first they knew was when I brought the forms in for them to sign. Thankfully they did sign, and I was all set to report to HMS *Ganges* in Shotley Kent on 16 October 1969 to commence training.

The recruitment officer in Manchester must have been pissing his sides laughing because it would be about two fucking years before I even set foot on a ship, never mind going to sea on one and being in some far-flung place sitting in the sun with a beer in my hand.

From leaving school in July to joining in October, I worked at Pauldens in Manchester City Centre (now known as Debenhams). I earned five pounds a week; my first wages in the navy was one pound a week. It wasn't the last time I questioned whether I had made the correct decision or if I was off my rocker.

Just after I left school, I received a letter from Radcliffe College saying I had been accepted. They gave me a date to come down to enrol, but bollocks to that. It was a bit late because I had decided a life on the ocean waves was for me.

On a cold, miserable Thursday morning, I was on my way to the Manchester recruitment office to meet up with the others at 9.00 am. I'd collect my rail pass and head off on my journey to start a life in Her Majesty's Royal Navy.

When I turned up at the recruitment office in Manchester, there were about a dozen other lads there. Most looked much older and bigger than me, which wasn't hard because I was only five feet seven and a skinny little runt. Everyone else had relatives with them to see them off, and some were surprised I didn't have anyone with me. I didn't see the point, and because my brother, parents, and mates were working, I thought it a waste of time to drag someone to the middle of Manchester just to say goodbye.

Shortly after meeting everyone, there was a roll call followed by a pep talk by one of the recruiters. We made our way to Manchester's Piccadilly train station to first catch the train to London. Then we'd head across to Liverpool Street and get another train to Ipswich. Like me, most of the lads hadn't been much farther than Blackpool. I certainly hadn't been on a train as big as the one from Manchester, to Euston in London. The only one I had been on was the Bury to Manchester train which only had two carriages. This one was a monster by comparison, and I was amazed that it had toilets and a buffet section. I must have looked a right tit as I stood there gawping at the size of the fucking thing. I had seen big trains on the telly before, but this was the first time I had actually got on one. Little did I know then that over the next few years, I would be on that train dozens of times, but I was gobsmacked the first time I was on it, we sat near each other, and I was next to a lad from Bolton called Paul and one from Salford called Sam, Sam looked the oldest and he was going to try his luck at getting some beer from the buffet bar. I wasn't a massive beer drinker at the time because I was only fifteen, but when he asked me if I wanted a couple of beers, I wasn't going to say no as I didn't want to look a right wimp. Fifteen minutes later, he returned with a big cheesy smile on his face and dished out a couple of the cans to me and Paul. I thought, *'Happy days'*. I felt dead grown-up at having a fag and a can of beer and going to serve in the Royal Navy.

When we arrived at Euston, there was someone to meet us and take us across London to the other station. I don't remember how long it took to get from Piccadilly to Euston, but it seemed like hours and hours – nothing like the 2 hours 40 minutes it takes nowadays. I'm not surprised we were met by someone to guide us across London because the underground is a right nightmare the first time you use it. I should imagine the real reason though, is that he didn't want us lot getting pissed up and missing the next train.

The train to Ipswich was pretty scruffy and run-down compared to the one from Manchester, and this train journey seemed to drag on as well. When we arrived at Ipswich, we were all knackered but in good spirits. Outside the station, there was a big single-decker dark blue bus with big white painted RN letters on the sides. After a name check, we got on the bus, and reality set in. I remember the bus was not built for comfort because the seats were rock hard. We were all dead quiet and lost in our own thoughts on the journey to Shotley Gate, where HMS *Ganges* was. I thought, *'What the fuck have I let myself in for?'* I know where the term '*signing your life away*' comes from because that was what it seemed I had done. When I think back now, signing up for twelve years at such a young age seems crazy, but at fifteen it seemed such a great idea. For the rest of the journey, I thought to myself, *Twelve-fucking years*. This was not the same feeling I'd had during the days and weeks leading up to my joining, when I was a care free and a cocky little shit, bragging to everyone that I was going away to sea to serve my country.

The closer we got to the establishment, the more my bravado left me. For want of a better expression, I was shitting bricks. There was no turning back now; I had to man up and get on with whatever was going to happen next.

Chapter 4

HMS *Ganges*

HMS *Ganges* was a huge, sprawling shore establishment which, if you believed the hype, turned boys into men. It was in operation from 1905–1976. Although there had been other seagoing ships called *Ganges,* and there has been other training bases for boy sailors, the uniqueness of this establishment was that it could train so many young navy recruits at the same place.

That was where all young sailors under the age of sixteen were trained. During part of that period, it was also known as Royal Navy Training Establishment Shotley. In 1927 it was named HMS *Ganges.*

From 1973–1976 (when *Ganges* finally shut), they no longer trained just juniors because the school leaving age had changed to sixteen. Training for sailors lasted only a few weeks, unlike the twelve months we had to do and lads aged from 16 upwards were now trained there. Then the trainees went on to do their part two training at their specialized training establishments. Roughly 150,000 recruits were trained at HMS *Ganges* during its lifetime.

Shotley is just a few miles from Ipswich and lies next to the River Orwell and the River Stour. The next few months were going to be a big culture shock and a big learning curve for the lot of us. Most of the lads had never been away from home before and had never had to fend for themselves in any way. I knew the next twelve months were going to throw some massive challenges and surprises my way. Bring it on, as they say, because I had fuck all to lose. For the next few weeks, I would have to knuckle down and take all the shit I knew I was going to get thrown at me.

It was not long till we arrived, but it was not the entrance of the main establishment we entered. We went to a place known as the annex, and this would be our home for the next four weeks while the instructors did their best to get us ready to join the hundreds of other trainees at the main base. In the middle of the annex was a large parade ground surrounded by three mess decks (dormitories to all you land lubbers) and a dining hall. To one side of the parade ground was a mast that flew the White Ensign, which is the flag of the Royal Navy.

When we got off the bus, this was when reality hit me. I realized that life would never be the same again. We were met by a number of instructors. If any of us were expecting a nice friendly, warm welcome, we were soon to be disappointed.

None of the instructors seemed to talk – they just shouted, bellowing out orders. I wasn't sure who was shouting what to who. Other lads in our detachment, which was called No. 114 Recruitment had arrived the day before us. They were pissing their sides at our misfortune because they had already been through the welcome we were now getting. After a certain amount of confusion – well, to be honest, a load of fucking confusion – we fell in, one next to another. All the time, more orders were being shouted at us, but I did not have a clue what they were about. I naively thought to myself, *'Why don't they calm down for a minute and quietly explain what it is they want from us?'* I quickly learned the instructors didn't do quiet.

Each mess had a different name and the one I was allocated was Bulwark. Which was also the name of one of the biggest ships the navy had at the time. Once we got our beds and bedding sorted, we were escorted to the dining hall for tea. After being fed and watered, it was time for more shouting as we were told what to expect the next day. The fun and games would start properly in the morning.

There were about thirty lads in each mess. The beds were big iron things, and the mattresses were as hard as a plank of wood. The first night was really strange for me. Back home, I had always had my own bed in my own room. Now I was sharing a room with thirty strangers. It was dead hard to get to sleep that first night because the environment, the smells, and the noises were alien to me. As soon as I drifted off to sleep some fucker would start coughing and spluttering, oh, well; it was something I would learn to live with. It did take a long time to get used to everything because it was so fucking unnatural in those first few days and weeks.

The next morning, we were woken up at 6.00 am by a sadistic instructor bawling and shouting at us. He walked up and down the mess, whacking a big stick against all the beds. What a fucking racket it made. I soon jumped to the conclusion that having a big gob and no sense of humour was a fundamental requirement to be a Royal Navy instructor but I kept that information to myself as a matter of self-preservation.

The day started with a shit, shave, and a shower, never mind the fact that a lot of us at that age didn't need to shave. But if some six-foot instructor hovered over you, shouting down your ear to get a shave, then you had no option but to have a shave.

Then we went to the parade ground, fell in, and learned to march. You would think it does not take much to master the art of marching, because at the end of the day, all you are doing is putting one foot in front of the other and swinging your arms at the same time. Believe me, it is not as easy as it looks, especially at daft o'clock in the morning with some psycho instructor bawling in your face. Simply remembering left and right seemed a massive task at times. It was not all bad news. We got breakfast at about eight o'clock, and then it was off to the barbers to get our haircuts. Well, that is what they said we were going to have. In reality we all ended up with shaved heads, and it probably took the barber less than a minute to get rid of my curly locks. Then we were issued with our kits. I think it was a case of one size fits all, because fuck all seemed to fit me properly. We were not allowed to wear any civilian clothes, and so we parcelled all our stuff that we'd arrived in and posted them back home. Then it was back on the parade ground for more abuse – sorry, I mean instruction in the art of marching.

We were given ID cards and navy numbers. Mine was D114292M. I can remember that, but never my National Insurance number, which Cath thinks is weird. We then had lectures on how to wash, shave, and clean our teeth properly and other such rudimental exercises. Over the next four weeks, we learned to wash and iron clothes, how to sew, and how to polish boots. We learned how to march, double march, stand to attention, stand at ease, and salute, as well as how to tie and untie knots, and how to scrub floors on our hands and knees. It was an extremely tough regime and was very tiring. It must have slipped the Manchester recruitment officer's mind to tell me how intense the training was going to be. I was hoping for a game of football at the weekend, or going into Ipswich or Harwich for a bit of time out, but there was no chance of that happening till we got to the main site. We wouldn't get any leave for the foreseeable future – another thing my glorious recruitment officer forgot to mention.

Ipswich were playing City a couple of weeks after I arrived, and we drew 1-1. A great result but I was gutted, Ipswich playing City just down the road, and I couldn't go. We couldn't even listen to the game or watch City on match of the day because we didn't have a telly or even a radio in the mess.

The one thing I remember enjoying at that period was the assault course, especially when they threw flash bangs and smoke grenades at us. The only explanation I can give for enjoying something as hard and knackering as an assault course was that it broke up the monotony of the routine stuff we did every day. If we thought the training at the annex was bad, we got the shock of our lives when we marched through the large, imposing gates for the first time at the main establishment, which was to be our home for the best part of the next twelve months. There were guards on both sides of the gates, and they looked like fucking giants. They had slight grins on their faces as if to say, 'Hello, suckers.' The parade ground looked absolutely massive and was many times bigger than the one we'd left behind at the annex, in the middle of it was a 143-foot mast, and dozens of young sailors who were climbing it stopped for a minute to give us loads of abuse. My new mess was called Ashanti, and it was in an area called the long-covered way. Everywhere we went as a group, we had to march. If we were going to be late or if the instructor had a cob on, we had to double-march.

I was going to train as a chef, and so I was given my title, junior assistant cook second class. Fuck me, I couldn't have got any lower if I had tried. Talk about a confidence builder! We were called Jack Twos for short. It was better than being called Jack Shit, I suppose.

Even though being a chef was my chosen profession, I only spent two hours a week learning to cook. We had to go to school three or four times a week to pass an exam in English and maths because we all had to be of a minimum standard. The rest of the time, we were tying knots, marching, saluting, washing, and ironing. I don't remember seeing pictures of fucking ironing boards at the recruitment office back in Manchester. We spent a lot of the time in the swimming pool and at the gym and doing cross-country running to get us fit. Fuck me, I wanted to be a chef, not a fucking Royal Marine Commando. We also had to go on sailboats and go rowing on the big cutters. That was frigging hard graft. People used to volunteer to go on them – they must have been nuts. I only went on them when we had to as a group.

There was a cinema, and we were allowed to watch a film once a month. I used to enjoy the swimming, but it was very demanding when we had to swim a couple of lengths in navy-issue overalls because they became very heavy as soon as we got in the water. It took a lot of getting used to at first, and it was knackering, but it was something we all had to do, so we had to grin and bear it. The cross-country run was quite tough at first, but the more times we did it, the easier it became. One lad took a shortcut and climbed over a metal fence. Unfortunately for him, he slipped, and the spiked bit of the railing went through his leg. He was in agony, and a few of us stayed with him till the medics arrived and freed him from the railing. He was in hospital for a couple of weeks and got back-classed to a new recruitment.

One piece of uniform I dreaded wearing was the seaman's jumper. It was made out of the most uncomfortable material known to mankind, and I am sure wearing something made of sandpaper would have been more comfortable. The smartest of all the uniforms was known as number ones, and that was what we wore when on parade or on leave. The bell-bottom trousers had to have seven creases in them, representing the seven oceans. The creases had to be ironed into them an equal distance apart. That was very hard to achieve, especially at the beginning of our training, but once we got the hang of it, it was not too bad, and the end result was we all looked dead smart.

The training was a very strict regime, and at times bullying was pretty common. Some instructors seemed to enjoy getting under our skin. The worst was the verbal bullying and abuse they used to hurl at us; after a while, it became tiresome because I suppose we became a bit immune to it. Living and training in those sorts of conditions was really stressful at times, and it was hardly surprising that arguments and fights broke out, Once when we were about to fall in to march to the parade ground, I got smacked on the side of my head. Talk about seeing stars. I managed to mutter, 'What the hell was that for?' The lad just smiled. I never found out why he whacked me, but I think he was just stressed out, and I was the smallest in the group. I would not have minded so much, but I got on with him OK; it was Paul, who was on the train with me when we'd gone from Manchester to Ipswich. He bought himself out after three months, so obviously the training, conditions, and stress got to him a bit more than it did to the rest of us.

Our clothing was always immaculate. We seemed to spend half our time polishing our boots and shoes, or washing and ironing. All the clothes had to be folded to the correct size of the navy handbook, with our name showing and stowed in our locker, which always had to be left open so the instructors could see if it was up to standard. We regularly had kit inspections, where we laid our kit out on our beds. If anything was out of place, the bastard doing the inspection would launch the kit at you or throw it halfway down the mess. Then you had to sort it all out again. It was depressing and demoralizing because so much time and effort went into getting it up to standard. Even if it was up to standard, it could get launched at you anyway depending what mood the fucker was in. Sometimes, just for spite they would tip your bed over as well.

In the 1960s and 1970s, if people of our age were sent to a custodial sentence by the court, it was usually for twelve to eighteen months borstal training. I am sure the regime we were put through was tougher, and we were fucking volunteers. There would have been riots if borstal inmates were treated as poorly as we were. There were many times that I thought I must have been barmy for signing up for this.

The mess room, like our kits, was always immaculate. We spent many hours keeping it up to standard, and on Friday nights we spent ages on our hands and knees scrubbing and polishing the deck and the heads (bathroom) to get the mess ready for the divisional officer's inspection. The best mess when the captain did his rounds won a cake. I'm sure they just gave the cake out in turns because every mess was of the same high standard.

Also based at *Ganges* were two Ham class minesweepers. The Ham class sweepers were named after English villages. HMS *Flintham* was named after a village in Nottingham, and HMS *Dittisham* was named after a village in Devon. We were supposed to have a go at going to sea on them as part of our training, but even though I went on them many times, I never actually went to sea on them. The first time I was on them was to get them up to spec for a cocktail party. I thought I was the main man strolling about the deck, thinking *'This is the life'* – until reality kicked in and I had to clean the heads and scrub the decks.

Come Christmas, we were given two weeks leave, and we had a special train to take us from Ipswich to London. That was a mission in itself to transport hundreds of young sailors from *Ganges* to London and beyond. It seemed weird to arrive in Manchester on my first home leave in my sailor's uniform, walking down Market Street with everyone looking at us. I remember all the old ladies wanted to touch our collars for luck. At least I got to go watch City play. I went to the home game against Burnley, but we could only draw, 1-1.

I was even luckier on my next home leave, which was in March. I went to see City beat United at Old Trafford, 2-1. There was so many City fans there that day it was unbelievable. We were all singing about going to Vienna because City were playing against Gornik in the European Cup Winners Cup Final a few weeks later. We won that as well.

As I said, the regime at *Ganges* was very tough and strict. We were never allowed to wear civilian clothes, even on the odd occasion we were allowed out on weekends we all ways went out in uniform. The punishment dished out to the trainees was quite severe. There were three types of punishment. The unofficial was dished out at the instructor's whim. For example, if you were a couple of minutes late getting out of bed, you were liable to have to run up and down the long-covered way with your mattress on your back. It was quite a distance, so you were knackered as well as humiliated, because all the other lads from the other mess decks would be shouting abuse and taking the piss. For other offenses, like getting out of bed after lights out, you could end up cleaning the heads with a toothbrush. Not having your shoes shined to the instructor's liking could have you scrubbing the mess deck with a hand scrubbing brush. The least severe of the official punishments was dished out by the divisional officer for being late on parade, smoking when not permitted, or not wearing the correct uniform. You would get up to a few hours extra drill, which would take place on a Saturday – usually the Saturday you were scheduled to get a few hours leave. The extra drill would be an hour at a time, so if you got awarded four hours, it was four Saturdays on the bounce. Most of the extra training would be done on the double, so you could sometimes be running for ages at time with a rifle above your head. If that wasn't bad enough, there would be other trainees there that would see you and take the piss. Once you had done the running, you thought you would get a breather, but oh, no – you had to hit the deck and do press-ups. At one stage I thought my middle name was press-ups. The hardest punishment was the commander's routine, where you did an hour of the above plus an hour of cleaning duties that usually consisted of cleaning the toilets, picking up cigarette stubs, and scrubbing pans in the galley. This punishment was dished out for offenses such as answering back to instructors, fighting, or coming back late from shore leave.

When I was there, one lad was sentenced to twenty-eight days in the Royal Navy detention centre at Portsmouth, which was a prison just for navy personnel. *World in Action* did a television programme about how brutal it was there, and following the programme, massive reforms ensued. Some of the most brutal punishments had long ago been stopped, but I am sure some of the instructors we had would have loved to bring back the cat of nine tails.

At this point, you might ask why we stayed in the navy. One reason is we had no choice till we had done at least three months; then we could apply to buy ourselves out. The other reason is we knew or hoped it would soon get easier. We also thought we wouldn't have to do much of this bullshit once we'd left *Ganges;* our dream was to serve in the fleet and go abroad. I was fucked if I was going to let some jumped-up instructors with big gobs and big sticks stop me. Plus, it was not all bad news, and I got on well with some great lads. We had some good laughs and a bit of banter, and because we were all going through the same shit, we supported and helped each other. It was this sort of camaraderie that saw us through the training.

One thing we enjoyed doing was climbing the mast. It was about 143 feet high and was designed like the masts on the old sailing ships. The first time we had to climb it, I was shitting bricks because it was massive, but I soon got into it. I never actually made it to the very top, which is called the button. I did managed to shimmy some of the way past the fourteen feet of the cow horns, which was the last section of the mast before the button. There was a safety net round the bottom of the mast, but I think that was just for show because if you fell from quite high up, no safety net was going to help.

In 1968 John Noakes from Blue Peter did a documentary about the mast, and he got as far as I did. Looking back, we must have been barmy. It was huge and dangerous, especially if it was windy, but to us it was something to do, and it was much better than marching or scrubbing the deck.

The day after my sixteenth birthday, on 7th March, City won the League Cup against West Bromwich Albion. With all the attacking power we had, it was down to two Manchester City defenders, who were also dyed in the wool City fans, to score the goals. Mike Doyle and Glyn Pardoe scored the goals for us. Out of the eleven players and one substitute, there were eleven English players, and the one Scottish player was defender Arthur Mann. In the final of the European Cup Winners Cup the same year, all the players were English. It was a brilliant achievement. City were also the last team to win the league in 1968 with all English players. We must wonder how come nowadays clubs in England in general, and City in particular, cannot produce the same quality players from our own shores. They instead spend millions on recruiting players from abroad. Teams abroad seem to have no problem recruiting quality players. Some of the bigger clubs in England are lucky if there are more than a couple of English players in the team. No wonder the National Team have not done well over the last few decades.

The only downside was that I did not get to watch the game, and I certainly didn't get a drink to celebrate. I had to wait to read all about it the week later, when my regular Manchester football pink (sports paper) arrived from home.

While still serving at HMS *Ganges*, our recruitment was selected to be the window ladder display team. It consisted of the riggers, which included me erecting a sixty-foot-high display unit.

A group of lads had to climb up ropes to music and perform a series of manoeuvres in between the units, which resembled the old window units of the 1950s and 1960s. Then they had to come down the ropes in formation. It was all very impressive, and we performed at many locations down the South of England, including Colchester. The highlight of the performance was performing at the Royal Tournament at Earls Court London, in front of thousands of people. That was some experience for a young kid in those days, but we did not have much time for sightseeing because we were either training, performing, or making sure our kits were immaculate. Even if we did go out into London, considering our wages and the price of stuff in London, we would not be out for long.

We had an open day at HMS *Ganges,* to which my parents came. We performed the window display on the day, and the lads also manned the mast to music. Both events wowed the families that attended.

After about six months in the navy, a lot of us were questioning what the training and displays were all about. Everything was so repetitive, and none of us spent much time training for our respective careers. Like trainees before and after us, we could not understand why we couldn't have more free time and more leave, and why couldn't we wear civvies when off duty. Fuck me, we were never off duty. Loads of stuff we did seemed totally unnecessary. Our views seemed to be born out many years later, when after the school leaving age rose to sixteen, the regime at HMS *Ganges* changed dramatically and for the better.

From 1973 to 1976, when *Ganges* closed, the trainees were only there for a few weeks before they went on to do their part two training at other establishments. HMS *Raleigh* recruits, who joined over sixteen years of age, also only had to do a few weeks training. It is no wonder the longer we were there, the more we thought it was a load of bollocks.

To be honest, our time up there couldn't end quickly enough. Most of the stuff we learnt there was of no importance to us once we joined the fleet. I had a mixture of emotions. Sometimes I hated it, and other times I really enjoyed being there and the things we did. After a while some of the stuff seemed so pointless, but I understood it was all about discipline: we were programmed to instantly obey an order no matter how stupid we thought it was. To be honest, that is one thing that is vital in a seagoing warship, but I don't think it took twelve months for that to sink in.

When we were on the rifle range, it broke the monotony of the normal day, and it was something I was good at and enjoyed. We used to go on the rifle range a couple of times a month, and although it was good fun and gave us something enjoyable to do, how those skills were going to help me with in a galley on a warship was something I did not comprehend. We were taught not just how to fire the guns but also how to strip them down and clean them properly.

Drinking has always been a big tradition in the Royal Navy. When sailors have been at sea for any length of time, there is nothing better than arriving in port to go ashore, let your hair down, and get wasted. Up until 1970, sailors in the Royal Navy were actually issued a tot of rum each day. A tot was on eighth of a pint and was mega proof. The petty officers could have their tots neat. The ordinary ranks had it with two parts water, making their daily ration three-quarters of a pint. Sailors under the age of twenty were not issued a tot, and there was no chance of them getting a tot by mistake because 'UA' was marked next to their name in the ration book, which stood for under age. Going back in the day before the rum ration, the sailors were issued with either beer or wine, the conditions in those days were extremely tough, and the navy probably thought because of the harsh conditions, it was best to keep the crew half pissed and happy all the time.

Over the years, the issue surrounding the rum ration was raised many times. Some in the Admiralty, the House of Lords, and the House of Parliament questioned the wisdom of giving young sailors – tasked with protecting the country, and being in charge of sensitive equipment, maintaining helicopters and planes, and being in control of guns, ammunition, missiles, and torpedoes – a glass containing three-quarters a pint of rum each day. The rum ration finally got abolished in July 1970. When I was still at HMS *Ganges* we all had to muster on the parade ground because there was a big ceremony commemorating the ending of the rum ration not only at HMS *Ganges* but at every ship and shore establishment within the Royal Navy. As trainees we did not really see what all the fuss was about, but to the older sailors it was a big deal because it had played an important part of their navy life. With the rum ration finally coming to an end, sailors over the age of eighteen and at sea were allowed to buy three half-pints of beer a day, but in reality they could usually buy as many as they wanted. A special stamp was issued to commemorate the event, and it could be purchase from the general post office in Portsmouth with the immortal words 'Last Issue of Rum in the Royal Navy, July 1970'.

One of the proudest moments of my life at that time came at the end of my training, when I took part in my passing out parade at HMS *Ganges*. The reason I was so proud is with all the shit they threw at us – the humiliation, the stupid regulations, the lack of leave and free time – I never gave in. The rules were that after three months of training, and then again after six months, you were allowed to buy yourself out. Although I was tempted to buy myself out, I was glad I never did. For one thing, I never had the money. I also knew that once I had passed out and left the Ganges, life in the navy would get better. Well, I could dream, couldn't I?

My parents came to see me at the passing out parade, and they were proud as punch. Just over a year earlier, I had shattered their lives by being arrested and charged under the Larceny Act. Now here I was, marching with my fellow recruits, the band was playing and I was looking very smart in my number ones.

After I left *Ganges*, my next establishment was HMS *Pembroke* in Chatham Kent – the Navy Catering Establishment. I spent the next six weeks doing more cooking there than I did in twelve months at *Ganges*. What really pissed me off though, was that the lads from HMS *Raleigh* who joined us on the same course, because of their age, had only done a few weeks' basic training. We had fucked about for twelve months. I could tell you about and tie every knot known to mankind, run round an assault course with my eyes shut, hit a bullseye with a rifle at one hundred yards, and swim a couple of lengths in a pair of overalls. But what use was that to me in the galley?

I remember we were a bit demoralized at first because we still couldn't wear civvies when we first arrived, but the lads from *Raleigh* could. It was not their fault, and there was no hard feelings from us. After a couple of weeks, we could also wear civvies when off duty or on leave. Going from being in the prison-like regime of *Ganges* to the more liberal *Pembroke* was unreal. There was even a bar we were allowed in because no one asked for ID. We didn't have to double everywhere; in fact, we were treated like humans, which was a great step forward from the previous twelve months.

It is hard to express the difference in types of establishments. At *Ganges* we were humiliated and abused for the slightest thing; we were the lowest of the low. I cannot remember the amount of times I had to stand to attention while some jumped-up instructor shouted in my face, telling me how shit at everything I was. 'You are a trog, you will always be a trog, and you will never fucking pass out.' Whether that was some sort of reverse psychology,

I will never know, but I passed out with flying colours, so '*fuck-em*'.

Once at HMS *Pembroke,* the regime changed dramatically. Even though it was still very much disciplined, it was much more relaxed than *Ganges*. We even had a pay rise, so we got about eight pounds a week, plus I was no longer Jack second class and was just called Jack. Another plus was when we started at *Ganges,* the navy had opened an account at the post office for us, and each week they had put ten shillings (fifty pence) in. When at *Pembroke,* we were given our post office account book with twenty-five pounds in it. Fuck me, I thought I was rich!

The two things I remember about that place was the first time I ever threw up after drinking. As I said before, I was never a big drinker, and at *Ganges* I had no chance of improving my skills. At the bar at *Pembroke,* they weren't arsed about your age; most lads were much older than me and were hardened drinkers. When they were drinking rum, I thought, *Man up, Don. Get in there and show them how it's done.* It wasn't long till I fucked off wasted, staggering back to my mess. Before I got there, I threw up behind a building. I always remember hearing the record by the group Chairman of the Board singing, 'Give me just a little more time.' There is some shit in your life you can't forget.

The other thing that amazed me was that we were allowed out every night and every weekend if we were not on duty. I think that when most ratings from HMS *Ganges,* went on to their part two training establishments, they must have thought, 'What the fuck was the last twelve months all about?' I really enjoyed my time at *Pembroke.* That was where I first learned to make cakes, bake bread and learn loads of new skills. I really enjoyed my time there, so the six weeks flew by.

We even had TVs in a lounge so we could watch Match of the Day on a Saturday without having to be in bed by 10.00 p.m. It was such a strange feeling to be treated like scum and shit for twelve months, and then like normal human beings once we left *Ganges.* Maybe other lads who were there at the time might have different memories, but these were certainly the recollections of the stuff I experienced.

I got my first tattoo while I was based at Chatham, I thought I was a proper sea dog, or an old salt, as veteran sailors are called. It was soon after that that I was on my travels again.

Chapter 5

HMS *Dolphin*

After leaving HMS *Pembroke*, I joined the Royal Navy Submarine Base HMS *Dolphin*, which was in Gosport and just over the water from Portsmouth. Whenever you joined a new ship or establishment, you had to take all your kit with you, and it just about fit into your kit bag and suitcase. I was five feet nothing and weighed less than Victoria Beckham, so carrying this lot was a huge challenge – in fact, it was a fucking nightmare, I looked like a typical drunken sailor even though I was stone cold sober. I staggered about under all the weight, and how I got to the submarine base at all was a bit of a miracle. I am sure the passengers on the trains and busses thought it was funny as fuck, with me trying to get on and off with all my gear. The fucking kitbag was nearly the same size as me. When I was about two hundred yards away from the mess, some kind-hearted submariner came to my aid. I don't know what he was fed on, but he carried it as though it weighed fuck all; he even bounced up the steps and plonked it on my bed. I met him a few times around the base over the next few months, and he always ribbed me that I was a weakling. Nothing's changed there.

Once I put my kit away, I got a brew from the NAAFI (Navy. Army. Air Force. Institute) which refers to cafés and shops on ships and shore establishments. I had a walk around to get used to my new surroundings, and I was soon in awe of the place, especially where the subs were berthed; it was truly an amazing sight. There were loads of sailors going about their daily tasks, and there were about a dozen subs there altogether. The smell of diesel and seawater was something that sticks with you for ages. Some of the older lads let on to me because they could see I was a fresh-faced, awestruck little runt. For someone who was not yet seventeen, it was exciting stuff. Over the months I was there, I never got bored of going down to see where the subs were berthed, having a look at what was going on, and watching them load and unload the torpedoes, which was a mission in itself. I could not help but be impressed with the skill of the crew carrying out that task. Watching the submarines going out to sea and returning to their berths was a great sight and was something I was never tired of doing.

The reason I was at HMS *Dolphin* was to carry on with my catering training in order for me to be up to the required standard for when I joined a seagoing ship in about twelve months' time. This was something else omitted from the recruitment officer back in Manchester. I could still see the pictures of sun-kissed beaches in faraway, exotic places. Instead of being in Gibraltar and lying on a beach with an ice-cold beer, I would be at Gosport for the next twelve months. If being at *Pembroke* was totally different from *Ganges,* this place and the regime was on a different planet altogether. Like HMS *Pembroke,* you were allowed to wear civvies and go ashore when off duty, without having to ask anyone's permission.

I was still a junior and not yet seventeen, so I had one or two restrictions placed on me, but they didn't give me any grief. I still had to do kit inspections now and again to make sure it was all up to standard and I hadn't sold any of it, but there was no more washing it by hand and drying it on the radiator; they had launderettes that we could use. We were no longer shouted at or abused 24/7; we were treated with dignity and respect, and older sailors helped us and took us under their wings. There was no marching everywhere we went, and no getting shouted at for no reason by sadistic instructors. I worked in both the petty officers' galley and the ratings galley, which was a fantastic experience. At long last I was glad I had joined up. I was doing something worthwhile and was enjoying my new environment while I learned new skills.

I was in a team with a leading cook and two qualified cooks. For the first time I really started to enjoy my life in the navy, plus I got another pay rise. I grew in confidence because I got praised if I did things well. I learnt a hell of a lot in those twelve months. Sometimes I had to deliver stores to the submarines, and I loved going on them, talking to the submariners, and dreaming of one day going to sea in one. The conditions in the subs were very grim, and due to the lack of space, everything was very cramped, but they had ingenious ways of placing things in every nook and cranny to store all the equipment. Although it was very claustrophobic, none of the submariners complained; they were all volunteers, and all of them loved the life.

When they were berthed alongside the jetty, they didn't eat or sleep on board the subs except for the ones on duty. They were billeted in their own mess and came to the mess hall, where we served them their meals.

I had only been there a couple of months when I went home on leave for Christmas and New Year.

City played Huddersfield on Boxing Day, and I can remember it was freezing. My mate Derbo came with me, and in those days you could get a bus straight there from the Woodthorpe Hotel, which was a pub in Prestwich near my house. The bus took us near the ground. We met quite a few lads that I knew from Prestwich at the pubs near Maine Road, and even though we only drew, I had a few pints and a good laugh. It was great to meet up with lads I had not seen for ages.

Whilst I was on leave, we also played Liverpool away. One of the other juniors at *Dolphin* was a lad called Phil. He was from Bury and wasn't a big City fan, but he enjoyed his football, so we decided to go to the game. I had never been to Anfield before but had heard it was a scary place for away fans. We were chuffed to bits when we saw the football special train went from Manchester, Victoria Train Station. The train was absolutely packed with City fans. When we arrived at the Lime Street train station in Liverpool, there were a few scallies giving us abuse, but because there were hundreds of us, they couldn't do fuck all except try to act hard. In reality, they looked like a load of dickheads.

We walked to the ground, stopping for a few beers on the way. When we got to the ground, there was a few Scouser's near our end up to no good. I have never been a fashion guru, but I had recently spent my hard-earned money on the latest fashion in clobber: a black Harrington jacket. My mate and I were looking to see which turnstile to go in. A couple of young Scouser's approached me and said, 'Give us your Harrington Jacket la' I looked at them, unsure if I had heard them right. One of them repeated it. Well, if he wanted, it he would have to rip it off my back because I wasn't going to hand it over to him. I didn't want a fight, but because there was nowhere to run, I called his bluff and shouted at him to fuck off. At the same time, I kept walking with my mate a few yards to where the older Blues were. The Scouser left me alone and went on his merry way, no doubt looking for some other unsuspecting fan to rob.

The match finished 0-0, which never was a bad result at Liverpool. On the way to the ground, all the City fans were together, but while leaving the ground, everyone split up into smaller groups. Phil and I kept to ourselves, and about forty yards in front of us was a group of about twenty-five older City fans. Suddenly they were attacked by a group of about sixty Liverpool fans for absolutely no reason other than they were City fans. Phil and I didn't get hit because they must have either thought we were not worth attacking or were a couple of Scouser's. Either way, it was over in seconds, with the City fans scattering. One fan was in a bad way on the floor, I managed to get him to his feet and half carry, half drag him to a nearby pub, all the time thinking they were going to come back and give us both a good hiding. Thank fuck they did not, and I got the landlord to phone us a taxi. I got a quick rum as well to calm my nerves, hoping the fuckers were not waiting for us outside. Luckily the coast was clear. When we arrived back at the Lime Street train station, there were a few scuffles going on, but the police soon got on top of it, I soon found my mate Phil; he had ran most of the way to the station but never got hit. The lad I'd picked up was also reunited with his mates. The sign at the ground said, 'Welcome to Anfield.' What a fucking joke.

In the same season, we also played West Ham United at Upton Park. They were another set of fans with a scary reputation, but that didn't stop me or another mate nicknamed Spider (his last name was Webb) from going. We took the train from Portsmouth to London and then made our way to Euston Train Station. We were there at about 11.30am and enquired about what time the football special would be arriving from Manchester, only to be told there wasn't one. Any fans coming would be on the normal service train. It wasn't cheap on the Manchester to Euston train, so I didn't think many would be on it. We went in the Royal George, the nearest pub to Euston. Later on a few City fans came in, and we had a chat. I didn't know them, but they were all sound lads. When they asked me how I got to London, I felt really proud and six feet tall when I told them I was in the Royal Navy and was serving at the submarine base in Gosport. I am sure they thought I was full of shit at first because I did not look old enough to leave school, never mind serve in the navy. After a couple of drinks with them, we left to go to the game.

We got to the ground at 2.30 p.m., and if there were any City fans about, they were keeping low profiles because I couldn't see any. Just before kick-off, a group of about sixty Blues started singing. We joined them, as did more and more City fans. Obviously this brought lots of attention, and we were quickly surrounded by West Ham fans. I thought we were going to get battered because apart from legging it across the pitch, there was nowhere to go. I don't remember any physical violence, which I was very pleased about, only a lot of abuse and piss taking. I'd had twelve months of piss taking and abuse at HMS *Ganges,* so that was water off a duck's back to me. After the game, which was a 0-0 result, Spider and I kept a low profile as we made our way back to Euston. Even though by then I had been on the underground system a few times, it was still pot luck if I got on the right tube or not.

Spider was a very good football player, and before he joined the navy, he was a junior footballer with Swindon Town. If he hadn't joined the navy, there was a good chance he could have made it as a professional footballer. He invited me to his house in Swindon for a weekend on a couple of occasions, because it was quicker than going up to Manchester. I jumped at the chance. The first time we went, we hitched it because money was in short supply. I remember for quite a distance we got a lift with a load of hippies in the back of a van. They were dressed weird but they were friendly enough, and it was nice of them to give us a lift.

On the Saturday, Swindon were playing away at Bristol, and Spider's mates were going. We went with them on the football special, had a few beers, and got in the ground without any mither. Once in the ground, it was a different kettle of fish. Even though there were hundreds of Swindon fans, the Bristol lot were well up for a fight. We stood next to two massive Swindon fans and were pretty much left alone. In those days, violence at football grounds was rife. There was little in the ways of segregation, and the policing of games left a lot to be desired. At half-time I was drinking a lovely cup of tea until a Bristol fan kicked it out of my hand and threatened me with violence. Fortunately for me, I spotted the two massive Swindon fans and stood with them. The little shit who wanted to kick the living daylights out of me did not fancy his chances now that I was with my new best mates.

Another occasion I went to Swindon was in pre-season. I can't remember who they played, but a game is a game, so we went to watch Swindon in a friendly on a lovely afternoon. Spider's mates made me very welcome again, and I had a good laugh with them and a few drinks. It was another smashing weekend leave.

Southampton is not too far from Portsmouth, and I had the weekend off when Chelsea played them in the league. I had never been to Southampton before, so Spider and I went to watch the game. There were loads of Chelsea fans there because it is easy to get there from London, and it was a great atmosphere and a great game. Chelsea went on to win 3-0. In those days, Chelsea were a team well worth watching because they played some great football. If I wanted to watch the Southampton and Chelsea game nowadays, it would be impossible to turn up and pay to get in; I would need a membership card and would have to buy tickets in advance, plus a ticket would cost a fortune. In those days, for the vast majority of games at most grounds, you could just turn up and pay to get in. It did not cost much to watch football at most grounds in the 1970s.

Whilst based at Gosport, it was not long before we had a run-in with the local lads. I didn't have a problem with them, but their problem with us was that we were in the navy and were in their pubs. One run-in we had with them ended when someone jabbed me in the side of my head with the pointed bit of a man's umbrella. It was not worth moaning about, and though it bled a little, it did not need any stitches. The police were about and collared the group who attacked us. I had no intention of pressing charges, so the police had no option but to let them go. It would not have done my street credentials any good to admit to be being assaulted by an umbrella. Quite often we used to see them knocking about, and it wasn't long before they thought we were ok and not full of shit, so most of them got on with us. I think it also helped that I did not press charges when I got whacked with a brolly. They were all big Portsmouth fans, and we often went to see the Pompey games with them. One of the lads I got on well with was called Frank, he and his close mates were sound lads.

One game was against Birmingham City. The Brummies' brought loads of fans down, and fortunately there was segregation in place. There were loads of the usual banter between home and away fans, but unfortunately the police weren't too keen on us having a laugh and ejected some of us from the ground. I didn't know the lads who got thrown out with me, but they were quick to spot I had a different accent. At first they thought I might have been a Birmingham fan, but after telling them I was in the navy and a Man City fan, I thought all would be OK. It didn't defuse the situation as much as I would have liked it, and I thought it was on the cards that I might get filled in by them. Lucky for me, Frank and some other lads from Gosport also got slung out a few minutes after me, and they vouched for me. We didn't get to see the rest of the game, so we went back to Gosport to wait for the pubs to open.

At the submarine base, we were getting more time off and had more money. The other juniors and I drank a bit more regularly. On one occasion we were in the George and Dragon, a pub not far from the base that was mainly frequented by submariners and the ship's company from HMS *Dolphin*. Fortunately for us, the landlord wasn't strict with his opening and closing times, so it was dead handy for a drink most of the day. On one occasion I thought I was Jack the lad, and before I went back to base, I finished my drinking session with a double rum. I walked back with three older lads, and it was the first time I could not remember getting back. It was a bit frightening in the morning, and I thought, *'How the fuck can I not remember?'* That was the first of many occasions when I couldn't remember a night out or getting back to base. I also remember being rough as fuck in the morning and wanting the day off. There was no chance of that happening and I got little sympathy from the rest of the chefs. In fact, the bastards took great delight in my discomfort, and every time I legged it to the heads to throw up, they would take the piss. I swore I would never drink again, and as soon as my shift was finished, I went back to the mess, got my head down, and felt very sorry for myself.

I hadn't been at the base too long when I made the decision to apply to become a submariner. My initial request was turned down because I wasn't even seventeen years of age, but I was determined to try again.

I was on home leave for my seventeenth birthday, and I went for a drink with my mate Derbo. City were playing at home to Wolverhampton Wanderers, so we went for a drink in Whitefield before the match. Before we knew it, it was gone 2.00 p.m., so getting to the game on time wasn't going to happen. Bury was only fifteen minutes away on the bus, and they were playing Bristol Rovers, so we decided to go and watch the *Shakers* play instead. We did not have membership cards or tickets like you have to now a days but we just strolled up and paid to get in. We stood with the Bury fans, and I knew some of them from when we used to watch Bury when we were at school. One of the older lads resented the fact I was a City fan and started gobbing off at me. Not wanting any hassle, I started to move away. The bastard then pushed me, and because I was off balance, it sent me flying down the steps. I just can't remember the exact words I said to him, but it was along the lines of, 'Stop being a dickhead. Why don't you just fuck off?'

Before I could move on, the police arrested the pair of us. I could not believe it. I hadn't intended to watch Bury in the first fucking place! I explained to the police and also to the police sergeant at Bury exactly what had happened, but they could not care less. I had not even raised my hands, and in fairness to the other lad, he hadn't even swung a punch. He'd just pushed me. Fuck me, I had been pushed harder on the school playground. To get arrested for this was a complete joke. We were both charged with breach of the peace, which I found out was the lowest of the public order acts you can be charged with. No doubt the police got a bonus that day. Even though I was in the navy and it was my birthday, they didn't change their minds about charging me. At least I had a bit of luck: they let me out after a couple of hours, and I was able to meet up with Derbo and the lads for a drink. I got really pissed to celebrate my birthday and drown my sorrows.

The date I had to go to court was when I was due my next lot of leave, thank fuck. I thought I wouldn't have to tell my parents because they would have gone ballistic, and I wouldn't have to tell the navy either. I thought it crazy from the police's point of view to arrest and charge me. My main thoughts though were, *Thank God my parents and the navy are not going to find out that I was arrested.* Well, that's what I thought, anyway. I duly went to court, pleaded guilty, and got a ten-pound fine. I paid it straight away and thought that was the end of the matter. How wrong I was.

About three weeks later, my divisional officer called me into his office. He had been informed by the courts about my arrest, and the fact that I had pleaded guilty and had been fined. He then read the riot act to me. He was annoyed and disappointed – not so much that I was arrested, because he said shit like that can happen. What he was mad about was that I didn't tell him, if I had, he would have got me legal advice and would have advised me to plead not guilty. As sod law happened, now that he knew about me being arrested and fined, he had to punish me for bringing the navy into disrepute. I got another fine and a stoppage of leave for a week. I will never forget that birthday in a hurry. He was not in the best of moods, so I thought it wasn't the right time to ask about reapplying to join the submarine section of the Royal Navy.

Apart from the odd hiccup, life at HMS *Dolphin* went really well. There was a bar on the site, so if we wanted a drink and didn't want to go out, it was dead handy. I got to know many people and learned lots of stuff from more experienced chefs. We had a few perks too. From time to time, we had to help out with the cocktail parties the officers hosted. That was great because the stewards always sorted us out with a drink or two. Also, from time to time I had to do other duties, and I took my turn a couple of times per month as part of the evening patrol of the base. That was a piss take. I was given a tin hat, a wooden stick with a bit of brass fastened to the end, a torch, and a whistle. I had to walk around the insides of the perimeter to make sure no one who shouldn't be on the base got on the base. I used to shit myself. There I was, only seventeen years and patrolling on my own in the middle of the night. I was never sure who was supposed to come to my aid if I was attacked and I had to blow my whistle.

One building that stood out at HMS *Dolphin* was the Royal Navy's Submarine Escape Training Tank. It was a hundred-foot deep water facility primarily used to conduct submarine escape training. All submariners in the Royal Navy have to be trained in the escape procedure. Such was its worldwide reputation as a centre of excellence that submariners from many different countries trained there. The Tower was also privately hired by civilian diving clubs to practice deep diving training.

I often tried to talk the instructors into letting me have a practice, but they said there was no fucking chance. Three crew members of the submarine Artemis would be extremely grateful for the training they received, and the 1st July 1971 will stick in my mind forever. Spider, Phil, and I had been ashore to buy some new clobber because we were going out that evening to sample a few drinks and then head to a nightclub in Portsmouth. We were just getting ready to go back out when the shit hit the fan. The submarine Artemis had sunk while berthed up alongside at Haslar Creek at HMS *Dolphin*. You may be thinking, 'He is winding us up. A submarine sinking while tied up at a naval base? That can't be right!' I kid you not. Even though nobody in their wildest dreams could have imagined a submarine sinking while moored up, policies and procedures were in place in case the unthinkable happened. The base was soon in lockdown, and no one was allowed off the base, so that scuppered my plans for a night on the tiles. What made it even more embarrassing for the navy was that the Artemis had just undergone a very expensive refit, and it happened at the submarine services headquarters.

The Artemis was an A-class submarine which first came into service in 1946. She was 280 feet long and weighed 1,360 tons. She was being refuelled when water started gushing through the hatch. The torpedo bay at the rear escape hatch had also been left open so that power cables could go to the control room. It took only fifteen minutes to sink in nine metres of water, leaving three crew members trapped inside. There were also a group of sea cadets on board as well, but the duty petty officer managed to get them out before going back below to try to shut what hatches he could, and to see if anyone else was trapped. There were two other ratings on board, but because of the amount of water coming in, they had to shut themselves in the forward compartment. An amazing rescue operation swung into action. I and many other chefs stayed up all night making soup; bacon, sausage, and egg butties; tea; and coffee for the hundreds of people who took part in the rescue. TV crews and loads of press were allowed into the restaurant area, and we fed them all night as well. After about thirteen hours of being trapped, all three were safely rescued and emerged through the forward escape hatch. For a seventeen-year-old kid like me, it was pretty exciting stuff to watch such an operation unfold and also be a part of it. The sub was never brought back into service and was scrapped a few years later. Three people did get a guilty verdict at the court martial that followed the incident, but no senior officers were on board at the time, and no senior officer was charged with any offense. There is an old saying that the shit always falls to the bottom. It was a PR disaster and a shambles for the Royal Navy. I would have to wait a few more days till I could go out in my new clobber to the pubs and clubs of Portsmouth.

While at HMS *Dolphin,* some of the submarines that were based there were to take part in exercises with the French Navy, and they were to be based at Brest, which was in Brittany in the North West area of France. An advance party had to go across to set up the accommodations, get transport and communications sorted out, to man a liaison and transport office. They also wanted two chefs to go as well because they were not sure the submariners would take to well to the local French cuisine. It was to my utter surprise but total delight that I was to be one of the chefs selected to go with the advance team. Fuck me seventeen years old and getting paid to go to France! I had never been abroad before, so I was delighted to go. We went in a convoy of Royal Navy busses, trucks, and Land Rovers. Even though the busses were still uncomfortable, it was a small price to pay for three weeks in France. Everything was smooth and efficient, and we were soon on and off the ferry.

We arrived at the huge naval base in Brest to prepare for our submarines arriving. As it happens, my services as a chef were not required because the French were upset at the thought that their food would not be to our standards. In order to avoid any ill feelings, the French chefs were left on their own to cook the food. I wasn't arsed because I was in France, and they were not sending me back. Instead, I was allocated other duties, one of which was getting up early and making one of the officers a cup of coffee in the morning. Mainly I was a passenger in the Land Rover, delivering letters and parcels and taking sailors to and from the submarines. I had a fantastic three weeks and loved every minute of it. I thought this was what being in the navy was all about.

When it was time to go back to the UK, one of the submarine chefs took ill and had to go to hospital. I was asked if I could take his place in the submarine. Too right I would! But after a bit of deliberation it was decided they couldn't take the risk because I wasn't yet eighteen, and I hadn't undergone training in the submarine escape training tank. I was gutted, but hey, shit happens. On the bright side, I had a great sun tan after three weeks in France.

As soon as I got back to the UK, I put in another request to become a submariner. Once again my request was declined. My divisional officer, Lieutenant Stewart, explained that it would be in my best interest to get the experience of a seagoing ship. Once I had the experience, I could reapply then. I still had about three more months to go at Dolphin, and I was raring to go to sea because travelling to France whetted my appetite for adventure.

The great thing about being based at Gosport was it wasn't far to London. If City were playing there, I could usually get to see them. Arsenal had a great team at the time, Highbury was an awesome ground, and the fans didn't have a scary reputation like others in London did. I watched City play at Arsenal loads of times, and it was probably my favourite ground in London. It was dead easy to get to from Euston, and when I went to games in London, I usually went to Euston to either meet mates I knew were coming. The Royal George was a decent pub and was just outside the station and I usually met someone in there that I knew.

One of the best games I went to see in London was Chelsea against City in the FA Cup's third round at Stamford Bridge. As I got off the Portsmouth to London train proudly wearing my City scarf, I was staggered to see hundreds of Arsenal fans queuing up to get the train to Portsmouth. That was who they had drawn in the cup. What a dickhead I was. I knew they were playing Pompey because Frank and his mates were going to it, so why didn't I click they would be on the platform to get their train? I would have hidden my scarf if I had realized. In order to get out of the station, I had to walk through them all. I braced myself for loads of abuse and a couple of slaps, but my fears were unfounded. They were great and let me through with no hassle. Many commented on how they hoped City beat Chelsea. I found out later that there was massive crowd trouble before, during, and after the game at Portsmouth, so maybe they were not all so nice after all.

I made my way to Euston to meet my mate Johnny, who had some money that my mum had given him for me, because as usual I was a bit skint. Then it was off to the Royal George for a couple of pints. I later met up with my brother Bob and some other lads whom I knew. Unlike the West Ham game, when there weren't many City fans there, because it was a cup game there was about eight to ten thousand Blues at Stamford Bridge, and we went onto win the game 3-0, which was a great result considering how good a team Chelsea were at the time.

Later on in the year, I went to Chelsea again for the semi-final of the European Cup Winners Cup Final. It was a night game, and I was home on leave in Manchester at the time, but wild horses would not stop me from getting to that game. Piccadilly Train Station in Manchester was awash with City fans, with trains departing to London every fifteen minutes. There were estimates of up to twenty thousand City fans being in Stamford Bridge for the game. We got beat 1-0 but didn't think it was a problem because we had the return leg to come at Maine Road, and we thought we would easily overcome the score line. Unfortunately it was not to be, and we got beat 1-0 at our ground as well.

While at HMS *Dolphin,* I got to watch loads of football, which was great for me and was a big change from when I'd been at HMS *Ganges.* I only managed the odd games when I was in Manchester on home leave. One of the strangest games I went to was a friendly at Port Vale before the season started. I was home on leave, and Port Vale was near Stoke and was not too far away from Manchester. Derbo and I, along with loads of others from Prestwich and Whitefield, went on the train. There were hundreds of City fans there, and it was a great atmosphere in the pubs near the ground. Port Vale never usually got big crowds, and their fans were not known for football violence, so crowd trouble was the last thing we expected as we entered the ground. We climbed up the steps to the end we had been allocated, and we quickly realised all was not calm and the shit was hitting the fan big time. There were hundreds of Stoke City fans in the stands, ready to kick off with the City fans. If we were playing Stoke at Stoke's ground, I would have expected trouble, but for that many fans to turn up at a ground where they were not even playing stretches anyone's imagination to the limit, and of course they were not there to watch the game but to cause havoc and fight with the City fans, which they did for most of the game. There was little or no policing at the game, and there was virtually no segregation, so fans could wander around the ground whenever they wanted. I have no recollection of what the game was like or the score; I was simply pleased to get out of the ground in one piece. The next time I went to Port Vale's ground was many years later, and I am pleased to report there was not a Stoke fan in sight. The daft thing is those sort of incidents did not put most people off from going to the games.

After nearly twelve months at HMS *Dolphin*, my divisional officer called me into his office for a meeting and asked me what I thought about joining a Royal Navy frigate in Hong Kong in three weeks' time, I was gobsmacked when he told me that I would be flown to Hong Kong. The ship would then visit Singapore, South Africa, East Africa, Bahrain, Gibraltar, and other far-flung places before returning to Plymouth six months later. I could not believe what I was hearing. He had a big grin on his face because he knew I would jump at the chance. He also signed me off for two weeks home leave; that would give me a couple of days when I got back to HMS *Dolphin* to sort out my kit and get all the travel details sorted.

The next day I was in Manchester making everyone pig sick and jealous after telling them where I was going. The great thing about the navy was that they would sort out all the details for me; all I had to do was turn up at the right place and at the right time, I did not even go out for a farewell drink with the lads at *Dolphin*, or even with Frank and his mates in Gosport, because I did not want to do anything to mess up this opportunity. I said my farewells over a few cups of tea in the NAAFI.

CHAPTER 6

Joining HMS Achilles

The flight to Hong Kong was on a Royal Air Force flight from RAF Brize Norton in Oxfordshire. Here I was, seventeen years of age and on my own, travelling halfway around the world to join my first seagoing ship. At long last the stuff the recruitment officer had told me in Manchester two years previously was about to come true. This was the first time I had been in an aeroplane, and the RAF planes were certainly not built for comfort. There was no drinking alcohol on the plane, and I remember my ears kept popping and they were killing me. After a few hours we landed at an island in the Indian Ocean to refuel, and we were able to get off the plane for three hours to freshen up and get something to eat and drink. That was the first time I came across a lovely drink called Tiger Beer. I was with some older lads, but the problem was I tried to drink as quickly as them. They were also having gin, and it wasn't long before I was steaming.

On the way back to the plane I threw up near the steps as I was getting on it much to the horror of the RAF officer, because bits of my sick splattered over his shiny shoes. As soon as I got back on the plane, I went to the toilet, locked the door, and threw up again. Soon someone was banging on the door because they couldn't take off until I sat down. When I came out, I must have looked a right state, and they were ready to throw me off the plane because I was too pissed. Fortunately some of the older lads said they would look after me, and they convinced the flight crew I would be OK. Thank fuck for that. I would have been up shit creek without a paddle if I had got kicked off, because I did not have a clue when the next RAF plane would land – or indeed, whether they would have let me on. All's well that ends well. Next stop: Singapore. We would stop there for a couple of hours, and then Hong Kong here we come. Well, that was what I thought.

When we got off at Singapore, I was told a navy liaison officer wanted to see me. I thought, '*Oh, fuck. I'm in the shit now for being drunk and throwing up*'. I was relieved to find out it wasn't for that, but to inform me that I wouldn't be going to Hong

Kong after all because the ship was in Singapore. How the hell did that happen? Thirty-six hours previously, I was at HMS *Dolphin* being told the ship was in Hong Kong. Apparently it had been in Singapore for a few days. Talk about lack of communication! I said my kit bag was still on the plane and asked if I get it off before the plane left for Hong Kong, because I needed my stuff, but he said because it was labelled for Hong Kong, it was going to have to go to Hong Kong; I would get it in about four days. It was not my fault, so I did not give a shit. On the plus side, I would not have to struggle carrying my kit onto the ship. I might not be going to Hong Kong, but Hayho, Singapore was a good substitute.

The first thing that hit me about Singapore, or Singers as it was known to the older sea dogs, was the heat as it was stifling hot, and I was sweating buckets within minutes. As we approached the dockyard where the ship was docked, I was dumbstruck by the sight in front of me. When I first saw Royal Navy ships in Portsmouth, the hairs on the back of my neck stood up because it was a fascinating sight to see ships of all shapes and sizes looking immaculate with the White Ensign flying. Here in Singapore there were ships from many different countries, and the sight was amazing. I stood watching as hundreds of people went about their duties, and it seemed so unreal.

England still had a large presence in the Far East with army and navy bases in both Singapore and Hong Kong. Even though the British forces were preparing to withdraw from Singapore, it still played an important role for the Royal Navy in terms of keeping a presence in the Far East.

I was soon welcomed on board my new ship, HMS *Achilles*, which was a Leander-class frigate. Amongst other things, it was equipped for antisubmarine warfare. The mess deck took me by surprise, and I couldn't believe how a room so small would be able to allow so many people to sleep there. I quickly realized Royal Navy ships were not designed with the comfort of the crew in mind. There was much more space and comfort than on the submarines, though. The galley was also very small and nothing like I had ever worked in before. It didn't bother me because I was on one big adventure. Another nice surprise was the fact we had a laundry, which was run by three Chinese people who would do you're washing and ironing for a small charge. Where were these guys when I had my kit inspections?

I was still not eighteen, and so when I was on shore leave, I had to be back on the ship by 1.00 a.m. That was never going to be a problem because the heat and the drink drained me well before then. While in Singapore, we went to sea for a couple of days to take part in some exercises. When the ship returned, it went into dry dock for about a week for routine maintenance and a makeover. We were put up at HMS *Terror*, the Royal Navy base in an area called Sembawang. It was great for me because there was no cooking for a few days, so it was a nice, relaxing time. There were regular inter-forces football matches which had to be played in the evenings because of the heat, as it was still very warm and sticky. It was a great way to relax, and the standard was pretty good. I never got picked to play, but I don't think I would have lasted five minutes in that heat. The beaches were fantastic, and the street food in Singapore was delicious even though I did not have a clue what I was eating half the time; I think that was half the fun about it.

One place that was very popular with servicemen, sailors, and visitors from all over the world was an area called Bugis Street. It came to life late at night and was frequented by Kai Tais. These were the equivalent of the lady boys from Bangkok, and many unsuspecting punters got more than they bargained for when they went for a night of passion with them. The hotels were great to visit, relax, and have a drink, but they were far too dear to stay at. I loved my time in Singapore. Looking back I should have done more sightseeing and taken more photos. That was the same regret I had in nearly every country I visited over the years. After nearly three weeks in Singapore, we set sail, and I resumed my seagoing adventures.

One of the most unusual places we visited on the tour was an island called St Helena. It is a small tropical island in the middle of nowhere in the South Atlantic. Its population at the time was only about 4,000, and it was about 2,500 miles from Brazil and nearly 1,200 miles from Africa. At the time there was no airport, so the only way on or off the island was by boat. The nearest land to it is the Ascension Islands, which is just over 800 miles away, so it is a fair old journey if you want to leave. To this day, I don't know why we went there. We were only there for about six hours, and because I was one of the chefs on duty, I couldn't go ashore. I remember all the locals turning out to look at the ship; it wasn't every day that a Royal Navy frigate dropped in to say hello. St Helena was where the British exiled Napoleon about two hundred years ago.

Our ship had a crew of 240. There were two petty officers and nine chefs to feed them. Two chefs plus a petty officer served the officers, and there were about twenty-four officers. Then there was one petty officer and seven chefs to feed the rest of the crew. It was very demanding but enjoyable work. Besides working in the galley, there were plenty of other duties for me. We used to practice fire drills because if a fire broke out, we all had roles to play to make sure it didn't spread and was put out swiftly. If a major fire broke out, there was little chance of other ships coming to our aid any time soon. Man overboard exercises were performed regularly because if someone went over the side, depending on the temperature of the sea, they wouldn't survive long; the quicker they were rescued, the better their survival rate was. When at action stations, where it was simulated we were under attack or mounting an attack ourselves, I was to help load shells into the gun turret. That was very tiring in hot and cramped conditions, and it was noisy as fuck when the guns went off. I nearly shit myself the first time they went off, but I just had to grin and bear it and like everything else I had to do it was not long till I got used to it. The shells were quite heavy, and occasionally I would drop the frigging things. Good job the foot wear I was issued with included proper safety boots, otherwise my feet would have suffered some serious damage. It was also reassuring to know that even when I dropped the shells on the floor, they could not detonate. That was a big fucking relief! We also took part in all sorts of exercises with other ships, submarines, and aeroplanes, so we were never bored.

I used to enjoy being on the upper deck on my own, having a brew, staring out at the sea, and wondering what I could spot. If we were exercising with submarines, I never got bored of watching them coming to the surface or submerging; it was so graceful. It was also a bit special to watch the sunsets and sunrises in different parts of the world. It was a very relaxing way to spend a bit of downtime, chilling out and watching the world go by.

On Saturdays, everyone looked forward to the football results, which were piped out through the ship's tannoy system. There was always plenty of banter amongst the different rival fans. Another highlight was the mail drop, when an RAF plane would literally drop the sack of mail into the sea near the ship, and then we would launch a boat to pick it up. I was not that bothered whether or not I received any letters; the main thing I looked out for was my copy of the *Manchester Evening News* football pink, with the results of previous week's games and all the news, gossip, and scandal of the football and sporting icons in Manchester and the UK.

When Royal Navy ships are at sea for any period of time, vital supplies run out sooner or later because there is limited storage space. On many occasions, ships operate hundreds of miles away from land and cannot simply pull out of operations or exercises to top up on their supplies. Over the years, the practice of replenishing ships at sea, or RAS for short, has been developed to a fine art. It is a very hazardous operation, but the skill of the crews make it look very easy and straightforward. A supply ship will travel at the same speed and course as the ship that needs supplying and come alongside at a distance of thirty to forty yards away. A course so close to each other represents a massive challenge, so excellent communication is vital because a slight steering error by any of the ships could lead to a collision. A line is sent over from the supply ship, and then a rig is set up so the supplies can come across. This operation can take place in all weathers, in rough or calm seas, and in daylight or darkness. Most of the crew are involved and muster on the deck. As the supplies come on board, they pass it to each other to get it below decks and stowed away as quickly as possible. Sometimes this can take two or three hours, depending on how much stores are coming on board. At the end of a RAS, everyone is well and truly knackered, but they cannot stop for a rest because then they have to carry on with normal duties. When being replenished with fuel, a similar procedure takes place, except the fuel hoses will be attached straight to the fuel nozzles and get pumped directly into the fuel tanks. The risk of an explosion while this is taking place is very real, and safety procedures have been devised. Ships also practice at breaking away in the event of an emergency. Wherever Royal Navy ships are, the supply ships of the Royal Fleet Auxiliary are usually not far behind; they are like floating warehouses and stock vital supplies.

The Christmas after I joined HMS *Achilles* saw us as one of only four Royal Navy ships at sea over the Christmas and New Year period. In all, we were at sea for six weeks on Beira patrol. Beira is a port in Mozambique, and our task was to stop oil from getting into Beira so it couldn't be piped by land into Rhodesia (now Zimbabwe). The reason for the blockade was that Britain and the United Nations wanted Rhodesia to go under a majority black rule when it gained independence, but Prime Minister Ian Smith rejected this. The Beira Patrol lasted from 1968 to 1975 with about seventy-five Royal Navy ships taking part at one time or another.

The use of force was not allowed under the rules of engagement, and so the navy had little or no power to stop the tankers going in. All in all, it seemed a waste of time, effort, and money. In all the years the patrol lasted, less than fifty oil tankers were intercepted, and most of them were allowed to go on their way. On the plus side, being at sea for so long gave us a chance to save some money and get a great suntan. There was also time to play deck hockey on the helicopter landing deck. I could think of worse places to be. Deck hockey was a great way of staying fit, and I also took part in the keep-fit classes that ran now and again as it made a nice change to break the daily routine up, plus it kept me fit.

One of the places we visited on that trip was a big South African naval base near Simons Town. From there we took a train to Cape Town, home of the famous Table Mountain and very strong brandy. It came as a bit of a shock that everything was segregated for black and white people. The black people were not allowed to sit on the same chairs at the train station, go in certain carriages on the train, or go in the same pubs or restaurants as the white people. Even the beaches were segregated. It seemed very odd at the time.

Another place we visited was Mombasa, a port in East Africa. The hotels and beaches were out of this world, and to this day, I don't think I have seen better beaches. The water was so clear and refreshing. You had to have a lot of money in those days to visit and stay in the hotels in Mombasa, because package holidays were still in their infancy.

We never stayed in the hotels, but we used their restaurants, bars, swimming pools, and showers. The staff were not bothered as long as we were buying food and drinks. I don't think the guests were too happy, though, because they had paid a fortune for the privilege of their holiday, and then we turned up like we owned the place. There was an all-weather football pitch nearby where we would play in the early evening, when it was a bit cooler.

One morning after I finished the early shift in the galley, I was volunteered to be one of the security guards to go with an officer to collect money from the finance department at the navy offices in Mombasa. There I was with my wooden stick and armband, with the letters NP for 'navy patrol', and I am supposed to protect the officer from any attackers! I must have looked a right tit. At least it was not dark, like when I did the patrols at HMS *Dolphin*. This time I was not on my own, but I was still was not eighteen, was five feet nothing, and weighed less than ten stone. I don't think my presence was going to deter anyone who was determined to relieve the Royal Navy of its property. On the plus side, I had a very nice time being driven round Mombasa by a Royal Navy officer, taking in the scenery and chilling out. When we stopped at a seafront hotel for a drink and something to eat, I didn't think life could get much better. We all had a great time in Mombasa but after a nice relaxing week it was time to set sail again.

After another four weeks on Beira patrol, we were on the last leg of our tour and were due to sail back to Plymouth, to arrive in March. One thing that was very popular with the crew was when the order 'hands to bathe' was given. This meant that the ship would stop its engines, and we could all go in the sea for a swim. Lookouts would be posted, and a rifleman would be out in a safety boat that was launched in case any sharks turned up. The safety boat would also assist if any of the sailors got into difficulty. It was a welcome relief from our normal duties to get in the sea for a dip. 'Hands to bathe' is a navy tradition that goes back through the centuries. Back in the day, ships did not have showers or spare fresh water to wash with, so it was a way of keeping the sailors clean. At that time, I loved swimming and was a decent swimmer, but I was still a bit apprehensive about getting into the sea miles from shore, not knowing whether any sort of marine life would suddenly come to pay an interest in us. I soon disregarded those concerns as I launched myself over the side into the sea. Getting into the water was the easy bit, but in order to get back on board, we had to climb up scrambling nets, which is a mission in itself.

On the way back to Plymouth, we took part in more naval exercises before stopping in Gibraltar. What a place that is! It's a British overseas territory located on the south coast of Spain. It was just like being in Britain, but it was a lot cheaper and very sunny, the main beach was brilliant but got very busy. Gibraltar was one of my favourite destinations, and I went there many times. The police were in British police uniforms, and the telephone and post boxes were red – exactly the same as in the UK. Spain has always contested Britain's claim to Gibraltar, and when we were there, the border with Spain was shut. It remained shut for many years. There was a big naval base there in those days, called HMS *Rooke*. We spent a few days there, which gave us chance to get the ship looking smart inside and out for our return to our home port. It was exciting times for the ship's crew; the vast majority had been away from their homes and families for twelve months and were looking forward to being reunited with them. I was looking forward to going home as well, plus City were playing Everton away and Chelsea at home while I was on leave.

We arrived back in Plymouth a few days after my eighteenth birthday. Looking back at the last six months was a watershed in my life. The places I had visited, the sights I had seen, and the people

I had met was something I would not forget for a long time.

It did not even enter my head to reapply for the submarine branch of the Royal Navy I had just had the most exciting six months of my life, and I wanted more of the same. There were huge changes at that time taking place in the navy. Because the navy was reducing its role around the world, the result was that the navy was getting smaller. Another change was that the minimum time people could join from the age of eighteen was reduced from nine years to three years. If I wanted to, I could leave the navy at twenty-one years of age. That thought never occurred to me because all I wanted to do was get back out to sea and see more of the world.

I went home on leave on the Friday, and on Saturday Derbo and I went to watch City away at Everton. I was a bit surprised to see only a few City fans at the train station; Derbo had been telling me the season before, City had thousands of fans at Goodison Park. Once we arrived in Liverpool, we had a few beers and then got to the ground just before kick off. There were a few hundred City fans there, but it was nothing like the following from the season before. The main thing though, it was the first game I had been to for months, and we won, which was a big bonus. After the game, there was a big mob of Everton fans waiting for the City fans to come out. I could see there was going to be trouble, and I didn't want to get involved in any fighting in case I got arrested again. We jumped on the first bus that came, but unfortunately we didn't check where it was going and ended up in Kirby, a very rough area of Liverpool. Fucking hell, it was out of the frying pan and into the fire. We hardly spoke in case they clocked we were from Manchester and gave us a smack. It wasn't too long though till we jumped off it, and got on the right bus, and ended up where we needed to be, at Lime Street train station.

Both Liverpool and Everton supporters had a bad reputation for slashing opposition fans with Stanley knives. On the two occasions I had been to watch City play in Scouse land, although they were not the friendliest of fans, there was no evidence of anyone getting slashed by knife-wielding thugs.

Before I had to return to my ship, City were playing Chelsea at Maine Road. In that era, Chelsea had some brilliant players, and I loved watching Charlie Cooke, Peter Osgood, and Chopper Harris.

City won that game as well, so I was a happy lad. As I prepared myself to go back to Plymouth, I think Derbo and my other mates were glad to see me go. I could not shut up talking about my last six months at sea and all the places I had visited. I think I bored them to death.

Plymouth was a great place to be based. It was a very friendly and a great place to stay, because it had been heavily bombed during World War Two, lots of it had to be rebuilt, there were plenty of bars and clubs to keep us entertained. One place I loved going to was an area called the Barbican. It was a place that seemed to have been set in time, with cobbled streets and plenty of bars with character. If we were off for the weekend, we would get a carry-out of beer and cider and go to Plymouth Hoe, which overlooks the sea. It was from here that Sir Francis Drake spotted the Spanish Armada, and legend has it he finished his game of bowls before taking his fleet out to do battle with the Spaniards. One of our haunts in Plymouth was a pub called the Castle, which is on Union Street, the main drag in Plymouth. There are loads of pubs and clubs down there, and that was where many off-duty sailors and marines spent their time. Andy Morrison mentions Union Street in his book, and he reckons the only people who go there late on a Saturday night are either too pissed to care or are looking for a fight. Well, we were usually pissed when we were down there, and we got into one or two fights, but I'm pleased to say I never got arrested in Plymouth. It used to kick off a lot with the marines, who were psyched up all the time; they used to spend a lot of time in Northern Ireland, and when they returned to their base, they came into Plymouth. It did not take much to wind those fuckers up, and my mate Gibbo saved my bacon once when a few of them were giving me a hard time as I was leaving a night club. That night Gibbo was a man on a mission and sorted the situation out. Thank fuck for that, because I thought I was in for a bit of a right fucking kicking.

I used to know a few of the marines quite well, and some of them used to drink in the Castle. Their whole lives seemed to revolve round them going to Northern Ireland, and they could not wait till they went there, I thought they must have been fucking barmy, but it was what they were trained to do. I was trained to feed people, and they were trained to kill people Oh well. I suppose someone had to do it. It was probably pretty hard to switch off, and if they spent all week practicing different ways to inflict serious damage on people, it stands to reason on a Saturday night after a few beers, it would not take too much to put their skills into practice. I must say I was glad I was not on the receiving end too often, but most of them were sound lads, especially when sober.

I went to watch a few Plymouth games whilst I was down there, but the one game that stands out was against Santos from Brazil. It was a friendly game and at the time Plymouth were in the old third division. Santos were a brilliant team, and their star player was the one and only Pele. A lad called Martin and myself, who I knew from *Ganges*, went together to the game. Before the game against Santos. It was the only thing in Plymouth everyone was talking about; the whole city was excited at the visit of a brilliant team and arguably the best football player in the world.

After a few drinks, we got near the ground. The queues were unbelievable, and it took ages till we got a half-decent view. The attendance was put at thirty-seven thousand, which was unheard of for a club in the third division. We found out later that the Santos president demanded more money to play the game, and it only went ahead after the president accepted the promise of more money. If the game had not gone ahead, I am sure there would have been a riot of epic proportions. The problem was that on the previous game, Santos had played Fulham, and only eleven thousand fans had turned up. The agreement was that Santos took half the gate receipts, and Santos were disappointed because it was not a great deal of money. The president of Santos then decided to negotiate a set fee with Plymouth regardless how many turned up but when he saw the size of the crowd he demanded more money for Santos to play. Plymouth had no option but to pay up but they were not at all happy about the situation. Two of the other stars of the team were Edu and Alberto and they were both brilliant players and both were Brazilian Internationals

Much to everyone's surprise and delight, Plymouth were up 3-0 at half-time, Santos then put a master class of football on and scored two goals, with Pele getting a penalty. Plymouth though went on to win the game 3-2, so the crowd went home happy. Getting to watch both Santos and Pele play in those days was a once in a lifetime experience, and that was why thirty-seven thousand fans packed into the ground to watch it.

One important role for the navy at that time was what is commonly known as the Cod War. The Cod War was a series of disputes between the Icelandic and British governments over fishing territorial rights. For many years going back centuries, British trawlers have fished in Icelandic waters. When the Danish government, who governed Iceland in the nineteenth century, claimed an exclusion zone, the British trawler owners didn't recognize the limit and continued to send the trawlers to Icelandic waters. There were many clashes between Danish gunboats and the British trawlers. The dispute was never resolved and rumbled on until the start of the First World War, which more or less ended the dispute. It flared up again in the early 1950s but ended with a victory for the Icelandic government. The term Cod War was what the press and media called the dispute. None of the disputes could be called a war in the normal use of the word.

I was on board HMS *Achilles*, and we were in the port of Reykjavik, in Iceland, when the dispute flared up again in the 1970s. Talk about being in the wrong place at the wrong time! We were not very popular with the locals because fishing played a massive part of their economy, and to them our ship represented a hostile government. I remember we used to get loads of abuse, and loads of kids came to where we were berthed and spent ages giving us loads of stick. One thing that struck me about Iceland at the time was it was only dark for a couple of hours. At other times of the year, it was the opposite.

When the Icelandic patrol boats began enforcing the fishing limit, they tried to cut the British trawlers' nets, which were very expensive to replace. In one month alone, eighteen nets belonging to the British fishing fleet were cut, forcing the trawlers to leave the territorial waters. They then demanded the protection of the Royal Navy. The captains and crew of the Icelandic patrol boats were very skilled and brave seamen, and they were not intimidated by the presence of Royal Navy frigates and tugboats, and they were not afraid to ram the navy ships. While we were on fishing protection duties, one of our roles was to help any trawlers in distress. We had nothing but respect for the crews of the trawlers because the seas were usually very rough, and it was in freezing conditions that the fishermen were on the decks day and night in the hope of getting a decent catch. I remember on one occasion, a trawler had engine problems, so a team of navy engineers and mechanics went on board to resolve the issue. The fishermen were so grateful they gave us loads of fresh cod. I will now share my ignorance with you: even though I was trained in gutting and filleting fish, I never realized cod was so fucking big. They were massive! When you see the cod in the chippy, it has already been cut up to portion size. When I had cooked cod in the navy, it was already filleted. When I'd come home from leave, I used to tell everyone that if it wasn't for me and the navy, half the chippies in Manchester would be shut down. They didn't have a fucking clue what I was talking about, and they thought I was barmy when I told them I was a Cod War veteran. Our ship was never rammed, but many other frigates were. To be honest, the ships that the navy had at the time were not designed for the task in hand. The ships were designed for many tasks, but fishery protection was not one of them. Some of the British warships also suffered damage from ramming the Icelandic patrol boats, and some of the frigates were fitted with specialist rammers. Looking back now, it seems crazy how the dispute escalated.

There were serious political implications to it as well. The 1970s were the height of the Cold War, and Iceland was a member of NATO and had a huge American and NATO base at Keflavik. The Icelandic government threatened to close the base and also implied that they would withdraw from NATO. In the end, the British government backed down. They had sent dozens of Royal Navy ships to the area, suffered millions of pounds' worth of damage to the ships, and in the end had nothing to show for their efforts. On the downside, hundreds of trawler men lost their jobs because Icelandic waters were where a large part of the fishing fleet spent their time. There was a half-hearted campaign for everyone involved to receive a medal for the campaign, but it was never going to happen. Places like Fleetwood, Hull, and Grimsby suffered a massive economic loss because of the decision to withdraw from Icelandic waters. As with the Beira patrol, the massive effort, skill, and determination from the crews of the Royal Navy wasn't matched by the government of the day.

After finishing fishing protection duties, the ship went in dry dock for a three-month refit. All the chefs from the *Achilles* were asked, if during that time, we would like to gain experience by working in a five-star hotel. The other chefs and I thought it was a no-brainer: six weeks at a five-star hotel, or six weeks at the navy base in Plymouth? We jumped at the chance. Charlie and I were teamed up together. Charlie was a petty officer cook, and we went to work for six weeks at the Imperial Hotel in Torquay. We didn't fancy staying in the workers' quarters at the hotel, so we rented a flat while we were there. Well, it was described in the estate agents office as a flat, but it bore no resemblance to any other flat I had been to. It was a room in a cellar, but at least it was clean and cheap.

It was the first time the navy had worked with hotels. We would get a different outlook on how things were done in a top hotel and hopefully get some good tips from the hotel chefs. We were determined to make a good impression. Well, I made a great impression, all right, but not in the way I had hoped. The first night there, we decided to join the other hotel staff in their private bar. After a few beers, I got the round in and was short-changed by a fiver, which was still a fortune to me in those days. I remember being nice and polite at the beginning and explaining I was five pounds short. The response was not what I was looking for. The barman told me to come back in the morning once he had checked the till. I told him if he didn't give me my money, I would jump over the counter, rip his fucking head off, and take the money out of the till myself. I was still a short-arsed, skinny little runt, and he didn't take my threat seriously and promptly banned me from the bar. He and another barman kicked me out. Not the flying start I wanted. I went to see him in the morning and got my fiver back because he had made a mistake, but because I'd threatened him, the bastard still barred me. If he could have added up properly and given me the correct change, there would not have been an issue. Oh well. It wasn't the first time I had been banned from a bar, and it certainly would not be the last.

Torquay is a fantastic place, and it was even better in the summer when we were there. Working in the hotel wasn't always a barrel of laughs; to the head chef, we were simply free labour. He had no intention of teaching us anything, and he wanted us to do all the shit jobs. I knew I was nowhere near the standards of a chef at a five-star hotel, but that was why I was sent there: to learn new skills, not to do the washing up, take the rubbish out, and clean the yard. I did my best to keep out of his way. One of the chefs there was called Harry, and unusually for a lad from Manchester, he was a united fan. He took me under his wing whenever he could, and I got on all right with him. I enjoyed my time at Torquay. It was a nice change from the normal routine, and it was great to get away from the naval discipline for a while. The lads from the hotel played football quite often, and I would join in with them now and again.

When I returned from working at the hotel, we were billeted at HMS *Drake,* a navy establishment in Plymouth. Every now and then I had to go out on patrol in the evening with the navy police. On one such occasion, there was a bomb scare in one of Plymouth clubs. It was at the height of the bombing campaign by the IRA. We had to help evacuate the building. With all the drinks lying about, I thought, *'It's a bit rude of me not to help myself to a few'.* When I went back outside, I got an almighty bollocking by one of the patrol for doing a disappearing act, but all's well that ends well. There was no bomb.

Whenever the ship was abroad, there was always a patrol made up of the ordinary ranks. I remember when we were in Haifa in Israel, and I was on joint patrol with a petty officer and members of the Israeli defence force. We were in their Jeep, which had a machine gun fitted to it. The Israelis were armed, but the petty officer and I had only a whistle each, not even a stick. Like now, there was plenty of tension and trouble between the Israelis and the Palestinians, and all Israeli police and troops were armed. We had to go into the bars to make sure the lads were behaving themselves. I thought it was a bit provocative myself, but who was I to argue? Inevitably when I saw the lads from the ship whom I knew, I managed to get a few drinks down my neck. While on patrol, we had a break at one of the Israeli soldiers' house. His mum and dad made us something to eat, and the dad plied me with a brandy type drink, the petty officer with me wasn't too happy at the amount I was drinking, but I thought it was disrespectful to refuse, so I got stuck in to help do my bit to improve Israeli and British relations. I was such a thoughtful lad at times. What did seem odd to me, but perfectly normal to them, was that the army Jeep with a machine gun on the back was parked unattended on the road outside the house while we inside having a drink and enjoying the local hospitality.

Another time I was on patrol was in Malta. The ship used to anchor in the harbour, and in order to get ashore and back, we got on boats called dghajsa, pronounced 'dyso'. They were the traditional Maltese boats and were painted in very bright colours. One of my duties was to be on the shore, and if anyone was too pissed, I had to stop them from getting on the dghajsa. One of the stokers was absolutely steaming, but his mates were looking after him and didn't want to see him on a charge, so I turned a blind eye. He got on the dghajsa no problem, but as he tried to get on the gangway to get back on board the ship, the dozy fucker slipped and fell in the water. Luckily his mates managed to swiftly pull him on-board without too much fuss. I was quizzed about it the next day, but no action was taken against me or the lad, thank fuck for that.

Malta was one of my favourite places to visit. It has a great climate, it has nice beaches, and the people are very friendly. Malta was awarded the George Cross for its efforts during World War Two.

There is a place called the Gutt, which was as rough as fuck, but it was great for a night out with the lads. There were plenty of nice beaches and bars, and there was an all-weather football pitch on which we could play. We had some great times there.

Whilst on the *Achilles*, we spent a lot of time showing the flag around various places in the UK and the Mediterranean. Once we were berthed in Liverpool, and my mum, her friend, and my brother came to visit me on the ship and take me back to Manchester for weekend leave. I gave them a tour of the ship, and then we went to my mess for something to eat and drink they could not believe how small our living and sleeping quarters were.

The lads in the mess plied us all with drinks and my mum, her friend and my brother really enjoyed the hospitality. I remember my brother looking round the galley and he could not fathom out how we could cook for so many in such a small place.

One place we went to show the flag was Cardiff. We had a surprise visit from Anne Aston, who was the *Golden Girl from the Golden Shot*, a very popular TV series in its heyday. I am not sure why Anne was in Cardiff, but she came on board with a couple of other people; I was told they were actors, but I hadn't heard of them. My claim to fame is that I cooked her a cheese omelette, and she assured me it was delicious. They invited us to a nightclub with them, but it wasn't my cup of tea, so I only had a couple of drinks and then went elsewhere.

Whilst we were in Cardiff, England were playing Wales, and we were given tickets to go and watch the game, but we had to go in uniform. It was not a wise move because we got loads of stick and abuse from the Welsh fans. My hero from City, Colin Bell, scored the only goal so England won 1-0. I missed the goal though as I had gone for a beer.

A few days later, I was home on leave and went to watch City play United at Maine Road. City won 3-0, and Colin Bell scored two, thank fuck I didn't miss them, and all in all it was a great week, hobnobbing with the stars and a freebie to watch England and I also saw City batter United.

Another place we visited was Sweden. We visited twice, and I remember it was very expensive there. Whenever we visited a place, the officers usually hosted a cocktail party for the local officials, mayors, police chief, and other high-up dignitaries. I used to volunteer for these because it was a chance to get a few free drinks before going ashore. It was around that time that I and the other chefs had one of our proudest moments on board by winning the fleet cookery competition. It was a fantastic achievement and gave us a great sense of pride. The navy had hundreds of ships of all shapes and sizes, so it was no mean feat to win it.

On the same tour, we visited the German port of Lubeck. One of the chefs whom I worked with was killed in what was officially called a tragic accident. We never got to the bottom of it, but many felt there was foul play involving a couple of bouncers from one of the clubs. I think for convenience and political reasons, it suited the powers to be in the navy and the officials from Lubeck to class it as an accident. There was no formal enquiry or investigation, and it was very hard to differentiate fact from rumour because no witnesses came forward.

When someone died on the ship, the person's belongings were auctioned off, we paid silly prices for stuff, and most of us didn't bother to collect what we had paid for. That way we managed to raise a good few quid for the lad's family, plus they got his belongings to do what they wanted with them.

My time on HMS *Achilles* was due up after three years on board, but the ship was next going on a twelve-month tour to some great places like Mombasa, Singapore, Hong Kong, and Japan. I applied to have my stay extended, and I was chuffed to bits when my request was accepted.

Just under three years after I'd first joined HMS *Achilles* in Singapore, I was to set sail for the Far East again, visiting other countries on the way. For the first few months, we were doing exercises with navies from other NATO countries, and we visited Gibraltar and Cape Town in South Africa, Cochin in India, and Karachi in Pakistan. While in Cape Town, I got another tattoo. This time it was of an eagle and a lucky horseshoe. Most lads in the navy who have an eagle tattoo usually have them covering their backs. I was too much of a shithouse to have it on my back because I don't think I could have stood the pain. Plus, because I was a skinny little fucker, it probably would have looked stupid. I settled for a small one on my arm, and I am happy to say it doesn't look stupid, but it still bleeding hurt. Thank fuck I did not have it on my back – I probabley would have fainted.

Cochin was OK, and I remember having my first prawn curry there. Well, they told me it was prawn. Whatever it was, it was very tasty. Cochin is a port city on the south-west coast of India. It has always been an important trading centre and was one of the first European colonies in India. Over the centuries, it was occupied by the Portuguese, the Dutch, and the British. It is also the home of the Indian Navy's Southern Naval Command. Fishing and tourism play a big part in the local economy, and the climate is pretty good most of the year. The beaches are not bad, but they're not a patch on the ones in Mombasa. Although there was some poverty when we visited, the people were very welcoming and friendly, and they liked their food very spicy. I have never been back to India, but places like Cochin and Goa are now very popular with British tourists. I have heard great reports about the place, but the downside is that the elephants wander about on the beaches and have a dump all over the place. Oh well; you can't have everything. There is always a downside to something that is good. It is one thing to stand in a bit of dog shit. It is a different matter altogether to stand in something that an elephant has just dropped. Fuck me, it just does not bear thinking about.

Karachi is located on the Arabian Sea. It sounds very inviting, but the waters around the coast were very badly polluted when we were there. I would dread to think what exotic diseases you would catch if you fell overboard in the harbour. As we were approaching Karachi and sailing towards the harbour, we were greeted with a thick, yellow smog and a disgusting, horrible smell. It was unreal. I have heard that some places in Pakistan are really nice, but I got the shock of my life when I visited Karachi. What a fucking shithole. It is the worst place I have visited in my life. God help the people who live there, because it is such a dump. But nothing would stop us from going ashore and enjoying ourselves. As soon as we left the ship, we jumped into a taxi and asked the driver to take us to the best restaurant or hotel; we wanted to have the best that Karachi had to offer. Something must have been lost in translation. Either that, or his relatives owned the place he took us to. It was a run-down place that was as scruffy as fuck, with live chickens wandering about. On the drive there, we passed dozens of beggars, and many were badly deformed. The plight for them must have been heart breaking, and the sad sight of them stayed with me for a long time to come. I have always maintained

I could enjoy myself anywhere in the world as long as I had a drink in my hand, because it's was you make of it, but Karachi beat me hands down. None of us remotely enjoyed it, and after only a couple of beers, we got a taxi back to the ship and never went ashore again.

Everyone on the ship was glad when we left the port and set off on our travels. Our next port of call was Mombasa before we headed for the Far East. We had left Plymouth about three months earlier, and all the time we were at sea had been pretty tough because we were taking part in exercises. There was not much relaxation time when off duty, as on many of the exercises the crew did six-hours on duty and six-hours off duty, so the crew and ship was at a maximum state of readiness. Many times during the six hours off duty, action stations were sounded, or there was a fire drill. It was a very demanding and exhausting, so sleep was at a premium. The plus side was that the captain was more than happy with the way the crew completed all the challenges, and we knew that after Mombasa, there were hardly any exercises. The ship and crew would be in a more relaxed state as we prepared to show the flag at various countries in the Far East.

It was not long after we left Karachi that we landed in Mombasa. I had been there before and was telling all the lads where the best hotels were, what the bars were like, and how great the beaches were. It had been nearly three years since I had last been there, and it was fantastic to be ashore there once again, sunbathing on some of the best beaches in the world, swimming in brilliant blue water, visiting the hotels, and using their facilities. The last few months had been tough going since we had left the UK, and we viewed the time we were spending chilling out in Mombasa as a well-deserved break – or in navy terms, R and R, which stands for rest and recreation. We were certainly going to make the most of it. Although I loved it at Mombasa, I could not wait till we got to Hong Kong, because that was where I should have first joined the HMS *Achilles*. At least my kit had gone there.

The pop star Rod Stewart was also in Mombasa with his then girlfriend, Dee Harrington. He was staying at a beachfront hotel about a mile from where we hung out. Some of the lads met up with him on a couple of occasions and got on great with him. Although I had heard of him and knew a couple of his songs when he was the singer in the band The Faces, I was not a big music lover, and so I did not make an effort to meet him; I did not see the point as I was having a great time with my mates. He agreed to play in an inter-ship football game, and by all accounts he was pretty good. I could have played but thought it only fair to let the lads who were knocking about with him play. I had intended to watch the game, but I was having a great time in a couple of the bars, and in the end I never made it to the match. Oh well, never mind. These things happen. Rod became a real icon with the Royal Navy when he recorded the hit song 'I Am Sailing', and it was the theme tune for the award-winning TV series *The Ark Royal*, which was about the Royal Navy's largest aircraft carrier as it went about its duties around the world.

Three days before Christmas, another inter-ship football game was organized, and I was playing midfield for the A team against the B team. Everyone was in high spirits; the worst of the exercises were behind us, and we were having a few great days before setting sail for more adventures in some great exotic countries, showing the flag and maintaining a Royal Navy presence in the Far East. At least, that was what I thought I would be doing. The football game was going well, and at half-time the score was level, 1-1. Just after half-time, I had the ball, and a lad went to tackle me but mistimed his challenge. The tackle left me in agony, so I was carried to the side-lines to watch the rest of the game because I could not carry on. After the game finished, my injury had not got any better, so when I returned to the ship, the ships medic took me to sickbay and gave me an X-ray. He said my leg was broken. *Oh, fuck me*, I thought. *'What a fucking sickener'*. My next thought was, *'am I ever going to get to fucking Hong Kong?* A couple of hours later, I was dispatched to the Katherine Bibby Hospital in Mombasa. To make matters worse, one of the lads who came with the medic to look after me as my helper had had a bit too much to drink and accidently kept steering the wheelchair into all sorts of objects, sending more pains shooting up my leg. At least, I hope it was a fucking accident. What a dickhead. That evening I had more X-rays to confirm what the ships medic thought, and I had a plaster of Paris put on. There were about twenty other patients on the ward, mainly sailors from different parts of the world. I didn't sleep well that night because I was in pain and was very uncomfortable. I felt very sorry for myself.

In the morning, my divisional officer from the ship came to visit me and to give me the bad news that I would not be returning to the ship. It was estimated my leg would be in plaster for at least three months; then there would be a bit of time doing rehab. I was expecting the news, but it was still a sickener to be told. I appreciated that he came to tell me in person. He explained that I would probably be in hospital for about ten days, and then they would put me in a hotel while they sorted out a flight to take me back home to the UK. I got a visit from loads of the lads, and that helped cheer me up a bit. The day before the ship was sailing, Dutchy, Flash, Gibbo, Charlie, and George came to visit and left about five crates of beer, hundreds of fags, a couple dozen cigars, and a bottle of rum, chocolates, crisps, and peanuts. Nice one, lads. The bloke in the next bed was getting on my nerves. I think he was just trying to be nice, and he didn't speak English, but he kept offering me figs and raisins. I wasn't in the mood and wanted to be left alone.

What a small world we live in. One of the senior nurses was from Prestwich. Although I never knew her, she knew people whom I also knew. There were many English and European staff at the hospital.

The next day, I decided to drown my sorrows and got stuck into the beer. I even had my own fridge at the side of my bed. After I had a few cans, I thought I would get my own back on the bloke in the next bed, and I started mithering him and asking him if he wanted peanuts. When he started ignoring me, I flung a load of peanuts at him. The nurses were not amused with my antics, and after that the bleeding spoilsports rationed me to only six cans of beer a day. After a couple of days, they started showing me how to use the crutches. These fucking crutches must have been from the

Ark, because they were big, clumsy things made of wood, not the trendy ones you get nowadays. At first it was dead hard and knackering, but I slowly got the hang of it. I soon became the ward porter's mate because I gave him a few cigars in return he gave me extra beer.

The view from the hospital was great, and I spent a lot of time out on the veranda soaking up the sun and having a few beers. Life wasn't too bad after all. After about ten days, I was transferred to the Outrigger Hotel, which also serviced the adjoining yacht club. I was given my own bungalow, which was situated near the bar and restaurant and overlooked the swimming pool. The manager explained to me that all the food at meal times were paid for, but if I had any drinks or food out of meal times, then I would either have to pay for it. Alternatively, I could sign for it, and at the end of my stay they would bill the navy. Happy days! I got really drunk the first night there and didn't get up till late, so I thought I would put what the manager said to the test. I ordered a bottle of beer and a steak buttie for a late breakfast, and lo and behold, I didn't have to pay cash; I simply signed for it. Altogether I ran up a bill of about a hundred pounds, which taking into consideration that my accommodation and all my meals were free, and that I paid cash for some drinks, it took some doing to go through that amount back in 1973. I was always one to rise to a challenge, and I thought I might as well go for it big time and make the most of it. It would not be long before I would be back in the freezing cold in England.

It was many months later when the navy contacted me about the bill. Instead of me having to pay it back all at once, they just took some money each week out of my wages. I felt pretty pleased with myself because I felt vindicated in running up a tab. I always remember when I was called in to the chief petty officer's office to be told they had received the bill. He said, 'One hundred pounds in ten days in a free hotel? You must have had a fucking good time?' There was nothing I could say to that.

Even though I could not go swimming, I spent my days round the pool and then getting a cab into town to hit a few bars. If the bar at the hotel was still open when I got back, I finished off with a nightcap. On one of the nights, I was talking to a bloke who was staying at the hotel, and he asked me if I fancied going shark fishing with him sometime. In for a penny, in for a pound. I said no problem and then forgot all about it because the drinks were flowing.

I wasn't in bed long when there was a knock at the door. It was about 6.30 in the morning, and the bloke I had been talking to was standing there looking pleased with himself, I thought, *'What the fuck does he want?'* He went on to explain he had pulled a few strings and had managed to hire a boat to go shark fishing, and we were leaving in half an hour. What a fucking nutter! We were at sea for about five or 6 hours and caught fuck all. To make matters worse, I was rough as fuck and I couldn't stop being sick.

Once we landed back on shore, the manager of the hotel told me the navy had sent a car for me to go for a hospital appointment to check my progress and to see if I was fit to fly. Shit, I had forgot about the appointment. If I was declared fit to fly, they would arrange for me to be flown back to the UK. I wasn't ready to go back yet because I was having the time of my life, so I did a bit of self-inflicting damage to the plaster so that when I did visit the hospital again, they would have to stick a new plaster on, giving me a few extra days at the hotel.

One day I was lounging about when five or six sailors based in Mombasa and their wives turned up for a few drinks. I took an instant dislike to the women because they were talking to the staff and waiters like they were shit. I wasn't too keen on the blokes either because they knew I was in hospital on my own over Christmas, and they never bothered dropping by to see if I needed anything. Plus, they never came round with my wages or my allowance of duty-free fags, because they were part of the Royal Navy liaison department. Visiting people in hospitals and making sure they got paid was certainly part of their remit. They could see I wasn't happy, so they invited me back to their place for a BBQ. I thought bollocks to that – I would rather be on my own. I didn't take them up on their offer because I knew if I went, I would probably lose my rag with them.

One night I was in the one of the bars in town, and I got so drunk I forgot my crutches. Luckily the bar staff knew which hotel I was staying at and sent my crutches to the hotel in a taxi the next morning. I found out later that a porter and the duty manager had to get me out of the taxi and carry me to my bungalow.

Finally it was the day I had to fly back to the UK. First I had to fly to Nairobi, and then I'd head to London, where I would be met to be driven to the navy hospital in Gosport. It wasn't too far from where I was based when I was at HMS *Dolphin*. I couldn't bend my leg, so I was seated near the front where there was extra leg room, plus they gave me something to rest my leg on. Most of my kit was still on the ship; the lads were going to put it all in a kit bag, and then it would be flown back. All I had was a suitcase with a few bits and pieces. When we arrived at Nairobi, a stewardess was waiting for me with a wheelchair. I got her to take me to duty-free before I got the flight to London. The flight went quite quick because I had quite a bit to drink.

When I arrived in London, I must have looked a right sight. It was freezing, and I was wearing shorts, a T-shirt, a straw hat, and one flip-flop. A Royal Navy ambulance was waiting for me. The driver had an assistant to give me a hand, and as soon as we left the airport, I got the duty-free out. The assistant joined me in the back for a few drinks. I fell asleep after a bit because I was half tired and half pissed. The next thing I knew, we'd pulled up at Haslar, the Royal Navy hospital. It wasn't long till all the help and care I'd had up till then went out of the window. I was now back to the navy regime. The next day they put a new plaster on and said I could go home on two weeks' leave. I asked a nurse if she could order a taxi for me, but the miserable bitch just told me where the phone was. When the cab came, no one gave me a lift with my suitcase, the wankers. I hobbled past loads of staff, doing my best not to fall over. It was hard enough walking with the old wooden crutches; it was even worse carrying a suitcase. No one lifted a finger to help. I thought, *'What a load of tossers'*.

After my two weeks' leave, I was sent back to Haslar. There were no duties for me there, so I had to hang about there, bored shitless with about five other lads who were in a similar position. There was no chance of them letting me recuperate at home; the navy did not operate like that. More is the pity. After a few more weeks, I got a new plaster and was a bit more mobile. The new plaster was only up to my knee, so I was discharged from the hospital and sent to the navy barracks in Portsmouth, HMS *Nelson*. I was put on light duties in the regulators (police) office, mainly brewing up for everyone.

I had my twenty-first birthday while there, and I went out for a few beers with a lad I knew from training called Yorkie. What a big mistake that was. We were in a pub called the Ideal when Yorkie got into a row with some lads. I tried to calm it down, but I got a slap as well as him, and I also got thrown out onto the pavement. Then came my crutches, which landed on me head. I never saw Yorkie again and thought *'Fuck this for a lark I better do one'*. I went to a few pubs on my own and then went to the Chinese restaurant for something to eat, but by then I was steaming, and so I fell asleep in the doorway of the restaurant. The police were called and couldn't wake me up, so I was arrested for being drunk and spent the night in a Portsmouth nick. Happy twenty-first? I don't think so. It was not long before I went to court and got a ten-pound fine. A couple days later, I got called in to see my divisional officer. He gave me a right bollocking for getting arrested, and then he promoted me to acting lead cook (equivalent of a corporal in the army). How mad was that? It took a bit for that to sink in, plus it meant a pay raise. Every cloud has a silver lining, as they say. This was nearly three months after I'd left the *Achilles,* and my kit still hadn't turned up. I wondered if it had gone to Hong Kong again.

A few days later, City were playing Queens Park Rangers in London. Derbo and some other lads I knew were coming down for the game, so I arranged to meet them for a drink before the match. There were a few thousand City fans at the game, and I bumped into quite a few other lads I knew, including Paul Holt, a massive City fan from Hillock Estate. After the game – surprise, surprise, we got beat – some QPR fans came round looking for trouble, if there was one club in London where you would not expect any trouble, it was QPR, but as I discovered over the years, every football club has its fair share of pricks. One of them came up to me and said in a broad cockney accent, 'Don't worry – we don't fight cripples.' I thought what a knob and told the dickhead to fuck off, and I also tried to hit him with my crutches but failed miserably and lost my balance. I nearly ended up on the floor. Thank fuck I didn't, or the lad would have pissed his sides laughing. I was glad when the lad fucked off, and the other QPR fans quickly disappeared as well.

Not long after that game, City were playing Leicester away, so I decided to go there because I still had a couple of free travel passes to use. I had never been to Leicester's ground before. Like most grounds at the time, it was pretty grim and run-down, and it was nothing like the ground Leicester now have. I got the train to Leicester and had a few drinks with some City fans before the match. It was another ground where there were loads of City fans, and it was a great atmosphere. Pity we got beat 1-0. At some grounds where I went to watch City in those days, there were thousands of City fans in attendance, but at other grounds there were hardly any. I enjoyed it more if there were loads of Blues at the away games, because City fans have always been friendly with a great sense of humour, which guaranteed a good laugh and a great atmosphere even if the game was shit and City got beat, which was quite often. Not long after that game, it was time to say goodbye to Portsmouth, and I was off on my travels again.

Chapter 7

HMS *Osprey*

With my leg well on the mend, the navy decided I had been having life a bit too cushy in Portsmouth and decided it was time for me to have a new posting. I knew it would be too much to ask to get a seagoing ship because it was only three or four months since I had left the *Achilles,* and the general rule at the time was a couple of years on a seagoing ship, then around twelve months at a shore base. I would have been more than happy spending all my time on seagoing ships, but hey, that's life in the Royal Navy. My new posting was the HMS *Osprey* which was a navy air station situated in Portland, Dorset, which is not far from Weymouth down the south coast of England. It was also known as Royal Navy Air Station Portland, and it was used to train helicopter crews in anti-submarine operations.

It was to be my first posting as a leading cook, and I was extremely nervous because I hadn't had any leadership or supervision training. Also, I was not fully qualified to be a leading cook because I was still awaiting to go on the course where if I passed, I would get my City and Guilds and be a fully qualified leading cook. If I failed, I would be demoted straight away with all the embarrassment and humiliation that would bring me. What's more, I had not been is a galley or done any cooking for over four months, so there was massive pressure on me, and the last thing I wanted was to embarrass myself. Talk about being thrown in the deep end!

When I arrived at Weymouth train station, it was about tea time. I thought there was no point going to the base yet because I did not think I would know anyone there, and I would be bored shitless on my own at a strange base. I figured I might as well have a few drinks in Weymouth. My kitbag had still not arrived back from the *Achilles*, so I only had a suitcase to cart round with me. Well, one drink led to another, and I arrived at the main gate of HMS *Osprey* rather drunk just before midnight. As my luck would have it, there was no one on duty who knew which accommodation block I was in, and there was no duty stores accountant to sort a mattress and bedding out for me. The guards on duty were friendly enough and said I could put my head down in the cells and get my accommodation sorted in the morning. There I was the first night at my new base, sleeping in the cells. The bonus was I was not going to get a charge sheet when I woke up.

After my breakfast, I reported to the offices to register and to find out where I would be working and where my accommodation was. I was surprised when I was given the opportunity to stay in a bed and breakfast in Weymouth and commute each day. It sounded great, but I did not really fancy getting the bus to and from the base each day and because I was now a leading cook it would not be long till I got a room of my own on the base, so I opted to stay on site at HMS *Osprey*.

When off duty, there was not a lot to do apart from playing the odd game of football and drinking, so I ended up spending a lot of time in Weymouth in the bars and clubs. There was a belting pub in Weymouth called the Black Dog, and they sold a mad drink called parsnip wine. It was an acquired taste, and I acquired it with a fucking vengeance. A few of the bars in Portland sold it as well. I am not sure what proof it was, and I'm not even sure it was legal, but it was strong as fuck. Just what the doctor ordered!

After a few weeks at HMS *Osprey*, I got sent on the catering course. If I passed, I would then be a fully qualified leading cook. If I failed, I would suffer the humiliation of being demoted. Only the Royal Navy could act arse upwards like that. The course was back at HMS *Pembroke* in Chatham, and it was to last six weeks. Out of the ten of us on the course, only one other besides me passed outright. Five failed, and three others were allowed to retake some of what they failed on because they came close to a pass. To say I was chuffed to bits would be a massive understatement. It was a fantastic confidence booster for me because the possibility of getting demoted had been hanging over me. The pressure was now off me, and I could relax a bit more. I was always confident of my catering skills, but I wish they had waited till I was fully qualified till I got promoted. It still sounds a barmy way of doing things.

Back at *Osprey*, it was still pretty boring off duty, and I wished I could get another seagoing ship pretty quickly. I would rather be at sea or visiting other countries. The longer I stayed at *Osprey*, the more I drank, and I had a few run-ins with the authorities both on and off the base. One occasion was when it was a lovely summer afternoon, and a few of us had been drinking in the bars at the seafront. We got a carry-out and went on to the beach to soak up the sun and have a couple of beers till the pubs opened again. After a relaxing time on the beach, we headed back to the seafront because the bars were reopening for the tea time and evening trade. As we were about to cross the road, I saw an old oil lamp lying on the floor. It was the sort the council workmen used to light when they had been working on a hazard; the lights were used to highlight any potential dangers such as holes. I did not know why it was dumped on the pavement, but I thought even though it was a bit of old scrap, it would look great once cleaned up and painted in my room back at the base.

As we were crossing the road, a coach came towards us at speed, and he was not showing any signs of slowing down. We shouted some abuse at the driver because he'd just missed us. The driver stopped the coach and got out to confront us. I was the nearest, and so he had a go at me. A bit of a scuffle broke out, and someone said the police had been phoned, so I hung about till they arrived. After they spoke to the driver and then to me, I got the shock of my fucking life. I was arrested and charged with theft, assault, and criminal damage. The theft was the old lamp, the assault was on the driver, and the criminal damage was for his glasses. What a fucking joke. I had never heard as much bollocks in my life. One minute I was minding my own business and crossing the road, and the next I was banged up in the police cells. This time I did inform my divisional officer, and he arranged for a solicitor to act on my behalf. I pleaded not guilty to all three charges. When I first met my solicitor there was something about him that filled me with confidence, and it was not going to be long to see if my faith in him was misplaced.

It was about eight weeks later when the case was heard in Weymouth Magistrates Court. It was not too long into the case when any neutral observer quickly realized the case against me should have never come to court, and the only person who should have been in the dock was the coach driver. As my solicitor rightly pointed out, it was the driver who stopped the coach, it was the coach driver who got out, and it was the coach driver who confronted me. It was his actions and his actions alone that caused the confrontation. Under cross-examination, the coach driver could not come up with a credible explanation as to why he'd taken the action that he did. The policeman who'd arrested me was ripped apart in the witness box by my solicitor; he agreed that under the terms of the theft act that I had been charged with, nothing had been stolen. He also admitted he did not know who the owner of the discarded lamp was and also had to agree that it was scrap and not worth anything. He could not explain why he did not take any statements from any of the passengers on the coach. There was also no proof of any glasses had been damaged because no photographs were taken, and no repair bills were produced, He also had to concede that my actions of waiting for the police to arrive did not seem to be the actions of a guilty man, there was only two other witnesses called by the prosecution, even though many other people had seen the incident unfold. The two witnesses, a man and his wife who owned a shop on the seafront, admitted under cross-examination that they did not get a clear view of the incident because they were nearly two hundred yards away. They also admitted they never saw me throw a punch or heard me threaten the driver.

In summing up, my solicitor expressed his dismay that the case was ever brought to court. He pointed out that it was the coach driver who was the instigator of the events, and he highlighted the fact that the police did not do a credible investigation. Despite the fact there were many witnesses, the only two they could get to support their prosecution was an elderly couple quite a distance from the incident, and he labelled them as a couple of nosey parkers. Because their case was so weak, my solicitor did not even call my witnesses. The magistrates only took about ten minutes to come back with not-guilty verdicts on all three charges. I was relived to be found not guilty, but I was still annoyed and disappointed the case had come to court in the first place. Oh well; all's well that ends well.

Being in Weymouth meant it was great to get to London whenever City were playing there. I went about four times for different games, and each time I usually bumped into someone I knew. On a couple of occasions, I met up with a City fan from Oxford who used to bring his young lad with him, and he loved to hear about my experiences in the navy. Going to watch City was a great relief from boredom because staying in Weymouth was doing my head in.

It was not long before I had another run-in with the police, and again I was in the wrong place at the wrong time. I had been in the Black Dog having a couple of quiet drinks on my own. It was a Saturday at dinner time, and the pub was full of locals. I knew most of them and they were a good set of lads. As I left the pub to go to another bar, a lad whom I did not know was harassing and giving some grief to three young sailors from HMS *Ganges* who must have been in Weymouth to do some training. They had not even been in the pub but were talking outside, and the lad was giving them grief solely because they were in the navy and in uniform. He was pissed and was a fucking bully. I intervened and stood up for the youngsters, telling them it was best to walk on to get out of the idiot's way. I thought that was the end of it, but no. The dickhead turned his attention to me and started a fight. Luckily I got the better of him, and then I walked away thinking to myself, *Why me?*

Not long after, I was still walking down the sea front when a police car stopped. There was a girl in the passenger seat, and she pointed me out to the police. The lad whom I had been in a bit of a scuffle with was her boyfriend. Fuck me – another trip to the police station. I tried to give them my version of events, but they did not want to know, and lo and behold, I had another fucking assault charge. The trial was about six weeks later.

I was out having a drink the night before the court case when the lad I was accused of assaulting came over to me. I thought, *Oh, not again,* but he was OK. He said he did not want to press charges; it was nothing to do with him, but it was out of his hands. During the court case, it emerged he had only recently been released from an eighteen-month prison sentence for a string of offenses, including robbery, theft, and assault. When he came to give evidence, I will give him his due. He admitted to being drunk, and he admitted to picking on the young sailors. He admitted to starting a fight me. I thought, *Déjà vu. Why the fuck am I in the dock?* A Royal Navy officer came and spoke on my behalf, giving me a glowing character reference. He explained to the court that under the circumstances, he would expect nothing else but for me to assist the young sailors, and he would have taken a dim view of me if I had not. My solicitor again made short work of the prosecution's case, and within a matter of minutes the magistrates found me not guilty. Again, I should have been overjoyed that I had been cleared, but I was equally annoyed because the case should never have come to court in the first place.

I wasn't really enjoying my time at HMS *Osprey*, and I pushed for a draft for a seagoing ship. I think many at *Osprey* would have liked to have seen the back of me as well. Besides the problems I had with the police, I also got into one or two scrapes on the base, and I had a bit of a chip on my shoulder. I was still bored and drank too much. One issue I had was with the sailors who'd joined for only three years; they didn't have the training discipline and commitment of the lads who had joined up to make a career of the navy. They were only in for three years and saw it as just another job. Those like me that did twelve months of navy training at HMS *Ganges*, when we were told to jump, we asked how high. When those who had only had a few weeks training and had only signed up for three years were told to jump, they asked why. There was a massive difference in attitude that I found hard to get my head round. They found it hard to accept the relaxed, informal ways they had on Civvy

Street just didn't work on Royal Navy warship or shore establishments. Some of them probably could not get their heads round me either. It was not all doom and gloom, though. Plenty of Royal Navy ships docked in Portland when they were having a break from exercises, and if I knew any of the lads on board, they would invite me on board for a couple of drinks. When HMS *Achilles* returned to Plymouth from the Far East, I went to Plymouth for a weekend and met up with my old mates. I was chuffed to meet up with them again, but I must say I was envious listening to their stories about where they had been and what they had got up to; while I had been to Portsmouth and Portland, they had been to Singapore, Hong Kong, and a host of other places.

Looking back, I probably did not have the right attitude at that time, probably due to the fact I did not want to be there in the first place. I was still a bit bitter about breaking my leg and missing out on a great trip. When I first joined HMS *Osprey*, I was probably trying too hard because I knew I did not have the correct training or qualifications for the job, and I had not set foot in a galley for four months. I seriously lacked confidence, and I hardly knew anyone there. It was hardly surprising I was well and truly out of my comfort zone.

It was great to get away from it all and go home on weekend leave. The weekend I had in mind was when City were playing United, and I was desperate to go. I managed to get the time off, and because I was a bit short of cash, I decided to hitch-hike it to Manchester. It was a right trek back in those days but, it was worth it to see City play. The best way for anyone in the forces to hitch a lift was to do it in your uniform. Many people who would never dream of stopping their cars to pick a stranger up might think differently about someone in uniform, especially if they or their families had been in the forces. Unfortunately, because of the IRA bombing campaign on the UK mainland, all service personnel were seen as targets, so we were advised only to wear our uniform when on duty. The next best thing for me to was to tie my sailor's hat on the handles of my bag.

During my time in the navy, I hitch-hiked all over the place, but never did I reach my destination as quickly as I did on that journey. I had not been out of the base for more than ten minutes when a very kind naval officer picked me up and dropped me off by a major road that leads up north. I must have been there less than five minutes when a lorry driver picked me up. I can't remember his destination, but when it was time for me to part company, he pulled into a lorry park, bought me something to eat and drink, and then spoke to the other drivers to see if any were going my way. Fuck me, it was my lucky day! One of them was going to Cheshire, and it was no problem for him to give me a lift, so I was chuffed to bits. Things were going far too smoothly for me at this point, and I thought at any moment now, Murphy's Law was going to kick in, but there was no such problem. Everything went as smooth as clockwork.

One thing about hitching a lift is after a short while, the conversation grinds to a halt. After talking about the weather, the state of the roads, and football, there isn't anything left to talk to a stranger about. I did not mind at all because it was great just sitting in the passenger's seat. Every time I looked at the signs, we were getting closer and closer to Manchester. We had another stop before getting to Cheshire, and the lorry driver bought me a brew as well. He dropped me off near Mere Golf Course and wished me luck. I was having a fag when a car pulled up, and a middle-aged bloke asked me where I was going. I told him Prestwich, and he said, 'Jump in.' Happy days! He was going to Salford, which (depending what part of Salford) is only a stone's throw away from Prestwich. He told me I was the first hitch-hiker he had ever picked up, and he only did it because his nephew was in the Royal Air Force. Top man. He dropped me off at a bus stop just a few miles from my house. From leaving the naval base to getting home, it took me about the same as if I had taken the train.

The next day, I met my mates and had a few drinks before going to Maine Road for the game. United were playing well at the time and were favourites by some in the media to win, but as always I expected the Blues to win. City played very well, and the game ended 2-2 – not the win we had hoped for, but at least we didn't get beat. To make it sweeter, one of our goals was an own goal scored by Jimmy Nicholl. My plan was that I was going to hitch it back to Weymouth at Sunday lunchtime, but I changed my mind, and after a few drinks I decided to get the coach instead, which left in the early evening. The coach returning to Weymouth left from near Portland Street in Manchester, I was always a bit nervy getting the coach from there because it was at Portland Street about eighteen months earlier that the IRA had planted a bomb on one of the army coaches going to Catterick and Darlington, killing and injuring many people when it blew up on the motorway. It was a long slog back to Weymouth, so I got my head down and managed to sleep most of the way, but my travelling wasn't quite over because there was another match I wanted to watch.

After I finished work on Monday, I was off to London to watch City play Norwich at Stamford Bridge in the League Cup second round second replay, because it was a replay it had to be played at a neutral ground. Nowadays it would go straight to extra time and then to penalty shoot-outs because it is all to do with the amount of games the teams have to play, and nothing at all to do with the amount of travel the fans have to undertake. I nearly missed the game because I fell asleep on the train as I was a bit tired, ok I may have had a drink or two as well. I made it only because I was spotted by a guard doing his checks before the train started its return journey, and he woke me up. Otherwise, I would have been on my way back to Weymouth, and that would have been a right sickener.

I managed to get to Stamford Bridge for half-time, and I couldn't believe it. I had missed City scoring three goals. Just my fucking luck to miss half the game! On the plus side, I still saw City score some goals, and I met a couple of great lads I knew from Whitefield, Eric and Billy. To top it all, we won 6-1. What a great long weekend.

Not long after that game, my divisional office called me in to see him My first thought was, *What shit have I got myself into now?* However, I need not have worried. He said my draft had come through, and I would be joining a seagoing ship in a couple of weeks. I was chuffed as fuck and could not wait to leave the shore base – and hopefully put my troubles behind me. I was looking forward to a fresh start.

Chapter 8

HMS *Devonshire*

It was not long after the meeting with my divisional officer that I got my wish to join a seagoing ship, and I was drafted to HMS *Devonshire*, a country-class destroyer. To be honest, I think many at HMS *Osprey* were glad to see the back of me. I was certainly glad to see the back of many there. The *Devonshire* was over twice the size and had twice the crew of HMS *Achilles*. I joined the ship in Newcastle, which was dead handy for me because I had a week's leave at home and so only had to travel from Manchester to join the ship. The reason the *Devonshire* was in Newcastle was that it was doing a goodwill tour, and part of the tour was to also visit Middlesbrough. On the second day on board, my divisional officer sent for me. I thought, '*That's nice*'. He is going to welcome me on board and wish me all the best. Like fuck he did. He had received a letter from my former officer at *Osprey* telling him what a pain in the arse I had been and the trouble I had been in. To be fair to him, he said he would not prejudge me and wished me well while on board. He also took on board the fact that the officer from *Osprey* couldn't fault my skills, professionalism, and commitment while working; it was simply my off-duty activities that caused them concern.

I knew one of the chefs from the *Achilles* and a couple of seamen from my time at the Nelson barracks. I soon settled in my new surroundings and kept my head down, and even though I went ashore a few times in Newcastle, I managed to keep under the radar and keep out of trouble, both on and off the ship. Well, at least I tried. One of the ship's regulators (navy police) spotted me in a chef's T-shirt without my leading hands badge sewed on. Fuck me, you would have thought I'd pinched the crown jewels. He was on my case after that.

After Newcastle, we went to Middlesbrough. I have to say straight away the people from Middlesbrough are the salt of the earth, but the place was a shithole. It didn't look like there had seen any investment for years, just like so many other places in the North, but we all had a great time. I had to laugh when I saw a load of MCFC graffiti sprayed on the walls on a couple of buildings following a previous visit from City fans. The ship's crew was made very welcome by the residents in both places, and hundreds of visitors each day came on board for a tour of the ship. We also visited a couple of places in Scotland, and then it was off to Hamburg in Germany.

By that time I was mixing more and more with the stokers because I didn't get on with a couple of the chefs and stewards in my mess. I was having a chat with Rattler, Dinger, and a couple of others in the stoker's mess. The *Devonshire* was based in Portsmouth, and they asked me had I been out there much and whether I ever went in the Ideal. I told them about my misfortune on my twenty-first birthday, and they started looking at each other as I told them about the night. Then they starting grinning like Cheshire Cats. The penny dropped: they were the bastards I'd had the confrontation with when I got flung out of the pub and my crutches landed on my head! They got me a couple of cans of beer and we all had a good laugh about it.

I was duty chef one night in Hamburg, and that meant I wasn't allowed ashore on leave. I was having a drink on board with the stokers before they went ashore, and they kept on asking me to go with them. At first I refused, but then I thought, *Fuck it. I've not been disciplined for a while, and I will keep a low profile.* An hour later, we went down to the bars. I said I was definitely going back at midnight, and then it was 2:00am and then 4:00am. I thought, *Oh, shit. I have the keys to the galley. I have to open up before five in the morning*. I managed to open the galley but really needed to go to my bunk because I found it hard to stand up, never mind do any cooking, Dinger, one of the stokers, volunteered to fry the eggs, so I left him and two other chefs to it. I thought, '*Never again*'. At least the others covered for me, and I wasn't put on a report.

When the ship was back in Portsmouth, Man City were playing Stoke City in Stoke at the weekend. Even though Dinger was an Everton fan, he said he would come with me. I phoned my mate Derbo on Friday to see if he was going, but he said he would not be going. Dinger and I got the train from Portsmouth to London and then got the Manchester train from London because it stops at Stoke. There were a few City fans on the train; most were originally from Manchester but then worked in London. There were also loads of United fans on it because the reds were playing in Manchester. But imagine my surprise when I found out a football special full of United fans had already left from London. These with me were the ones who could not get on it. For some bizarre reason, United have massive support in London. It has always been a mystery to me why someone from London would bother to support United if they have no connection with Manchester, because there are loads of great clubs in London to support.

We sat next to a couple of United fans who were in the Merchant Navy, so I was soon best mates with them once they got their duty-frees out. I was half pissed when I said goodbye to my new friends as the train pulled into the train station at Stoke. Man City had a massive following that day, and at the first pub I went in, I knew a load of the lads. Just before kick-off, I was getting served at the bar in the ground when I felt a tap on my shoulder. It was my mate Derbo; he'd come down for the game after all. After pinching a beer off me, he said he had only gone to the shops to get some fags and a paper, when a mini bus full of lads from Hillock estate saw him and talked him into going.

After the game, Dinger and I tried to meet up with Pete, a store accountant who'd left the ship a few weeks earlier and lived in Staffordshire. Dinger had his address, so an hour or so later out of the blue, we knocked on his door. His dad answered and explained that Pete and his brother had gone to Weymouth to watch Stafford Rangers play. Just our fucking luck; you couldn't make it up. Anyway, his mum and dad invited us in and made us something to eat. His dad asked us if we fancied a pint in his local British Legion. We replied, 'do bears shit in the woods?' It was music to my ears. I don't think

Pete's mum was too pleased when we all staggered back. Pete and his brother were still not back, so we got our heads down in their beds, and they'd have to kip on the couch. In the morning after breakfast, we had a couple of beers with Pete and his family, and then we were on our merry way back to Portsmouth. Another great weekend was had.

While I was berthed at Portsmouth, City were playing in Sunderland. One of the chefs, Woody, was a Sunderland fan, and he asked me if I fancied going up for the game and staying at his house. Too right I did. It was a bit of a trek, but we made a weekend of it, and I had a great time with his friends and family, who made me very welcome. Even though City were playing well at the time, it was still a surprise to me that we won the game 2-0. At the time, there was not much segregation for away fans at Sunderland, so any City fans who were there were probably like me, keeping a low profile. It takes a lot of will power not to jump up and cheer when your team scores, though.

Whilst the ship was in Portsmouth, I was home on leave when City were playing Newcastle in the League Cup Final. I had been to Wembley for an England match, but this would be my first time to watch City. Derbo and a few others were going to stay in London for the weekend. The lads I went with had a transit van with a couple of mattresses in the back. We were with loads of City fans, having a drink and a good laugh in Manchester City Centre, before we set off the night before the game.

We were having a great time in London till some Newcastle fans tried to pinch a Denis Tueart flag we had. Some of the Newcastle fans were great, but some were acting like scum, saying that they could say the same about some our fans. We won the game with Peter Barnes and Dennis Tueart scoring the goals. Tony Book, our manager, became the first person to win the cup both as captain and as a manager.

The crew of the ship got excited because we were going to be the first Royal Navy ship to visit the USSR in a long time. We were to visit the port of Odessa, which was in the Ukraine, and at the same time a Russian ship was to visit Portsmouth. It was a goodwill visit, and we were to be on our best behaviour.

I was surprised at the reception we received while we were there, and how nice the place was, and how friendly the people were. Each day hundreds of locals were allowed on a guided tour of the ship. I could not believe how many wanted to visit the ship. When in England and other countries we visited, the ship tours were very popular, but I'd never expected so many from behind the Iron Curtain would want to visit a British warship.

Before we arrived, I had preconceived ideas about the place and the people. How wrong I was. When we went ashore, we had to be in uniform, and the locals asked us for our sailor hats and blue collars for souvenirs. I thought, *Why not? I have more on board.* When we got back to the ship, the duty officer was surprised at our appearance because many did not have much uniform on, but at least he didn't put any of us on report. He would have looked a right tit if he had, because there were dozens of us who gave stuff away. The night before we left, hundreds of locals were waiting to say goodbye and wish us well on our journey.

I was in a great mood when I got back to my mess to get my head down. One of the stewards started taking the piss out of me for some reason. I had never got on well with him, but I usually ignored him. This time I reacted, and we had a bit of a scuffle. It was over in seconds, and not one of us had any marks on us, but I was put on a charge. What a wanker. These sort of arguments and scuffles were not uncommon, and over the years in the navy I had been on the receiving end of a few punches and slaps; I had also seen some people get a proper beating. These things happened from time to time, and usually the ones involved shook hands the next day, had a pint, and that was the end of it. It was virtually unheard of to report someone unless it got really out of hand, or if someone used a weapon. This fucker couldn't report me quickly enough, plus a couple of witnesses came forward, which again was unheard of; normally everyone was 'asleep' and didn't hear or see anything. For that offence I got demoted from leading cook to cook. At least I couldn't get a bollocking for not having my badge on anymore. I also got moved from the chefs and stewards mess to the stokers mess. These were all sound lads, and I felt more at home with them.

We were due back in Portsmouth for a bit of leave and a few exercises, and then it was all systems go as we headed off to Singapore, Hong Kong, and other places in the Far East. I thought, '*Third time lucky*'. I would get to go to Hong Kong.

Before that happened, though, we had a serious incident. When we were at sea not far off the Scilly Isles, our helicopter was attempting an evening take off. One of the straps was still attached to both the helicopter and the ship, and the helicopter flipped over the side. One of the helicopter crew members was killed, but fortunately the others were rescued. The tail rotor also smashed into the Sea Slug missile launcher and caused quite a bit of damage. Like on the *Achilles* when the chef had died, it had a demoralizing effect on the crew, but we are all professionals and had a job to do. We had to get on with it, as sad as it was.

When we were finally deployed to the Far East, everyone was back in good spirits, but in the back of my mind, I harboured thoughts about leaving the navy. I was getting more disillusioned with the navy, and after a lot of soul searching, I thought about applying to buy myself out. It cost about ninety pounds, and you had to give six months' notice. It took about six months for them to decide if you could go or not, so usually from your request going in to you leaving, it took about twelve months if your request was accepted the first time.

The straw that broke the camel's back was when we were visiting Lisbon in Portugal. The incident really pissed me off and finally made my mind up to leave. One of the lads I knew invited four of us onto his ship, which was a supply ship and was anchored off shore in Lisbon harbour. We got a tender or tug boat to Dave's ship. After a few beers it was time to get the boat back, but the sea had cut up rough, and the officer on the watch deemed it too dangerous to board the boat to take us back; we would have to wait until the morning. Happy days – back to the bar for a few more drinks. We were picked up at eight in the morning, and because we should have been on board by eight am we were all disciplined for being absent without leave. No one could believe they would be so petty because they knew where we were, and they knew we couldn't get back. How the fuck were we to know how bad the sea would be? Fuck me. The tender had come for us, but the officer of the watch would not let us get on it. No fucker in his right mind could have blamed us for that, but we all got disciplined and received a fine and some stoppage of leave. That was when I decided the navy and I were going to part-company.

After a couple more days in port, we set sail on what would be my final trip in the Navy. At last I would be visiting Hong Kong.

One night while we were relaxing and the ship was nicely sailing along, we heard an almighty explosion this was followed shortly afterwards by the officer of the watch announcing over the ships tannoy, 'Hands to emergency stations.' We knew it wasn't an exercise, so we grabbed our life jackets and went to our positions to wait further instructions. We soon found out that there had been an explosion in one of the boilers, and we didn't have much power. It was pitch-black, freezing cold, and with high winds. The sea was a bit rough, and we were miles from land. We hoped and prayed we didn't have to abandon ship because I did not fancy a couple of hours in one of the life rafts. We were also starting to feel the cold because most of us only had on thin cotton shirts. This was something else the recruitment officer forgot to mention to me back in Manchester.

It was a few hours till everything was under control. The firefighters and damage control team did a magnificent job. We were all trained in firefighting and were prepared if our turn came to fight the fire, but it was sorted without our help. The ship was very badly damaged, and it didn't take a genius to work out we wouldn't be going to Hong Kong anytime soon. We ended up going to Malta for repairs, and we were there about two months till we were ready to go back to Portsmouth.

I really loved going to Malta because I had been there a few times when I was on HMS *Achilles*, but I was a bit disappointed that I was not going to visit Singapore and Hong Kong as my last trip in the navy. A couple of months in Malta wasn't to be sniffed at, and it wasn't long till I bumped into some old mates. Dave 'Flash' Gordon from the *Achilles* was attached to the Royal Navy base at Malta, and a lad nicknamed 'Hammer' from Hillock Estate was at the RAF base. It was great when I got invited to their respective bases because the drinks at the bar were duty-free.

For some strange reason, like in London there was massive support for Manchester United in Malta. One of the bars we were in had a big United picture on the wall. I was determined to rip it off the wall but was persuaded not to by the barman and his big Alsatian dog. Fucking spoil sports.

One night before heading back to the ship, I decided I wanted to get a Manchester City tattoo. It seemed a good idea at the time. It was midnight when we got to the tattoo shop. Unsurprisingly, the tattooist was in bed, but that did not deter me in my quest. We threw stones at his upstairs window, where he lived. I am not sure if he welcomed our visit or not, but he let us in anyway. I explained I wanted a footballer with a blue shirt and socks, with the words 'Man City Super Blues'. All went well till I realized he didn't have any blue ink. In my drunken state, I pointed to what I thought was a similar colour. When I woke up in the morning, I realized it was green. Oops.

When we eventually arrived back in Portsmouth, the ship was put in dry dock for another refit. It wouldn't be long till I left the navy because my request to buy myself went through a lot quicker than I'd expected. I had to leave the Devonshire and go to Nelson Barracks to prepare for my discharge. I was leaving the ship on Friday and City were playing West Ham United on Saturday in London. Before I left, I decided I would have a leaving do with the lads and stay in Portsmouth on Friday, and then I'd go watch City in London on Saturday. I had booked a room in a navy-run hotel in Portsmouth for Friday night. Dutchy and George from the *Achilles* met up with us, and the duty-frees were out early. Then we visited a few bars in Portsmouth. I was soon a bit the worse for wear, so a couple of the lads took me back to the hotel. For some reason that I never found out, one of the lads started rowing with me and gave me a smack in the mouth. My lip was split, and blood poured out. The bloke who ran the place phoned for the navy police. The lad who hit me had fucked off sharpish, but I was in a bit of a state, and my clothes and a towel were covered in blood. I was given stitches for my wound and was then placed in the cells of the navy barracks for the night. Fuck me I thought I was the victim! The next morning, the duty officer interviewed me, and I told him I was going on leave for two weeks and not long after that I was leaving the navy. He also took into account that it was me who was attacked, and he decided to take no further action. I was free to go.

I had a bit of a hangover, but at least I could go and watch City play, and I wasn't on a charge – or so I thought. After the game, I went home to enjoy my last leave before leaving the navy for good. Whilst at home, I carried on applying for jobs, even though I wasn't in a mad rush to start work. I fancied a month or two off because my intention was to join the Merchant Navy or work on the oil rigs. It didn't prove to be as easy as I first thought.

Whilst on leave, the regulator from the *Devonshire* phoned me at my mum's house to say I had to return to the ship. They were going to charge me after all. I thought, *'What the fuck?' I was attacked and had stitches!* I had left the *Devonshire* and was due out of the navy in a few weeks. Talk about wanting a pound of flesh.

When I went back, my punishment was three days' stoppage of leave and three days' extra work. Then they gave me another two-week leave. Work that out if you can, because it did not make any sense to me.

When I again reported to Nelson Barracks, they said if I wanted, I could forfeit the two-weeks leave and could be discharged in a couple of days. I jumped at the chance before I got into anymore shit. I did not see the point of travelling to Manchester, having to come back to Portsmouth, and then go back to Manchester. My mates asked me where I was going for my leaving do. There was no fucking chance of another leaving do because I wasn't taking any more chances. *Civvy Street, here I come.*

Chapter 9

Civvy Street

I had arranged to meet my mate George so we could travel together to London. He was going on leave to his house in Durham and was meeting his girlfriend, Sue, who was in the Wrens she was travelling up from Plymouth to Euston. It would be a couple of hours till she arrived, so we had a few drinks in the station bar then got some cans of beer from the off licence. She wasn't too pleased when she arrived to find us both pissed up and surrounded by empty cans. It was the first time I had met her, so I said hello and goodbye at the same time and beat a hasty retreat, leaving them to it.

Being out of the navy took some getting used to. In all of the forces, your routine is mapped out for you each day. I wasn't yet working, and so I thought I would chill out and relax. I was still hoping to join the Merchant Navy, but my applications weren't meeting with much success. I was hoping to join through Salford Docks, but they were going through a closure programme, so I soon realized I wasn't going to get much luck going down that route. My attempts at getting on the oil rigs were also hitting a brick wall. Things were soon going to get a whole lot worse for me when I got arrested again a few weeks later. Talk about being in the wrong place at the wrong time. I was beginning to think that was the story of my life.

It was the Friday before the FA Cup Final between Man United and Liverpool at Wembley. I and some of the lads were in the Junction Pub, on the border of Prestwich and Whitefield. We were having a good laugh and a bit of banter with some United fans who we knew. Suddenly the mood changed, and a group of about twenty United fans came in the pub. As it turned out, they were from Wales, and they were picking up someone nearby. Most of them had on big Doc Martens boots (bovver boots), and the majority had white butcher's coats on with various slogans written on them, like 'Stretford end boot boys', 'Red army', and other such nonsense. No one could fathom out why they were in the pub, or why they were dressed like someone from the time warp.

It wasn't long till they were pissing everyone off in the pub; even the local reds were having none of it. Soon a few punches were thrown and scuffles took place. I came out of the toilet to get smacked in the mouth by one of the gobby ones. I grappled with him, and we both ended up outside where all sorts of mayhem was taking place. Another lad threw him off me just as a bottle smashed on the wall just above my head. I beat a hasty retreat and went back in the pub, and it was soon over. The United fans from Wales scarpered in their minibuses, and everyone else scattered.

I got another pint and was having a chat with the landlady. We were both astonished at what had just gone on and were trying to work out why it had happened. About ten minutes later, the police turned up, and the lad with them said he witnessed me throwing a bottle that injured his mate. I was the only one in the pub and had a blue shirt on, so there was no one else to blame. The landlady and bar staff pleaded my innocence, but the police were not interested in what they had to say. I was handcuffed and put in the back of a police van. I still thought the police would realize a mistake had been made and I would soon be on my way home. My hopes were short-lived when, after a few more minutes, the door of the police van opened and about six others said it was me who'd thrown the bottle. I thought there were rules about identification of suspects instead of saying to the witnesses, 'Is that him?'

I was charged with malicious wounding, which could carry a heavy prison sentence. I was shitting myself. My life went on hold for the weeks leading up to the trial, and I was worried sick. All thoughts of joining the merchant navy or going on the oil rigs went to the back burner.

The trial lasted two days, and it started in chaos. There were no separate rooms for both sets of witnesses, so the court staff had to open an office to put the prosecution witnesses before any problems arose. As the trial started, I grew more confident. The prosecution case started to collapse straight away. Even though it was obvious they had all got together to collaborate, under cross-examination their story didn't hold water. They were embarrassed when my solicitor insisted they tell the magistrate what clothes they had on that day before the final, and why they needed to wear butcher's coats and bovver boots if they were only going for a quiet drink on a Friday night. They could not agree whether it was a bottle or a glass that was thrown, and they couldn't agree whether it was thrown with my left or right hand, or whether it was thrown straight at the person or was lobbed in the air. They also had to accept that it was very hard for anyone to believe their version, because amongst all the chaos of more than thirty people fighting and scuffling in a dark car park, the chances of all the witnesses all looking up at the split second the bottle or glass was thrown and seeing where it had landed were extremely slim. My solicitor said there was more chance of winning the jackpot on the football pools than their story being true.

The police didn't come out smelling of roses either. They could not explain why they didn't take statements from any independent people, like the landlady or bar staff. If they had, I am sure I would have been exonerated that night. Fuck me, that would have meant doing real police work to find out who did it. My solicitor asked where the bottle or glass was now, and whether it had been dusted for fingerprints. They couldn't answer. They also accepted they were not sure what the object was that was thrown. My solicitor had heard enough and asked for the case to be thrown out. I think the Magistrates did not want to embarrass the prosecution by halting the case there and then, so they asked me to give evidence. At the end of the trial it was only a matter of minutes till I was unanimously found not guilty and was exonerated yet again.

Now, you might be saying to yourself that there is a pattern emerging here – besides me having a drink and being in the wrong place at the wrong time, that is. Three serious cases, and three times I was unanimously found not guilty. If on all three occasions a minimum police investigation took place, or the prosecution had studied the cases with a bit more thoroughness, none of the cases would have gone to trial. I was bitter with the United fans from Wales, as it was them that had started the trouble. They were prepared probably because they felt they could get compensation to tell blatant lies under oath, knowing that if I got found guilty, I could have been sent to prison.

With that out of the way, I again applied for jobs. To be honest, I didn't realize it would be so hard to get a decent one given my experience and qualifications from the navy.

The next turning point in my life came later in the year, after I'd gone to watch City at Maine Road against Bristol City. I went to my local pub later in the evening, and that was where I met Cath, who is now my best mate, the love of my life, and most importantly my wife and the mother of our two lads. We are still together thirty-nine years on. Miracles do happen! She was and still is my guiding light who has supported me through thick and thin during all of our time together. I can still though remember our first row, after saying that it wasn't much of a row because Cath got into a huff and went home and left me in the pub. Can't say I blame her. I had been to an away match at Nottingham and was a bit worse for wear when I met her. Then I got worse as the night went on. Oh, well. They say true love never runs smooth.

Even though I could get to more City games, I found it hard to get a job as a chef. In the end I got a job at the local hospital as a domestic porter.

I was still in touch with a couple of lads from the navy, and I went to Everton to watch City play. I met up with my old mate Dinger and also went to Liverpool to watch City. I also met up with Rattler, but I didn't wear my Harrington jacket.

Not long after that game, England's under twenty-ones were playing at City's ground, and Rattler and his brother Dave were going to it. I met them in Prestwich, and Dave was doing the driving. I wasn't watching where he was going because I was busy talking to Rattler. Before we knew it, even I didn't know where we was because we had gone past the ground to an area I was unfamiliar with. I never lived it down because we had to ask some old bloke the way to Maine Road. I felt a right wanker.

I was still working at the hospital, but I knew it wasn't the job for me because I wasn't using my skills and talents, and the job was very demoralizing for me. A lot of the lads I knew from Prestwich were working in Haarlem in Holland at the time, which was about thirty minutes from Amsterdam. They were earning good money, and there were plenty of jobs. After a lot of soul searching, Cath and I agreed I should give it a go for a month or so. She knew I was unhappy with the job I was doing. As it happened, I went for five weeks, came home for three weeks, and went back for four weeks. Each week I saved more money in Holland than what I earned in a week in England.

I also had the bonus of watching City when I was there. The first time was a friendly against Alkmaar, and the second was a European competition against Enschede Twente. I met a great City fan in Haarlem called Johnny Waters. He still lives there, and I am still in touch with him. On the way to Enschede, a mate of mine called Kev Beesley and a load of other City fans I knew from Prestwich and Whitefield got on my train. They had arrived in Holland after getting the overnight ferry to Rotterdam. There were thousands of City fans in Holland for the game, and they were having a ball. Most were staying for a few days, and many had a night or two in Amsterdam. The game ended 1-1, so all the City fans were happy and parted well into the night, taking advantage of the liberal licensing hours in Holland. Many explored the red light areas and the coffee shops, where not much coffee was drunk but much wacky baccy was smoked.

After my stint working in Haarlem, I had only been back in Prestwich a couple of days when I got a job in a local bakery, working six days a week for poor pay and very unsociable hours. I was surprised I stuck at it for so long because I could have got nearly as much money on the dole and about three times as much working in Holland for fewer hours. After eleven months I bit the bullet and once again returned to Holland to work for a month and save some money.

When I came back to Prestwich after my final stint in Holland, I felt luck was turning my way. The day after I returned, there was a note in the local job centre window saying Prestwich Hospital wanted two assistant cooks for six weeks, to cover the Christmas period. I was up there like a shot. There was no interview as such; the assistant catering manager asked when I could start, and he was delighted when I said the next day. That was the end of working abroad, and I worked at Prestwich Hospital for the next thirty years.

The hospital had its own football pitches, and we used to play friendlies against any team who fancied a game. Once we played the prison officers from Strangways Prison in Manchester. I was just running back to my position when one of the warders smacked me on the side of the head. Fuck me, I was seeing stars. I thought about retaliating, but he was a big fucker, so I didn't bother. It led me to think if he could punch the smallest player on the pitch when the ball was nowhere to be seen, then what would he be like with the prisoners? I bet the bastard shit himself a few years later when the riots broke out at the prison.

I now worked shifts, and this meant I had to miss many Saturday games, but I still kept a season ticket, just like I did when I was in the navy in the hope that once again we could get to Wembley and I could get a ticket.

One cup game I went to was Rotherham away in a replay. My mate was driving a van, and there were about a dozen of us going. Just before we set off for the game, a lad called Milky phoned me at home to see if I was going for a pint. I said we were setting off for the game, and considering he was phoning from near my house and I hadn't seen him for a bit, I said we would pick him up, have a drink in the van, and then drop him off. Milky lived in Radcliffe, but he had been visiting his family in Prestwich. He had been to the shops to get some nappies and powdered baby milk for his young 'un. We picked him up, and the beer flowed. We had been going for half an hour when Milky and I realized we had not gone to Radcliffe, but straight on the motorway on the way to Rotherham. Something must have got lost in the conversation when I told Pete to drop him off in Radcliffe. Milky was a lifelong Blue, and his missus had plenty of baby milk and nappies in the house, so he said, 'Fuck it. I will have to be late and might as well go to the game.' Little did he realize how late he would be?

We had a great win and celebrated with a few beers after the game in a pub near the ground. Then we set off back to Manchester. We hadn't been going long when the lads wanted a piss stop, so Pete pulled up at the services. The doors were locked, so we banged on the door to attract the staff's attention. Fuck me, it could have only happened because I was there. The fucking window smashed, and glass went everywhere. How the window smashed that easily is anyone's guess. We waited for the staff to come to explain it was an accident. Just our luck, the police turned up as well, and because we were football fans, they were not having any of it and paid no notice of what we were saying. For some strange reason, they only arrested six of us, and yeah, you guessed it: it was Milky and I who were amongst the six, as well as Kev and Ken and a couple more. *Fuck me,* I thought, *not again.* We asked them to let Milky go because he had the stuff for his baby in the bag, but no fucking chance. What a shower of tossers those police were. It was pot luck which six were arrested, so they could have easily let him go back with the others in the van.

Pete, the driver, drove the others back, so had to leave me and the rest of the lads to spend a night in a Yorkshire nick. The bastards let us out in the morning without charge. After interviewing us and taking statements from the staff at the service station, they accepted it was an accident. If they had spoken to the staff at the time, the matter could have been cleared up there and then. I maintain it must have been poor-quality glass, but at least we weren't charged, and Milky's nipper got the baby stuff, even if it was a bit late.

In 1981 Cath and I got married at St Mary's Church in Prestwich. If you watch *Coronation Street*, you will recognize the church because that is where the majority of weddings and funerals for the soap takes place. It is a beautiful church, and the sun was shining for us. Cath's dad was proud as punch while he walked Cath down the aisle. She was his eldest daughter and was the first to get married. Cath has a large family, and about a hundred came down from Scotland for the occasion. It was a great day and a fantastic evening. I had just took a mortgage on because we'd bought a house in Prestwich, so I had to start picking which games I went to. If I went to an away game, I would usually jump on a minibus from Hillock because Paul Holt and the lads usually organized one.

We joined the official Prestwich branch of the City Supporters Club, and they regularly ran coaches to away games, so occasionally we went with them as well. Our eldest lad, Steven, was born 1983, and Sean was born in 1985. I was going to fewer games at that time, but when they were a bit older, I started taking them to the reserve games and the Junior Blues meetings at the ground. Then they took it in turn to go to a match with me. I also managed to get an adult and a junior season ticket, so we started going more often.

Sue Wallace, who with her husband, Dave, produces the City Fanzine *King of the Kippax*. She sat next to us, and if one of their kids couldn't go, she would give me a ring so I could take both my lads.

Cath started feeling she was the original football widow because we were at the games and she was stuck at home – and when we got home, she had to listen to us go on about what a great game it was and what a great time we had. We used to say it was great even when we were shit and got beat. Cath came with us to her first game against Spurs at Maine Road. It was an evening game, and we went in a minibus. We were in great spirits as we won and on the way home we singing on the minibus and banging on the side window in tune to the City songs. Fuck me, the window fell out in the middle of Cheatham Hill, a pretty rough part of Manchester. The driver slammed on his breaks, and we pissed our sides laughing and burst into song: 'Where's your window gone?' He was not amused, but he was in a better mood when he found it wasn't smashed, and he could just slot it straight back in. Now that is what you call quality glass, not like the cheap shit they had in Yorkshire.

Although we were not an official organized supporters branch, the lads from Prestwich and Whitefield were great at organizing and arranging minibuses and coaches to away games, plus arranging to meet up for the home games. One trip I organized was Bradford away. It was the last game of the season, and we needed a result to get promotion. We should have sealed it the week before, but we could only draw with Bournemouth at home. A draw would do us at Bradford, so we were in high spirits and confident. At the time the hospital was looking at ways of making better use of their resources. One project they looked at was to hire out minibuses and cars at weekends when they were not in use. I hired a minibus and driver from the hospital. Derbo went to Bradford a couple of times to get tickets; we couldn't get any in the City end because they had soon sold out. The only minibus they had left was a hospital transport ambulance with 'Ambulance' written down the side and a blue light on top. Chris the driver was a big City fan. We had a spare ticket for him, so he was well chuffed at going to watch City and getting paid for it. Chris is still working at the hospital. In those days, inflatables at matches were all the rage, and because we were in an ambulance, we had an inflatable skeleton. As we approached the ground, a police car started to follow us. I don't suppose it was every day they saw a load of football fans going to a match in ambulance with an inflatable skeleton hanging out of the back. When we parked up, the police stopped us from entering the ground till they spoke to all of us. Obviously they thought we had nicked the ambulance, but Chris showed them the paperwork. Then they started getting petty by looking at the tyres in the hope they could pull us for something. When they got bored, they finally let is us in the ground – but not before arresting two of the lads for being drunk. Fuck me. If they had arrested every City fan who was drunk, hardly any would have got in the ground. The game was a cliff hanger, and we got the draw we needed for promotion. On the way home, as we were approaching a roundabout, Bradford fans bricked the ambulance, cracking the window. What a shower of twats. We could have been patients for all they knew. Needless to say, there were no police in sight. Remember the old saying, 'You can never find one when you want one'?

One evening game which I arranged the minibus was Everton away. It worked out cheaper than usual for the minibus, but we were not complaining, and we knew the driver, Dave, quite well. We hadn't been going long when we worked out the bus was going a different way than we expected it to go. I was near the back, so I shouted to Dave and asked, 'Where the fuck you are you going?'

He replied, 'where you fucking told me to go: Atherton.' Where the hell did he get Atherton from? I suppose if you're a bit thick, Everton and Atherton may sound alike. He got loads of abuse from the lads, plus we had a good laugh about it. We had to pay a bit extra and then set off again, this time in the right direction. Why the fuck he thought City would be playing Atherton is anyone's guess. I know we were pretty shit around that time, but we still were not that bad. Atherton is near Wigan and was not a million miles out of our way, so no great harm was done.

CHAPTER 10

Prestwich and Whitefield Supporters Branch

The Branch Pioneers

The following gave 100 per cent effort to either help form the branch or to support the branch. Without their input and dedication the success, we had would never have happened.

Mike and Joyce Burke, Paul Holt, Mario O'Dwyer, Keith Roberts, Aide Dickson, Neil McCaslin, Brian Livesey, Dave Mitchell, Paul Botty, Ian Ramsbottom, Dave Radcliffe, Phil Greggan, Gary Gowers, Little Oz, Paul Kerry, Moonchester and Moonbeam, and all the Dolly Dealers from the many race nights and charity events – we could not have done it without you all. A big thank you to Cath who gave me total support while being chairman of the branch and for putting up with all the mither, aggravation and endless phone calls.

Many others have also helped over the years and they can all be very proud of the part they played. Without the fantastic support of the people named in the book, the branch would never have been so successful.

The following is Mike Burkey's take on what it was like to be a P&W member during the Don Price era.

It was towards the end of 1993–94 season. Word got round the local pubs in Prestwich and Whitefield that there was to be a coach going to the last game of the season against Sheffield Wednesday. There was also talk that a local supporters branch could be formed. A Mr Donald Price took down names of those wishing to go to Sheffield Wednesday on an away day coach trip. In fact, it was so oversubscribed that two coaches and a minibus were completely filled. It was Saturday, 7th May 1994, and it was the first of many away games that the branch would put on. The first meeting of the Prestwich and Whitefield branch was arranged on that trip, and the venue, the Welcome Inn on

Bury New Road, was a great choice because it was a Joey Holts pub, and there was a free private room upstairs that we could use.

The match was memorable for the birth of the Uwe Rosler chant, which was sung with gusto both on the way to the ground, at Hillsborough, and in the pub in Brighouse afterwards. I am sure the Battle of Brighouse will be documented elsewhere in these pages, but suffice to say the inaugural trip of the P&W branch got off to a somewhat memorable start!

Other notable trips involved us having one of two minibuses stolen on the way back from a Newcastle away game, with half the lads left behind in the pub whilst the driver made two round trips to pick us up. We've had a coach completely break down and be rendered road unworthy outside of Brentford FC after travelling to the ground, only for the match to be postponed due to a frozen pitch. By the time a new coach was provided, it was past midnight, and we didn't arrive back in Prestwich until 6.00 a.m. – just in time for work! We've been driven the wrong way by Blind Eddie down the M6 on the way home from a 4-0 Quarter Final League Cup thrashing by Crystal Palace. We did the conga around a Beefeater pub full of diners in Nottingham. We've had bricks lobbed at the coach window at Stoke. We even had some trips pass off peacefully. Generally speaking, travelling with the P&W branch was anything but boring!

The camaraderie amongst the members was obviously forged through the away trips and the monthly branch meetings. In addition to all of this, Don would organise gentleman's mornings at Heaton Park Social Club prior to City matches involving comedians, exotic dancers, and copious drinking. We were a big, happy family by now, and we'd all let on to each other whenever we saw anyone from the branch at Maine Road. All this despite the fact that City were pretty awful during the formative years of the branch!

We mainly existed for beer, to be honest, and branch meetings would often be one big piss-up with the chance to grill some hapless soul from the club over a Q&A session chaired by Don. By now we were unwelcome at the Welcome Inn and had outgrown the British Legion, so our meetings were now at the bigger-capacity Heaton Park Social Club. It was on one such meeting that Alan Hill (assistant manager to Frank Clark) attended. I took the opportunity to fill my boots with beer, and at the end of the Q&A, I approached him for a private chat. He was a nice enough man, but his record at City was laughable, and I told him so in no uncertain terms. Needless to say, he (and Clark) got the sack shortly after, but I was glad that the branch gave me the opportunity to vent my spleen to him. No other club I could think of would have provided players and staff to supporters' meetings like City did to our branch during those years. However, the hard work put in by Don and the committee members kind of forced City's hand to comply. They probably got sick of Don's pestering! The club sure sent us some top-drawer names: Alan Ball, Gio Kinkladze, Kit Symonds, Uwe Rosler, Paul Lake, Peter Barnes, Bert Trautmann, Tommy Booth, Fred Eyre, Mike Summerbee, Franny Lee, John Wardle, and David Bernstein, to name a few. Not to mention Bernard Manning! They were mightily impressed with the packed turnout, although what they made of Don leading the branch to a chorus of the Invisible Man or an anti-United song at the end of each meeting is anyone's guess!

The branch grew to be the biggest of all the City supporters' clubs in terms of membership, and we regularly raised money for Henshaw's Blind School amongst other local charities, not only through collections at branch meetings but through family fun days and P&W football matches. We had a team of City all-stars come play us at Heaton Park and administer a thrashing via the wizardry of Peter Barnes, whom I had the pleasure of trying to mark! But the best match of all proved to be Don's final master stroke – the final game at Maine Road.

As a final summary, I would like to thank Don for all he did in the running of the P&W branch. He was the best leader the branch could have wished for, and his character and personality made it the big success it deserved to be. If it wasn't for the existence of the P&W branch, the world of following City would have been one of misery in the nineties. Instead, we were galvanised into feeling like we belonged to the club, and that they in turn were in it for us. Not only that, but he gave me one of the best days of my life and a place in the history books – but I'll let Paul Astley take up that particular story later on in the book.

'Cheers for that Mike'

Since the late 1970s and 1980s, Manchester City were a club going nowhere. Behind the scenes, the club wasn't making progress in terms of its commercial activities and professionalism. On the pitch we had our moments, but it was usually a case of one foot forward and then two or three back. We never looked like winning anything, apart from a good cup run when we got to Wembley in 1981. In fact, we were more likely to get relegated, and unfortunately over the years, we did that regularly no matter how poor the team was, how crap the football was, or how bad the facilities at the ground were. Once you were bitten by the Man City bug, you are hooked for life, and the fans stuck with City through thick and thin.

After saying that, many fans and supporters clubs were very disillusioned with the way the club was being run, wanting the late Chairman Peter Swailes to stand down. It was dark days for the club, and the straw that broke the camel's back was when popular manager Peter Reid was sacked. The fans started to increase their opposition to Peter Swailes, and there were plenty of demonstrations and a lot of discontent. Many of the official supporters branches were split in their opposition to the chairman, and many broke away. A rival organization was formed called the Manchester City Independent Supporters Club, later changing its name to the Manchester City Centenary Supporters Association.

Like many supporters at the time, I joined the independent group. By then I was organizing more trips and was thinking about forming an independent Prestwich and Whitefield supporters branch. This was back in 1994. The last game of the season was Sheffield Wednesday away, and I organized two coaches and a minibus so that well over a hundred fans from our area went. Most were up for the idea of forming our own branch. The game finished 1-1, and we finished sixteenth in the league. We were in fine voice and in great spirits when we set off after the game. We had arranged on the way home to stop for a few drinks at Brighouse, near Bradford in Yorkshire, which was only about twenty-five minutes away from Prestwich. The bar owners were pleased to see us, and everyone was enjoying themselves with about half an hour to go before we were to get back on the coach. I went on my own to get something to eat and phone Cath; her brother was with us, and she wanted me to keep an eye on him. I phoned home to report that all was well and that we would soon be home. As I walked back to the pub where most of the lads were, I could see and hear the police helicopter. I assumed they were looking for car thieves, and then I saw one of our coach's drive pass me empty, I thought he must be going to the garage for fuel. The penny still had not dropped. I walked round the corner to where the coaches were going to pick every one up, and I got the shock of my fucking life. The police riot squad were out in force by the remaining coach and minibus, and the lads were surrounded by the police, with their dogs and vans. The helicopter had its lights on, covering the area. What the fuck was happening? I had only left them for about thirty minutes.

I was the organizer, and so the policeman in charge wanted to speak to me. *Fuck me, here we go again,* I thought. He was OK and explained that what had happened wasn't started by our lot, but he wanted us out of Brighouse. They couldn't contact the other coach because the driver must have got cold feet and abandoned us, so over one hundred of us pilled on the remaining coach and minibus, and we got a police escort out of Yorkshire. A few of the lads had head cuts and a few bruises, but nothing serious.

Derbo explained what had happened. Most of the lads and the women with us had left the pub to wait for the coaches, but some were still upstairs in the Cheers bar. One of the locals shouted, 'Your coach is here.' As people drifted out, when there were only about twenty left inside, the locals locked the door and attacked the City fans left. Cath's brother got hit on the head by a bottle, so I thought no doubt I'd get a bollocking for not keeping an eye on him. No one got arrested, and no one got seriously injured. City did not get beat, so all in all it was a great day out, plus everyone was well up for us forming our own supporters branch.

A couple of weeks later, we had our first meeting at the Welcome Inn, near Heaton Park in Prestwich. The first meeting was to see how much interest there really was. It went better than expected, and eighty people turned up, many volunteering to take on different rolls within the branch. The next meeting saw more people attending, and officials from the independent supporters club came, addressed us, and explained their aims and objectives and what support they would give us.

We formed a committee, and I explained if we were to be successful branch and have regular meetings, we needed to get guests to the meetings, whether former players officials or current players from the club. Otherwise, the members would soon lose interest. We realized it wouldn't be easy, but we were up for a challenge and knew it was the way forward.

Thanks to the contacts of the Independent Supporters Association, we managed to get Tommy Booth to our next meeting. Tommy is one of City's all-time greats. I know the term legend is handed about like confetti at a wedding, but to us City fans, he is exactly that. He was born in Manchester and was brought up on a massive Blue supporting council estate of Langley in Middleton, which is on the other side of Heaton Park from Prestwich. Tommy and his family were lifelong Blues, and from an early age signed amateur forms with City in 1965. He stayed with City till 1981, winning many trophies and scoring important goals along the way. Any player who stays at the club he'd supported as a kid for sixteen years is always going to be held with the highest of regards to the supporters of that club. He was a terrace hero to all the fans who stood on Kippax Street at Maine Road. In every game he played, it wasn't long till the fans chanted, *'Tommy Booth, Tommy Booth! He's here, he's there, he's every fucking where! Tommy Booth!'* Even now, when he attends support club events, that chant went up, even at sportsmen's dinners at forty-five pounds a head. If Tommy is a guest, you can bet everyone in the room will stand up and sing that song. He is still a firm favourite with the fans after all these years. Tommy can still be seen on match days at the new stadium; he goes round the lounges and hospitality boxes, having a drink and a chat with the fans. He has no airs or graces, and he has time for everyone – kids, women, grandads, grandmothers. Everyone wants a photo and autograph with 'our Tommy' There have been many popular players at the club, but it will be very hard for someone to be more popular than Tommy. He is still in demand at supporters club meetings, and he will always do his best to turn up for any charity fundraising. His brother normally accompanies him, and neither of them will accept any money for transport or will have a pint bought for them. I remember one event I organized, and Tommy and his brother won a hundred pounds in a prize draw. He chucked the money in the fundraising bucket.

When Tommy finally left City, he went a bit further up the Motorway to play for Preston North End. When he finished playing, he became manager of Preston. He told me a story once over a pint how mental it was to be a manager at Preston at the time, because they were skint. They had no money, and there were far too many people on the board for anything to get agreed. The chairman simply appointed friends, and anyone who did the club a favour would have a place on the board. Tommy remembers a building company that did some work for the club. When the work was finished, the club could not afford the bill, so the owner of the company was appointed the newest board member. Is that crackers, or what?

Fans could listen for hours to Tommy's stories, and he never put anyone down or slagged off anyone. One of my favourite stories was when City played Everton in the semi-final of the FA Cup in 1969. In the dying seconds, Tommy volleyed in the ball to send City to Wembley, where they beat Leicester to win the cup. You can imagine everyone's delight. Every young kid in the country would have dreamed of doing that. After the game, Tommy and the other players went out and celebrated like mad, and when he got back home to his mum's house in the early hours of the morning, the neighbours were out celebrating and had put up banners giving him a hero's welcome. Everyone was out there except his mum. He will never forget her shouting at him, 'Tommy, where have you been? What time do you call this?' He might have been our hero, but his mum was certainly not letting it go to his head. It didn't get any better for Tommy in the morning. Both the press and photographers were outside his house, wanting photographs and comments. When Tommy finally emerged with a blinding hangover from hell, they wanted photographs of him heading the ball. After all, that was what centre halves did. I don't think the photographer knew Tommy had not scored with his head. He could not wait till they had finished so he could go back to bed.

He told that story the first meeting he attended with us at the Welcome. The meeting went well but would have gone even better if a couple of pissed-up dickheads whom I didn't even know would have shut up and stopped talking. At the break, they were spoken to by one or two of the lads, and they were then OK. When the meeting finished, Tommy came for a drink downstairs with us before he got off so he could get back to his local for last orders. Just as well he did, because it kicked off downstairs just after he left. Another dickhead took someone else's drink. Despite numerous warnings, the lad wouldn't give it back, so the other lad whacked him a couple of times. The dickhead ended up on the floor, and a couple of glasses got smashed as he banged into a table. We soon calmed it down and sorted it out, and that was the end of it – or so we thought.

The next day, I got a phone call to say we were no longer welcome at the Welcome. I complained that we had hired the upstairs room, and what had happened downstairs was fuck all to do with me. He wasn't having it and claimed a couple of lads were smoking joints, which was bollocks. Oh, well. No one said running a supporters branch was going to be easy. It couldn't get any worse, could it?

Changes were happening on and off the pitch in the 1990s. On the pitch, the rebuilding of the Platt Lane Stand and the Kippax Street, which was the large standing area, took place. The Kippax had to be done to comply with the Taylor report, and the Platt Lane Stand would have probably fallen down sooner or later. The investment in the club had been lacking over many years, and the result was it must have been the oddest-shaped stadium in the country. Every side of the ground was a different shape and size. The new stands came at a cost, and that was to the detriment of the team at the time because we couldn't afford the quality players we needed. Brian Horton had already replaced Peter Reid, and off the pitch Peter Swailes was eventually replaced by the fans favourite, former City and England star Franny Lee. Like me, many fans were sceptical about Franny's lack of experience running a football club, even though he was a very successful businessman in his own right.

While the club continued to struggle, the newly formed Prestwich and Whitefield Branch was going from strength to strength, and we devised a strategy for planning away rips and getting more guests at the meetings. The first game of the new season was Arsenal away, so we organized a coach and two drivers because we wanted an early start and a late finish. The game ended predictably: we got outclassed and got beat 3-0. When we got back to the coach, ours was stopped from leaving by the police. They searched the coach and found one unopened bottle of beer on it. How the fuck we'd missed that when we cleaned the coach, we didn't know. They said they would report the coach company and the driver. I don't know if they got fined or if anything else come of it, but the bottom line was we couldn't use that coach company again. On the way home, we travelled for about an hour and a half till we stopped at a pub. One of the lads had arranged it, and we had a good drink and a laugh. When we got back on the coach, most of us were wasted and fell asleep, much to the driver's delight. I woke up just before Manchester when Fitzy, who is a great lad but hardly ever speaks, said that the two lads in the aisle next to him, Chris and Craig, never got back on the coach at the last stop. I thought, *'Fuck me, it's a bit late to tell me now!'* Not many of the lads had mobile phones in those days, so there was nothing we could do about it. We hoped the lads would get back all right. We need not have worried. We were in the pub the next day having a lunchtime drink when they turned up in fine spirits. They'd hitched a lift from a lorry driver to Birmingham and then got a coach to Manchester. Unfortunately, they wouldn't be the last ones to get left behind on one of my trips.

Flynny, Eddie McGoldrick and Kit Symons at a Family Fun Day.

Paul Power, Asa Hartford, Paul Walsh with Don and Cath.

Andy Morrison, Gary Lewis, Colin Bell and John Wardle.

Don with Gerry Gow, Tommy Hutchinson and Bobby McDonald.

Don on parade and being inspected by
the Captain at HMS Ganges.

The last ever game to be played at Maine Road was by
the Prestwich & Whitefield Branch Football Team.

Moonbeam with Toni and Cath's Dad at Maine Road.

Don on his bike.

Don's first photo at HMS Ganges.

Don Chilling out off duty at HMS Ganges.

The Marauders Football Team with the P&W Branch President Chris Greenacre.

Neil Young after training young branch members in St Mary's Park.

Don photo with his mess mates and Instructors.

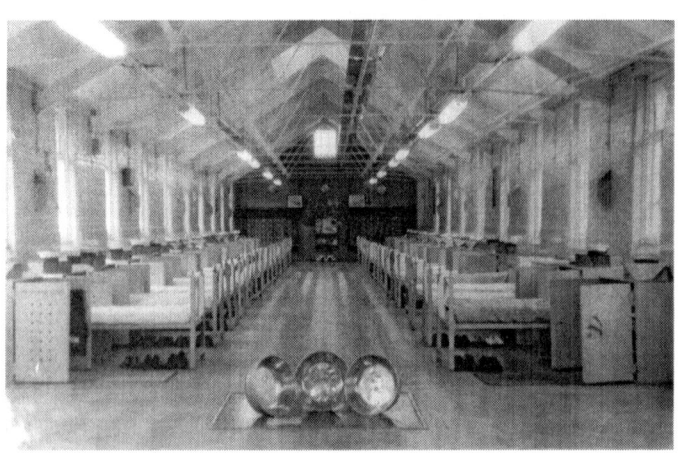

Mess Deck at HMS Ganges.

The Bee Hive City Flag.

Feyenoord Dutch Blues Flag.

Don off duty HMS Achilles.

Don with the Play Off Trophy.

Don and Ian Drinking competition before 'Tops off'.

Gio with Don & Cath in Amsterdam.

Eric Nixon singing 'Living Doll'.

City fans 'On Tour in Antwerp.

Don at The Navy Museum.

Don Off Duty on HMS Achilles
in the Indian Ocean.

David Bernstein, Andy Morrison and the Boxer Micky Gomez with P&W members.

Debs RIP Never Forgotten

Debs, Cath, Don and Ian at the Etihad stadium

Chapter 11

Royal British Legion

Because we were no longer welcome at '*The Welcome*' anymore we quickly found a new location for our next meeting: the Royal British Legion, adjacent to Heaton Park Metro Station. It was a bit run-down and the bar was quite small, but we were sure we could cope as long as they kept the beer flowing. The first couple of meetings were well attended as word spread, and we had Dave Wallace the editor from *King of the Kippax*, one of City's most popular fanzines, at the meeting for a question-and-answer session. We also had a quiz.

The next ex-player to attend was held in the same affection as Tommy Booth, especially to the older fans. It was the late great Neil Young, commonly known as Nelly. He too was a City fan, as were all his family. He was born not too far from Maine Road, and he scored some vital goals for the

Blues. It was a pleasure to meet him because he was such a humble person. He attended with his third wife, Carmen, who is such a lovely lady. Although he was hero-worshipped by the fans, he felt badly let down by City. Neil always maintained he had never wanted to leave City. He only agreed to leave City for Preston because it was obvious he no longer had much of a chance to start a game, and he was also promised a testimonial at City for all the years he had been at the Club. He always felt bitter that he never got that testimonial, and after a couple of years at Preston and then at Rochdale, he fell on hard times, which was such a shame for a City icon. He signed on the dole, and he must have been embarrassed as fuck by that because not long before he had been scoring goals to help us win the league. Neil had many jobs, including being a milkman, working in a supermarket, and being an insurance salesman. During that time, he went through two divorces. Fortunately after meeting Carmen, he got his life back on track and started a football coaching school, where he found enjoyment and fulfilment coaching youngsters around the Manchester area.

We were chuffed to bits when he agreed to do a special coaching session for the younger members of our branch. A couple of weeks later, it was back to my old stomping ground, St Mary's Park. Neil put the kids through their paces. To make the most of the day, we got the youngsters down to the Park early. Paul and Phil, two of our members, took them for an extra training session. Although they were not in the same class as Neil, they both knew their stuff because they both trained teams for the Prestwich Marauders. We thought it would add to the day. We had flags and banners up, and the whole setup looked pretty impressive. There was a buzz about the place when Neil arrived to start training the forty excited youngsters. To be honest, all the kids' parents were equally if not more excited to watch their hero in his element coaching the youngsters. It was a great couple of hours as Neil put them through their paces, and it was just as great for the parents to watch. He taught them good techniques in all aspects of the game. It was a great experience for everyone, and after the last session, we all went back to the legion, where we had arranged for Neil to present all the kids with a certificate and a medal. It was a fantastic experience for all the kids, and the parents enjoyed it as well. As a branch, we got a great deal of satisfaction about how well it went, and it meant a great deal to the kids. I got a great a buzz out of doing it, but I also felt a bit of a twat because for some bizarre reason, a couple of parents brought their kids in United shirts. I explained it was a City supporters do, and only kids whose families were in the supporters club could take part. One bloke was not having it and insisted his kid take part. I thought he was well and truly trying to take the piss, and he was told in no uncertain terms to leave. I did feel sorry for the kid because he should not have been put in that position, but his dad was obviously a prize dickhead.

For one game at Maine Road, as a branch we organized a private lounge in the new Kippax stand for our members. We invited Neil and Carmen as our guests. Neil was surprised (but we weren't) by the hero worship he was afforded from all the fans he met. Neil always came across as a very humble guy, and everyone wanted a photograph and an autograph with Nelly.

A few years later, and as Neil never got his testimonial, City supporters branches, fanzines, and websites helped organize a testimonial year where different branches would hold fundraising events and donate the money raised to Neil. At first he welcomed it and was pleased with the fans' response to him, he eventually though didn't feel comfortable that ordinary, working-class people were giving him money. Many branch chairmen, including myself, had to convince Neil we were only doing it because we felt he deserved it, and it was what we wanted to do the testimonial year proved a great success, and fans turned out in force at various events to show their support. Many former players attended the events so they too could show their support.

Unfortunately, Neil passed away in 2011. He will never be forgotten by City fans. Anyone who watched him play or met him at an event will have a lasting memory of him, and many fans also turned out for his funeral.

The branch was well up and running, and we had a few more people helping out. We were also doing a monthly newsletter, which we sent out to all the members. It was hard work but very rewarding, and Paul, Aide, and Bri Livsey played key roles in putting it together. Slowly but surely, we were getting more contacts with the club and local media. Now that we had had a few meetings and a couple of ex-players, we were now pulling out all the stops to get current players to the legion. Other supporters branches said it was very rare to get a current player to a branch meeting, but that didn't deter us, and we bombarded the club with letters and phone calls. Eventually after we pestered them for ages, we got a great response, but I think they only agreed in order to shut us up. When I told everyone that former City captain and manager Tony Book and Welsh goalkeeper Andy Dibble, along with England International Paul Walsh, were coming, the lads thought I was winding them up.

Although Tony didn't come to City till late in his career, he is Blue through and through. He held many positions at the club, some more than once. He is everyone's favourite, and he is affectionately known throughout the football world as Skip. No one has ever had a bad word to say about him. Tony didn't come into the football league until he was thirty, after he signed from Plymouth from Bath. The story doing the rounds was that Plymouth believed he was only twenty-eight when he agreed to sign but in actual fact he was older. Tony was then signed by City a couple of years later, and he soon became captain of the Blues and helped lead the team to a period of unrivalled success. Along the way, City became the first team to win a domestic trophy and a European one in the same season. Tony also became the first person to win the League Cup as captain and then as manager.

The club did the dirty on him a couple of times, and he was sacked as manager in 1980 but was soon brought back. He was again sacked in the late 1990s.

We held a night at the social club in Prestwich to recognize his services to the club. Tony was overwhelmed when nearly four hundred fans crammed into the place, and the top table was full of ex-players who turned up to pay tribute to Skip. The local Manchester radio station recorded the event and aired parts of the meeting over the following few days. Two of the ex-players who turned up were the two who'd attended the first meeting with him at the legion, Andy Dibble and Paul Walsh. Paul came up from London (where he is now a Sky pundit) especially for the occasion. Tony officially retired in 2008, but he is an honorary president of the club and the life president of the Manchester City Official Supports Club. Plus, he was introduced into the Manchester City hall of Fame in 2004 – the only person in the club's history to have all three honours bestowed on him at the same time. Even though Tony is now eighty-one, he doesn't show any signs of slowing down because he still makes regular visits to supporters meetings and charity events. He still does interviews, and of course he can be seen at the club most match days. It has been a remarkable career for a remarkable man.

Andy, or Dibbs as he was known, had a great start to his City career. He was a firm favourite with the fans when he signed from Luton. After a couple of seasons, he was out of favour and played in the reserves. He was loaned out to other clubs plenty of times before finally leaving City, when he signed for Glasgow Rangers. They played Celtic in the first game, and he kept a clean sheet. Rangers won 1-0, and he helped his new team to a ninth consecutive league title. The fans still have enormous affection for Dibbs, and even after leaving City many years ago, he is still asked to attend supporters events. He was our branch president for a couple of years till we lost contact with him and replaced him with the then young and hopeful Chris Greenacre. When Andy found out he was no longer our branch president, he phoned our house and spoke to my wife, pretending to be a reporter from the *News of the World* and wanting to know why he had been replaced. Cath was having a panic attack till Andy started laughing and told her who he was. I have met him many times over the years, and he still speaks fondly of his time at City.

When Paul Walsh first came to City, I must admit I was surprised that we'd bought him, because I thought he was too flash for our team. How wrong was I? Paul soon endeared himself to City fans with his fast, energetic, nonstop performances, plus he could score goals. He was only at the club for a couple of seasons, but played over fifty times, scoring sixteen goals. He was an exciting player to watch and was soon a fan favourite. The fans were stunned, as was Paul, when the club swapped him for Portsmouth's Gerry Creaney. All City fans were sorry to see him leave – and were equally disappointed that Gerry was his replacement.

The meeting of the three of them was a huge success. The fans thought it great that they could ask questions and have photographs and autographs with people they saw as heroes. Everything was pretty informal, and nothing was off limits. The strange thing is for most football fans, you can follow your favourite team for donkey's years and never get the opportunity to meet players who were in the first team. All three enjoyed the meeting and complimented us on how well we had organized the evening. That was probably more by luck than judgement, but we took the praise. I am sure that the first meeting with Tony and the players helped seal the idea with some at City that they should be more open to requests for players to attend meetings. Everything went smoothly, and so positive things could be said about the branch. We were rocking and rolling now. The question was, who would we get next?

Some at the club – like Margaret, one of the receptionists at Maine Road, and Gary Lewis and Liz from the Junior Blues – were brilliant with us. Having these people as contacts helped us sort things out with City a bit easier. Having to go all round the houses and dealing with some of the staff at City was not easy, and some thought we were a bit of a hindrance and were not as helpful and supportive with us as we would have liked. No one ever said it was going to run like clockwork, and we were on board for the long haul. We did not expect everyone to roll out the welcome mat for us.

As luck would have it, I was invited to the local radio station: Greater Manchester Radio, as it was known at the time. I had never been on the radio before, but I thought it would help raise the profile of the branch. Even though the other guest was ex-Manchester United player Paddy Crerand, I thought, *Why not?* It was a Sunday afternoon show; the presenter, Phil Trow, was going to be asking general questions about football; and fans were allowed to phone in to ask questions. I thought it would be interesting, to say the least. I did find it a bit odd that GMR didn't get anyone from City and opted for me instead. I was a bit nervous and wary because Paddy was an experienced radio and TV pundit, and I was a novice. Also, even though I had never met Paddy before, because of his United connections and the way he came across in interviews, I thought he was a gobby and an arrogant twat, but what did I know?

Nothing could have been further from the truth. He introduced himself to me straight away, put me at ease, and gave me a few tips. He didn't try to put me down, and he gave me a lot of confidence. I hate to admit it, but he was a half-decent bloke. The show went so well that it was extended for another thirty minutes, and the presenter and his producer was well pleased with how it went. I must have done something right because that was the first of many interviews I gave for them.

Derbo had come with me to the radio studio because afterwards we were going for a couple of pints. We were hoping for a drink or two in the broadcasting studio bar, but no such luck; we had a brew instead. We had time to have a bit of a look round the place, and it was a bit of an eye-opener seeing how everything ticks over at the BBC.

It became a lot of hard work to organize the branch's away trips and match tickets, and to get out the newsletter. I was extremely grateful for all the help the committee and others gave me, especially in the early days. One lad I hadn't met before the branch started was Aide Dickson. He was a lifelong Blue from Crumpsall, which is just down the road from Prestwich. He quickly became the branch secretary and took a huge burden off me. Another great helper at the beginning was Joyce. She was the first treasurer, but because of her increasing work commitments, she stepped down. Thankfully Keith was willing to take over. Neil started to sort the tickets out, so even though we were taking more stuff on, we were getting more organised and professional in our approach to the tasks in hand.

As Christmas approached, we decided we would take a double decker bus full of fans to watch the City players train and have a tour of the ground. Dave Leigh, the bus driver, sorted the bus out. Some of the girls sorted out a packed lunch for everyone. As agreed with the club, we would watch the players train, have a tour of the ground, and then go have our lunch in the City social club. There was also plenty of time to visit the souvenir shop. Everyone was in high spirits as we boarded the bus from Prestwich for a day to remember. Well, we wouldn't forget it in a hurry.

When we arrived at the training ground, we found out to our amazement that the players wouldn't be training after all that day. The night before, they'd had their Christmas party, and the players had been given the day off. The words 'beggars' belief' doesn't even begin to touch the surface of what we were thinking or saying. As a branch, we could have gone any day, but we went on the day the club told us to go. I thought, '*What a fuck-up*'. People had taken time off from work to come, and the kids were excited as fuck, but shit happens. We thought we would try to make the most of a bad situation.

We stayed for a bit at the training ground to watch the youth players train, and then we went for a tour of the ground. When the tour started, we were informed that the powers that be had decided we could no longer visit the impressive new lounges on top of the vast Kippax, which was a brand new stand and had not been opened that long. Fuck me, another broken promise. Never mind we were in the ground, and the kids and their parents were enjoying it even though the players were not around. People took loads of photos by the pitch, in the dugout, and in the chairman's seat, and everyone was still happy and in a great mood.

Then we got a bonus as we spotted City manager Brian Horton and his assistant, David Moss. They were soon mobbed and were busy having photos taken and giving autographs. Things were bucking up and were about to get even better. When our time was up in the ground, we went in the social club for our lunch, and we got another bonus. City favourite Uwe Rossler had turned up at the ground; he had come in to collect some kit. After being told we were in the social club, he swiftly came and joined us, and he too was mobbed and made sure everyone got their autographs and photos. What a guy! All in all, it turned out to be a brilliant day out even though it wouldn't be the last time a spanner got thrown in the works by the club.

I soon learned that not everything would go according to plan, but we had to carry on and make the most of it. The problem with organizing anything at the club was that there were too many people involved. For example, someone would agree to something with you, and then a couple of days later, you found that what you agreed was not going to happen. Sometimes we didn't find out until it was too late. We started working under the assumption that if it could go wrong, it would go wrong.

It wasn't long after that visit that Brian and David were to be our guests at the British Legion. What a boost for our morale! It was clear we were doing something right and heading in the right direction. Brian was a popular manager with the fans, but from the day he joined City, the press seemed to be out to undermine him. To make matters worse for him, not long after he became manager, the late Peter Swailes stood down as chairman, and Franny Lee took over. The speculation about Brian's future never let up because it was always assumed Franny would bring in his own man. Most fans thought Brian did a great job in difficult circumstances, and they felt Franny should have given him more support.

When Brian first got appointed to City, to their embarrassment the media led with the headlines, 'Brian Who?' That set the tone as to how he was treated by the press during his time with City. If they truly did not know who he was, they should be in a different fucking job – and if they did know, they should be ashamed of themselves. Oh, fuck me. A reporter being embarrassed or ashamed would certainly be a unique occasion. The first thing a journalist is taught is to never let the truth get in the way of a good story. Brian has never been a household name, but he has been in the game a very long time and has played over six hundred games in his football career, playing for Port Vale, Brighton, Hove Albion, Luton Town, and Hull City. In fact, Brian was team captain of the Luton team that played against City and won 1-0 to avoid relegation and to relegate City instead. He went on to manage Hull and Oxford United. As a City fan, I and most other Blues were disappointed by his appointment because we were expecting a more high-profile manager. After saying that from day one fans gave him our 100 per cent support, for want of a better description, Brian entered a shitstorm when he joined City. Brian was caught up in the middle of it, but to give him his due, he did his very best in the circumstances and impressed and won over the sceptical City fans.

There were mass demonstrations and protests before, during, and after most home games. The fans wanted Chairman Peter Swailes to stand down, and there was also a Forward with Franny Campaign, with many hoping that if Francis Lee took over, our fortunes would change. Brian had to put up with the all the shit going on around him. Once Franny did take over, hardly a week went by without the press speculating on Brian's future, and at most press conferences, he was always having to fend off those types of questions. Brian's and City's future looked brighter once Uwe Rossler, Paul Walsh, and Peter Beagrie started banging in the goals.

It was another great meeting when both Brian and his assistant, David Moss attended and they handled the questions brilliantly. We were all impressed with their commitment to the club, and we were equally impressed how he was handling all the negative press and speculation about his future. There were many youngsters at the meeting, and both the guests took time to have a chat with them, pose for photographs, and sign autographs. Even after Brian left City, not many City fans had a bad word to say about him. Over the years, he went to many City branch meetings, including ours a couple of times. He was our guest of honour when we had a sportsman dinner to celebrate ten years as a branch. Ironically, we decided to hold it back at the Welcome, where we had been banned ten years previously. From my point of view, our branch standing within the hierarchy at the club went up another notch, and that in itself brought another couple of challenges for us. First of all, some branches were not happy at our success getting players, managers, and staff to meetings, because they struggled to attract guests. But on the other side, many other branches used their connections to help us and gave us loads of support and encouragement. The second was there were so many people attending the meetings that the British Legion and the staff couldn't always cope, but those were the sort challenges that told us we were doing something right.

While at the British Legion, we had guests from the local paper, the *Manchester Evening News,* plus radio presenters from Greater Manchester Radio attending. This helped us get massive publicity for the branch, and it helped let people know what we were doing and what we were about. It increased our membership dramatically, and most of the guests who came from GMR were staunch City fans. GMR used to give our branch a plug, which was great for us, and quite often I was invited on the radio to give my comments and air my views about various subjects about City, whether it was about a recent match or what was happening within the club.

Paul Hince was the main reporter for the *Evening News* at the time, and he is also a lifelong City fan who lived the dream. He played for 'God's own club', as he often refers to the Blues in his articles for the paper. Paul was actually in the squad that won the title in the 1967–68 season, but he didn't play enough games to qualify for a medal. Paul's claim to fame was to score in his debut for City. Although he was at the club for a number of years, he did not play that many games for the first team, and after leaving Maine Road, he went on to play for a number of clubs, including Bury. After hanging up his boots, he carried on with his vocation as a sports journalist, becoming the City correspondent. He also later became chief sports writer and the paper's correspondent for the England team. He also had a weekly column in the paper that was both hard-hitting and hilarious at the same time. Paul loved coming to the meetings because he saw himself as a City fan that got paid for watching the team he had supported all his life, and he had the bonus of playing for them as well. I know he loves the Guinness and can polish off a good few pints every time he comes to a supporters meeting. As a journalist reporting on City, he had to have a thick skin because not everyone would agree with his point of view, but he used to tell me he wrote stuff as he saw it. He liked nothing better than winding up the then Manchester United manager Alex Ferguson, and also the United fans. He used to get under their skin at times, but it was all good fun even though the red half of Manchester did not appreciate it at the time. Paul could also upset the City players and the fans for simply writing the truth. If we played shit, as we often did, even the most biased reporter could not put a decent spin on those sorts of performance.

At the meetings, Paul could really relate to the fans, and the fans appreciated him sharing his inside knowledge of the club, which was second to none. One thing he told us that really pissed off the City players was when he used to mark their performance out of ten. If they were not happy, they would confront him about it or complain to his editor. He told us of one player who, after a couple of drinks in the player's lounge, got a grip of Paul because at the previous game, he was only marked with a four out of ten. The player told Paul that he did not have a fucking clue what he was on about, and the player demanded Paul explain why he only got a four. Paul kept calm, and with a straight face he told him in fact he was only going to give him a two, because he was fucking useless in the game, but the editor changed it so the player would not be too embarrassed. Paul said that soon shut the fucker up, but he did not tell us which player it was. We all had a good idea, though. I would have loved to have seen his face I bet it was a picture. I personally never took any notice of the players' marks because opinions differ. You can read a match report, and it does not tally with what you have just seen. I am sure at times all fans think the reporter has not even been to the match, or if he has, he spent the time in the bar. Over the years, I have had many a pint with Paul, and I am never tired of listening to his views, opinions, and stories.

When watching a friendly game in Ireland and having a pint with him, Cath could not find a phone. She wanted to give her mum a ring. Mobile phones were not in widespread use at the time, but Paul had one and came to the rescue. He lent it to Cath, and she rang her mum from Ireland care of the *Manchester Evening News*. Nice one, mate.

On another occasion, a few of us were having a night out at Belle View Dog Track, which is a stone's throw away from the Etihad Stadium. We used to go there now and again because the dog track and the *Evening News* used to do various promotions where we'd get in for nothing. Plus we were entitled to a free pint, chicken 'n' chips, and a first free bet. Lo and behold, we bumped into Paul in one of the bars, and we had a good chat and a laugh. I pissed my sides laughing when we told him it was great of his paper to do the promotion. He did not have a clue what we were on about, even though he worked for the paper. He and his group had paid to get in. I did not let him live it down for a long time. Paul is now retired but still does the rounds at the supporters clubs.

It wasn't long before our East German–born striker, Uwe Rossler, came to the meeting with ex-City player and youth coach Neil McNab. This was a tremendous coup for us because Uwe was a firm favourite with the fans because he scored goals left, right, and centre. Neil has always been held in high regards by the City faithful. The legion was soon packed. Uwe is another person who is so humble and grateful for getting a chance to play in England. The kids at the meeting looked at him in awe, and he was fantastic with them, posing for ages for photographs and signing autographs. The Guinness was flowing for Uwe, and he had a great time. Such is the esteem fans held for our star striker that they had T-shirts made saying, 'Uwe's Grandad Bombed Old Trafford,' with an airplane printed on them. It referred to the war, when Old Trafford was bombed.

Before joining City, Uwe had played in both East Germany where he was born, and in West Germany after reunification. He told us at the meetings how tough it was to grow up in the communist regime and how hard it was for people to adapt afterwards, but they were grateful for their newfound freedom. Uwe Rossler's brand of football was a throwback to the old days. He was a powerful centre forward who always gave 100 per cent effort for City. The fans instantly took to him, and he was at ease in the company of the fans. While at City, he became the first City player for nearly forty years to score four goals in an FA Cup game, which by anyone's standards is a fantastic achievement. Altogether, he played around 170 games and scored over 60 goals, including a cracker when he once came on as a substitute against United. He would have played more, and no doubt scored more, if it was not for some injuries and also some daft management decisions. The fans were sorry to see him leave the club, and he was not over the moon about leaving either. He played abroad for a while and then came back to England to play for Southampton and West Bromwich Albion, but he never had the same impact as he did at City.

He had to give up football altogether when he had cancer. Thankfully, he made a full recovery and was delighted with the messages of support from City fans. He then went on to manage in Norway before coming back to England and managing Brentford, Wigan, and Leeds. He did well at Brentford but struggled at Wigan and got sacked. Because of problems behind the scenes at Leeds, it didn't work out for him, and he got sacked there as well.

Uwe is still very popular with the City faithful, and he gets a great reception whenever he goes to watch City play or attends any supporters event. When City played Gillingham at Wembley in the playoff finals, Uwe was sat with loads of our branch members and had a great time. I was gutted when I saw all the photos they had with him; I sat somewhere else and did not see him. Our branch will never forget what a great bloke he is. In 2009 Uwe was admitted to the Manchester City hall of fame. Uwe has said many times he found his home in England during his time at City, and he has described his bond with City and the fans as unbreakable and the biggest achievement of his career. He has two sons: his eldest is called Colin, after ex-City player Colin Bell, and his youngest is called Tony, after ex-City captain and manager Tony Book. That sort of bond and his friendship with City and the fans is unbelievable, and his eldest son is also a member of the Manchester City Academy. No wonder City fans love him to death and would be over the old blue moon if he ever got a job in some capacity at the club.

Neil was at the meeting to look after Uwe, but we ended up looking after Neil because he got in a right state and was shit-faced by the end of the night. He didn't want to drink beer because he didn't want to keep going to the toilet during the meeting; his fucking bladder must have been worse than mine. I seem to put one pint in and then pee two pints out. Neil was on whiskey, which was trouble for him because all the fans kept buying him one, and they would not take no for an answer. I realize the Scottish people like a whisky or two, but Neil must have put enough away to launch a battleship. Neil was a cracking bloke; 'a tough little Scott who takes no shit' is how he was once described by the fans. City bought him in the early 1980s, and he stayed at City for about seven years. The fans loved him because he always gave his best, would not take any crap from the opposition, and always got stuck in. After he left City, he played for a host of other clubs before coming back to City as a youth team coach. He was a popular appointment, and it was during that time that we first met Neil and invited him to our supporters branch meeting. That was why he came with Uwe. At the meeting, Neil told it how it was, and the fans loved his stories told.

After one meeting, he came back to my house for a few more extra drinks. It was there that he told me how bad that the youth setup really was and what problems the club had as a whole. I thought, *'Fuck me. Here I am, pissed up in my own house with one of my idols from City, and he is giving me inside information on the club!*' He was clearly not happy the way the club was being run, and he was not the only one. Half the stuff the club was doing was shambolic. Cath took some photos of me and Neil in my house, but just my fucking luck, they never turned out. I blamed Cath for being pissed, but she is not having it and blames it on the fact it was a shit camera. She could have a point. I was not surprised when, not long after his revelations, he lost his job at the club. It was hardly surprising he'd lost his job because like Neil had said, it was a shambles. In the 1996–97 season we had five different managers. The only consistent thing about the club at the time was the loyalty of the fans. Neil had a great time at our meetings, and to this day he is still held in high regard by the fans.

Franny Lee, who was Manchester City's chairman at the time, and former City player Mike Summerbee also came to a meeting. Later on, they came to a sportsmen's dinner we organized. The sportsmen's dinner we organized was for a local charity, and we were pleased that both Franny and Mike had agreed to attend, along with many other ex-players. These sort of events, organized by the fans and attended by people at the club, were a great way of bringing the club and the fans closer together; they helped cement a decent relationship instead of an 'us and them' attitude, which is usually the norm at most football clubs. Franny loved the fans and had the club at heart. Many others like me thought that he simply didn't realize what he was getting into when he took over at City, and he didn't realize how big a fucking mess the club was in. Players were on big wages and were tied to long contracts, so it was hard to get rid of players even if the club wanted to. The other problem Franny had was when he joined the club, he made many promises and statements, but for many reasons he couldn't deliver. At the meetings, though, he was one of the lads, drinking a can of beer and eating pie and peas with the rest of us.

As a footballer, Franny had a very successful career. His first club was Bolton Wanderers, which was very handy for him because he was from West Houghton, which was not far from Bolton. The very first time I went to see Franny play, I was about twelve years of age, and he was playing for Bolton against Bury at Burden Park, which was a half-decent ground in those days. The Bolton fans loved him. Not only was he a local lad, but he always gave his all and did not know when to give in. He was an all-action player who could score goals. At the game, the Bolton fans displayed a large banner with the immortal words, 'Franny Lee – Alias God.'

City fans took an instant liking to Franny when he joined the Blues, and Franny was part of a very good City side at the time that went on to win quite a few trophies. He also went on to play many times for England. While still a footballer, Franny set up his own business, which was very unusual for players at that time. Players were on a decent wage compared to the working-class bloke, but most had to get a job when their careers finished. Franny was looking well into the future and ended up becoming a millionaire through his toilet roll business. While at City, he set a record of scoring fifteen penalties in one season, and he earned the nickname '*Lee Won Pen*' because most of the penalties were awarded for fouls on him. Many accused him of diving, but we didn't believe any of that shit. They were simply bitter at his success. Every one of those fouls was a genuine penalty '*honest*'.

Why Franny was sold when he was, is another strange decision made by the club, because we were doing well at the time. Franny did not want to leave, and he was still very popular with the fans. It was another in a long list of barmy decisions made by the club over the years.

I am not really sure what inspired Franny to become chairman of City, because he did not really have a lot to do with the club once he left in the early 1970s. Maybe it was a combination of the fact he was disappointed at how bad the club was being run at the time. Under Perter Swailes, the club was being ripped apart. Franny still had a lot of connections in Manchester, and in the end he was persuaded to help try to oust the present chairman. Very quickly the grassroots campaign group *Forward with Franny* became a driving force, and it was only a matter of time till he took over.

Although Franny went into this venture with his eyes wide open and did all the due diligence checks, I always thought he took on a bit more than he could chew. The club was in a much bigger mess than anyone had thought. Even though the situation was much worse than he had anticipated, he put his heart and soul into the club, especially in the first couple years. He was very accessible to the fans; I spoke to him on the phone many times and also met with him at the Platt Lane Training Complex for a drink and a chat. The first time he phoned me up, I nearly hung up on him because I thought it was someone winding me up and taking the piss. For me, Franny's biggest mistake was not giving Brian Horton his full backing from day one. Franny should have stood by him instead of sacking him and replacing him with his old mate, Alan Ball. That mistake annoyed many fans because Brian was a doing a decent job in difficult circumstances. Alan was not a popular choice because he had not achieved anything as a manager and did not look like a decent replacement. Franny had only been at the club a couple of years when a group of City fans, calling themselves '*Free the 30.000*' were formed. Their aim was to get rid of Franny. Fuck me, it could only happen at City, but it just shows what a shit state of affairs the club had got itself into over the years. What got on my tits was the same thing that baffled most other fans: most of the fuckers who had run the club over the past decades were successful businessmen in their own rights, but if they had run their own businesses like they'd ran our football club, they would have gone bankrupt overnight. It seems to me common sense goes out of the window when people are put in charge of a football club. Either that, or they simply did not give a shit because nine times out of ten, it was not their money they wasted. I never got involved in the campaign to oust him because I did not know at the time who would replace him, but I was not disappointed when he stood down. At long last, stability slowly returned to the club when Franny was replaced by the vice chairman, David Bernstein. Franny was well liked and popular, and it was a shame it did not work out for him. One thing he did get spot on was starting negotiations that would eventually see City leave Maine Road and move across Manchester to Eastlands. In 2010 he was inducted into the English Football hall of fame and was awarded the CBE in the 2016 in the New Year Honours list.

A Football Fan's Story

The legion was finding it hard to cope with the amount of people at our meetings, so many went to the local off-licence and brought in their own drinks. The woman who ran the legion wasn't happy, but I didn't give a shit. If she couldn't get her act together, it wasn't my fault. This wasn't the first falling out I'd had, and it wasn't to be the last. We seriously thought about going elsewhere for the meetings.

The first time I met Joe Corrigan was at a Junior Blues meeting at the social club at Maine Road. I took Steven and Sean when they were nippers. Joe had been a brilliant goalkeeper, and although he was no longer at City, like many ex-players he still held a great amount of affection for the club and attended various meetings and events. Joe was a huge bloke who was the typical gentle giant. He had a great sense of humour and a great laugh. He spent ages posing for photos and signing autographs for everyone at the meeting. Joe had a fantastic career during his time at City, but it was not easy for him at the beginning. He got a load of stick from the fans for some daft mistakes he made, but he soon won them over with some outstanding displays, and he went on to win many medals with the Blues. He also went on to play for England.

One game I will never forget was when we played Derby County away. The pitch was a mess with hardly any grass; it was more like a farmer's field than a football pitch. Derby was awarded a penalty, but there was a slight problem that ended up a big fucking problem. The white markings for the penalty spot had disappeared, so the penalty taker was not sure where to take it from. Joe, being the kind-hearted bloke he was, thought he would help out by pacing out the twelve yards to where the spot should be. Instead of the referee being grateful for Joe's help, the miserable fucker booked Joe because he thought he was taking the piss. We all thought that referee was a miserable twat. The solution finally came in the form of one of Derby County's groundsmen, who came running onto the pitch with a tape measure and a bucket of white stuff to mark a penalty spot. You could not make this sort of shit up, could you? And it could only happen with City being involved. After waiting very patiently, the Derby penalty taker blasted the ball past Joe, who could do fuck all about it. Derby went on to romp home to a 4-0 victory, so it was a bad day all round for Joe, City, and the fans. That moment was a farcical situation made worst by the referee acting like a dickhead.

My brother met Joe when Joe was on duty with the England B Squad, when they were on tour in New Zealand. My brother was living there at the time. Bob was just coming out of the pub by the ground when the England coach pulled up. As Joe was getting off the coach, he spotted that Bob was wearing a Manchester City scarf, so he went over and had a quick chat with him. It was a great gesture, and Bob was chuffed to bits because it is not every day you get a chance to meet and talk to one of your all-time footballing heroes on the other side of the world.

The first time Joe came to a meeting, I was having a chat with him before the meeting got underway, and I was quite surprised that he was not very complimentary about some of his former teammates. I naively thought they were all best mates because most of them were together for many years; I had the impression they got on great together. Nothing could have been further from the truth. When I mentioned one ex-player's name whom we tried to get to the same meeting with Joe, his exact words were, 'If that cunt had turned up tonight, I would have fucked off.' That took me by surprise, and I was chuffed to bits that the other player was unavailable. Then it got me thinking about my time at school and in the navy, and my years at the hospital. Just because you work together for so long, it doesn't mean you are the best of mates. Joe is another ex-player who is held in the highest esteem by City fans, and it was a big surprise there was no role for Joe on the staff at Maine Road.

Instead, for many years he was goalkeeping coach at our arch-rivals', Liverpool. When he was there, England beat Germany away 5-1. There were five Liverpool players in the England squad, so we contacted Joe and sent him three England shirts for the five players to sign. Joe arranged it for us no problem, and we used them for auction prizes at various sportsmen's dinners, sending the money to our nominated charities. Joe is still popular with the fans, and he still attends various events. He was unlucky with his England career because he played only nine times for the first team. At the same time Joe was at his peak, he was competing with two world-class goalkeepers, Peter Shilton and Ray Clemence.

It was always in the cards that Brian Horton was going to get the sack sooner rather than later. It came as no great surprise when he finally got his marching orders, but the way it was done did City no credit. There were rumours that he had been sacked, but the club denied it. Then Brian was interviewed, and he said he had not been told he was sacked; he had only recently met with some club officials, and as far as Brian was concerned, it was business as usual. The rumour mill went into overdrive, with every man and his dog being interviewed. Then someone at the club made the announcement that Brian's contract had been terminated after all. By now the media were in a frenzy, and when Brian was again interviewed, the club had still not told him. It must be bad enough to be sacked in the full glare of the media spotlight, but to have it done in that manner beggar's belief, and the way it was handled brought shame on the club.

With Brian now gone, once again we had the manager's job vacant. What made matters worse was that before Brian's replacement was made, Franny had made extravagant claims about the pedigree of the new manager. We were all led to believe it was going to be a top-class manager with experience winning trophies, and all our troubles would be over. Fuck me, were we disappointed when it was announced that Alan Ball was to be our new manager. Although Alan had been in the game a long time and his credentials as a player were impeccable, as a manager they left a lot to be desired. Alan was a great footballer – of that there is no doubt. He joined Blackpool as a youngster and played in the first team when he was only seventeen. After four years there, he joined a great Everton team, and they reached the final of the FA Cup only to get beat by West Bromwich Albion. He also won the First Division Championship. He then moved to Arsenal, where again he got to the FA Cup final, but this time they got beat by Leeds

DON PRICE

United. Alan will be most fondly remembered for his time playing for England, memorably as a member of the England World Cup team who beat Germany 4-2 in 1966 at Wembley. It was the first and only time England have won the cup. In 1999 Alan and four other members of the World Cup team was awarded the MBE.

Although the City fans were disappointed with the appointment, like all managers before and after him, we gave Alan the benefit of the doubt and threw our support behind him and the team. The team was playing badly. Well, 'badly' might have been an understatement. We had not won one game out of the first eleven we had played, and the fans' patience was wearing a bit thin. But give him his due: he came to one of our meetings.

I will never forget the first game we won that season. My youngest son, Sean, had won a competition in the *Manchester Evening News* Saturday sports paper, the *Football Pink,* and he was to be the club mascot against Bolton Wanderers. It was great for the whole family, and when Sean went out to warm up with the players, he got a tremendous ovation as he chipped our then goalkeeper to put the ball in the back of the net. Our goalkeeper at the time was a German called Eike Immel, but unfortunately he was not in the class of our most famous German goalkeeper, the legendary Bert Trautmann. Eike was nicknamed the Vampire by the fans because he was scared of crosses: the fucker would hardly come off his six-yard line. No wonder we were letting so many goals in. Sean, and all of us had a great day, and the club really looked after Sean. He had many photographs taken with the players, got a tour of the ground, and had a good chat with the captain, Kit Symons, as well as the referees and linesmen.

Whilst at our supporters meeting, Alan spelled out his vision for the future. He never ducked any questions and came across as very committed and genuine. But for us, all that mattered was what was happening on the pitch, and one win out of twelve did not bode well for the future. Like with Brian before him, it was obvious there were still massive problems behind the scenes that Franny had not managed to put right. We hoped Alan could put it right on the pitch, but we doubted it. We got thrashed twice by Liverpool twice in the same week and, the fans started singing sarcastically, *'Alan Ball is a football genius.'* It was a bit ironic: the worse the team played, the more the fans got behind the team.

Amazingly, the branch was going from strength to strength even though the team was shit. We were still getting quality guests to the meetings, and branch membership was increasing month by month. It was not all plain sailing, and a few of us were putting in a lot of hard work behind the scenes because there was so much to organize.

Many at Maine Road were still helpful and went out of their way, but a few were just as unhelpful. We never thought it would be all plain sailing and just got on with organising stuff the best we could. For certain games on a couple of occasions, we were given a load of complimentary tickets, so we were able to take kids and families to see the games. We would organize something to eat for everyone, and we'd organize transport to the ground and back so we could make it a great experience. On one occasion, the coach driver met us but then refused to take us. He said it was not the firm's policy to take people to football grounds. Obviously he was a tosser and a bitter Red, or he was simply thick. He must have been told where he had to take us to when he'd left the depot. He was a really rude, arrogant twat, and he mouthed off to us in front of the women and kids. Once I showed him the paperwork and got him to phone his boss, he reluctantly took us.

Gary Lewis and Liz Douglas, who were still in charge of the Junior Blues at the time, helped us out a lot. In fact, they must have been sick of the sight of me trying to blag prizes from them. Unfortunately, Alan could not get the best out of the players. Instead, it was the opposite, and after his first season in charge, we got relegated. A few months later, Alan was sacked. Unfortunately, Alan passed away in 2007.

No one was more helpful than the new club captain, Kit Symons. He was from a big working-class family, and his feet were firmly on the ground. I wrote him letters inviting him to a meeting, and he phoned me up at home to sort it out. At the time, loads of people didn't reply or got their secretaries to say no. Kit was great at the meeting and said he wanted to leave at 10.30pm because he had training in the morning. As if that was ever going to happen! We had a lock-in, and I forgot how many times I said, 'I've just phoned the cab company. It is on its way.' Kit helped us get many other players to the meetings, and he was always willing to support charity events. One such event, organized by the Rochdale branch, saw loads of players and fans playing Ten Pin Bowling at Pilsworth, near Bury. Loads of money was raised, and then we went for a scran with Kit and his missus, Lucy. Our Sean ordered something which he didn't like, so Kit swapped with Sean. Sean lived on that story for ages at school, and it was even better when Kit dropped off Steven and Sean at our house in his state-of-the-art sports car. I suppose it was better than going home in my Lada.

Cath, the kids, and I got invited to Kit's for tea one night. I had fancied a drink, so one of our other mates, Flynny, did the driving. I had visions of Kit and Lucy sweating over a hot stove when we got there. Not a chance. When we got to their house, they asked if we fancied a chippy tea. We all love a chippy tea, so Steven and Sean played computer games while Kit went off to the chippy, plus we had pickled eggs. What a man! The kids were buzzing because we had a great evening with them, and that was another story they lived off for ages. I bet some of their mates thought they were full of shit, but you cannot make up that sort of stuff.

One game when City were playing Portsmouth at Maine Road, I hired one of the suites in the Kippax for any branch member who wanted to come. Kit asked if he could have eight tickets for his mum, Lucy, and other mates coming from Portsmouth (the team he used to play for). Here was the captain of City asking me for tickets. Fucking brilliant! It was great meeting his mum, but I don't think she was too impressed when Kit dropped a clanger on the pitch and my mate Tommy started abusing him. I had to remind him who are guests were. Oops! His mum was a star like Lucy and took it on the chin. At one point I thought she was going to give him some stick as well! Kit used to get us tickets for the player's lounge, and on one occasion after a game, one of the defenders who wasn't playing that day came staggering across to us and asked how many bottles were in a crate of Budweiser. Kit thought there were twenty-four. 'Great,' the defender slurred. 'Only another six to go.' With that, he staggered off somewhere else. Mind-boggling, or what?

Kit was always the star of the meetings and family fun days. One meeting he came to was at very short notice. At six on the evening of the meeting, Kevin Bond, the reserve manager at the time, stopped Chris Greenacre and Paul Dickov (who were in the reserves) from coming to the meeting because they had a game the next day. What a joke, it was agreed by Alan Hill, City's assistant manager who was also attending; he said that they could come because he was also attending. Alan shit himself when he came in the room and saw that there were over three hundred fans already in the room. I told him the players couldn't come, and he must have felt a right dick because he was the assistant manager but Kevin Bond had overruled him. That was the sort of shit going on at the club at that time. My mate Flynny contacted Kit and called in a big favour. Kit came for the last hour and saved the day, and he saved Alan's bacon.

My family and I were privileged to be invited to Kit and Lucy's wedding at Portsmouth Cathedral.

It was a great day, nice and sunny, and we met loads of Kit's and Lucy's families. They were all down to earth and great with us. Kit and Lucy were in big demand with their families and friends, but they still took time to have a chat with us and make us feel very welcome. Both our lads had a dance with Lucy.

While we were at Portsmouth, it gave me a chance to show Cath, Steven, and Sean some of the places I had been when I was in the Royal Navy. It was the first time I had been back to Portsmouth since I had left the navy. We went on a tour of the navy dockyard and also went on a tour of HMS Victory which was Admiral Nelson's flag ship. We went over to Gosport, where the submarine base at HMS Dolphin was; it is now a submarine museum. There were also quite a few Royal Navy ships in the harbour, and the sight of them never fails to impress me. It was a great weekend all round. Cath, Steven, Sean, and I were so chuffed that we had been invited to the wedding, and we could not thank Kit and Lucy enough.

The last we saw Lucy was when Cath and I were in London for the final of the Royal Tournament at Earls Court. The last time I had been to the tournament was when I was representing the Royal Navy and doing the window ladder display. This time the Royal Navy was represented by the field gun crew. It is a pity that the annual Royal Tournament was stopped because it was a fantastic event, showcasing talents from armed forces from around the world. Some of the displays are unique and breathtaking, and the marching bands are a sight and sound to behold. Cutbacks within the forces forced the Royal Tournament to cease because it takes months to train personnel for these sorts of events, and because of all the commitments the armed forces have round the world, the personnel can no longer be spared the time they need to train and perform.

We met Lucy on both days we were in London, but Kit was on a training session somewhere with the Wales squad. Lucy made us a lovely meal, and I did my best to drink Kit's beer fridge dry but failed miserably. Over the years we lost touch, but to this day we still send each other Christmas cards, and we always looked out for Kit's results when he was playing and managing various clubs.

Last time we met Kit was after he signed for Crystal Palace. Aide and I managed to blag our way into the players' lounge to see him. City were playing down there, and I did not want to pass the chance up of saying hello. We must have been fortunate because the steward we asked to take us to see Kit was very obliging and helpful. Some stewards won't give you the time of day, so it was our lucky day. There are not many like Kit playing in the Premier League today. He might not have been the best player at the club, but he always gave it his best, and as a fan you cannot ask for more than that. Plus, he genuinely cared for the fans and was always popular at the different supporters events that he attended. Unfortunately, if things were not going great on the pitch, he was a target for the boo boys, and at times he got some dreadful stick from City fans.

More of us organizers and members were getting more pissed off at the legion with the way we were being treated. We felt after more than fourteen months of going, we were now being taken for granted. They probably took more money and sold more beer on one of our Tuesday meetings than they would do over six weeks of normal service, but they were acting as though they were doing *us* a favour.

The final meeting at the legion was a fundraising event for Paul Lake's testimonial year. We called it a day because the staff could not or would not cope with the amount of people that were turning up to each meeting. Paul was a City fan as well as a player, and he had been at the club all his life. A horrific injury cut short his career, and after months of operations and physio, it became clear that his life as a footballer was finished. It was such a shame because he had the footballing world at his feet. Fans also thought that Paul had been treated badly by the club; we felt he should have had the best specialist treatment money could buy straight away. Many other players who'd had similar injuries managed to resume their footballing career, but Paul had a couple of operations before he saw a top specialist in America. While he was recovering in America after one operation, some of the players did a whip-round so that his girlfriend could visit him, because the club would not pay for her to visit.

Tudor Thomas a life president of the club, was organizing Paul's testimonial year. Paul would be attending the meeting a little late because he was at evening studies at college in preparation for his exams. Tudor, fans favourite Gary Flitcroft, and future Captain Richard Edghill also attended. The place was packed, and the fans and guests were in top form. There was a lot of speculation that Gary would be sold; basically, City were skint and needed the money. He reassured us time and again that he would definitely not be leaving City. That was on Tuesday. On the Thursday he was sold to Blackburn Rovers for £3.2m Oh, well. What can anyone say about that? Typical City. Many of us believed that Gary genuinely did not have a clue he was being sold, or that if he did think it was on the cards he was going to leave City, he did not expect it to be that quickly.

Halfway through the meeting, the door opened, and in came Paul Lake on his crutches. Everyone in the room stood up and gave Paul a standing ovation that lasted nearly five minutes, and there wasn't many dry eyes in the place. Paul was visibly surprised at how many were there and at the reception he received. When he had recently been to his own branch, where he was president, there were only about thirty fans there. He had been expecting the same amount at our meeting. Paul was very articulate and a very down-to-earth bloke. He was fantastic with the fans and spent ages chatting with them, as well as signing loads of autographs and having photos with the fans. There were loads of kids in the audience, and Tudor did a competition. There was two winners, and our Sean won a great prize. He was to be a guest at Tudor's private suite at the ground for a future home game. I was also invited, and after a bit of negotiation, the entire family could go.

Before the game started, there was a bit of a misunderstanding. I thought I was to sit with Sean, but Tudor thought I was sitting in my normal seat with Cath and Steven. Before that though, we had a nice buffet in the lounge, and Tudor's grandkids took our lads for a tour of the ground while Cath and

A Football Fan's Story

I were left to help ourselves to drinks; Tudor and his wife were in the chairman's lounge having lunch. About fifteen minutes before the game started, Cath and Steven went to their seats. The players came out, and Tudor asked me where I was sitting. Obviously something had got lost in negotiations. I thought I was to sit with Sean, Tudor, and his wife. To his credit, Tudor didn't bat an eye lid and made sure we were all seated. Then he went off to find a seat for himself. What a fantastic bloke. At half-time, we had more drinks, and it was the dreaded Stella again. As the game was about to restart, I had just started another drink. He gave me the keys to lock the door for when I came out to watch the game. After the game, Cath and Steven came round to meet us, and we had another chance to have a quick chat with Paul Lake because after the match, Paul came in the lounge. He and Tudor were going to a hotel in Manchester for another testimonial event. What a great day out we had, and I can't thank Tudor and his family enough for their hospitality.

Paul's testimonial football game was against Manchester United. There was a decent crowd and a good atmosphere. Fair play to the United fans who came because there was a good turnout from them plus there was no trouble, and if anyone deserved a decent send-off, it was Paul. He had been a City fan all his life and had been at the club for a long time. It was such a shame what happened to him.

I don't usually do testimonials, but I thought I would make an exception for Paul. The only other one I went to was when I was in the Royal Navy. It was for Paul Hart, who was an ex-player who was also the manager of City for six months, but he had to finish early because of his health. I went because I was home on leave at the time. At the end of the match, I and a few hundred others fans were left in the Kippax and were about to make our way out of the ground after applauding the players off the pitch. A police sergeant started marching about and asking us to leave. I must not have been quick enough for him, and the bastard hit me in my stomach, causing me to double over with pain. I thought, Bastard! What the fuck was that for? Out of all the people in the ground. Why me? A lad who had seen me get punched, told me to report it and he would be my witness; he also had the policeman's number. I thought there was no point, and it was not worth the hassle.

It was not the first time I had been hit by a policeman at Maine Road. When I was about eleven, I got a crack while at the ground – and this was before the game had even started! As was the norm in those days, I and dozens of other kids sat on the Kippax wall with our feet dangling over the side where the pitch was. I was reading my match programme, and the officer told us to put our feet back over the other side of the wall. Again I must have not been quick enough for his liking, so as he walked past, he slapped me hard in the face. That's the story of my life, but if you think he could do that to an eleven-year-old kid in front of witnesses, I would not like to think what the fucker would do if he was really pissed off in a police station cell with a prisoner and no witnesses.

Another fundraiser I attended for Paul's testimonial year was a junior boxing match at City's social club. I was never really into boxing, but it was a night out and was for a good cause. The bouts were only for three rounds each, and all the kids had head guards on. They did not go half at it hammer and tongues. There were eight fights altogether, and it was a great night. There was also a three-course meal and a compare, and best of all, no kids were injured. Many people might not agree with lads so young taking part in such a tournament, where the objective is to punch the other person harder than he can punch you, but the kids seemed to enjoy it, and they would not have been there if their parents had not approved.

Paul is still well respected and recently had yet another operation, this time to replace his knee. Now he is in much less pain. For years Paul was an ambassador for Manchester City, but he left that role to take up a similar position for the Premier League. Since that meeting at the Royal British Legion, I have met Paul on many occasions, and he never forgets the reception he received when he attended the meeting. He is still a City fan through and through, and he still gets invited to supporters events because the fans still think the world of him. It was a special meeting, and it meant as much to the fans as it did to Paul.

Chapter 12

Heaton Park Working Men's Club

After the British Legion, we went a bit further up the road to what was then called the Heaton Park Working Men's Club but later changed the name to Heaton Park Social Club. The legion people were not happy, but they should have got their shit together because they knew how big the meetings were. In all honesty, it was time to move on because we were out growing the place – the branch was becoming huge.

The Working Men's Club suited us a lot better. It was bigger and more comfortable, plus it had a much bigger bar. Over the next few months, the branch really took off. The meetings were packed to the rafters each month, and the fans were coming from far and wide because they'd heard how good the nights we put on were. Many ex-players, current players, stars from Coronation Street, the Legendary Frank Sidebottom, radio presenters, *Manchester Evening News* reporters, Mick McCarthy (the Ireland manger), and our local MP Ivan Lewis also turned up. Past and present directors, managers, and chairmen were more than willing to attend.

The bigger and more successful the branch became, the more the backstabbers were out in force. That didn't deter us. If I had not had a thick skin when I'd formed the branch, I certainly had one now. I was a bit nervous before the first meeting at our new venue. No one could be too sure how it would work out and whether the members would take kindly to the move, even though it was in their interests to move and most of them were fed up with the way we were being treated at the legion. We need not have worried because even though it was a much bigger and better room, the place was soon full. Most important, the bar staff was on the ball and quickly served everyone.

Dennis Tueart and James H. Reeves were our guests to that very first meeting. At the time, Dennis was one of City's directors. Although born in Newcastle, Dennis went on to play for local rivals Sunderland and City signed him a few months after he had helped Sunderland beat Leeds United in the FA Cup. He quickly established himself as a firm favourite with City fans with his all-out attacking style of play, plus he scored many goals for the Blues. He will be forever remembered for his goal against Newcastle in the League Cup final with a spectacular overhead kick. With Peter Barnes scoring the other, we went on to win 2-1. There was a chant for Dennis at the time, which was, 'Dennis Tueart – King of all Geordies.' It was sung loud and long on that day.

Dennis had a break from City for a couple of years when he went to America to play for New York Cosmos. After leaving City for the second time, he ended up playing a handful of games for Stoke City. Then he finished the season off with City before going to Ireland to play for Derry City. His appointment as a director at City was welcomed by the fans, who were extremely disappointed when he was sacked as a director after the takeover by Thaksin Shinawatra. Dennis was well respected by the fans because he had a great rapport with them and went to many City supporters events. He had a great career with the Blues and also played for England. The night was a great success, and it was the first of many events that Dennis attended for us.

James was a considerable assist to our branch whenever he came to a meeting or events. He a lifelong City fan who was also a local radio presenter, and he was an in-demand after-dinner speaker.

James has tremendous contacts within the local entertainment circles, and he has many ex-players as his friends. There are few better than James at holding an audience and entertaining people on stage in front of a packed audience. Luckily for me and the branch, he lived around the corner from my house and attended as many meetings as he could.

He made a special effort to come and help me out if we had the chairman or the manager attending. His skills certainly enhanced the meetings, and he would never accept a fee. James also used his influence with his contacts to bring guests to the meetings, and on occasions he came with us as our guest to away matches. He was genuinely astonished how much some of the lads drank before games.

When we went to Cardiff for a European game against TNT, we organised a coach and stayed in Cardiff overnight. He thought we would never get there because it seemed to him that we couldn't go more than a few miles without stopping at a pub for a drink. As time ticked on towards the match, James got nervous. He said, 'We have come all this way. We won't see kick off at this rate!'

We assured him, 'No problem, James. We will get there in time.' We did, but only just. We won the game, and because we were staying overnight, we went round a few of the bars to sample the local hospitality and night life. Cardiff had certainly changed for the better since the time I'd visited, when I was in the navy. In the morning when we set off back to Manchester, James wasn't totally surprised that after only a mile or so, we stopped at the off-licence to replenish our supplies. He lost count of the amount of pubs we stopped off at on the way home, but he had a great time with us, and that pleased us all.

When we took him to Liverpool away, which was about forty-five minutes away from Prestwich, he couldn't understand why we couldn't go all the way without stopping at a pub. Thankfully, he was a quick learner, and it was a case of 'If you can't beat them, join them'. Quite often when City were playing away and we were not going to the game, James would come round to my house to watch the game with me and anyone else who popped round. He has now moved out of Manchester, but the branch will be forever grateful for all the help and support he gave us. In fact, it seems very strange when I watch the game at home and James is not there for a bit of banter.

At the end of each season, we held family fun day on a Sunday. They proved to be a spectacular success, with all sort of events happening. Usually there was a branch football match in the morning, or we had the youngsters in Heaton Park for some football training. On one occasion we had a football match against Man City Old Boys, and the star player for the Old Boys was fan favourite and former City and England international Peter Barnes. We also had players, ex-players, and club officials who attended. There were bouncy castles and hot food stalls. The fire brigade came down with a fire engine, much to the kids' delight. The local branch of the car company Peugeot sponsored the events for about three years on the trot. It was a very popular event, and several hundred people turned up during the day and early evening. We used to have all sort of fun and games, with local DJ Little Oz organizing the proceedings, and we always raised a good bit of cash for a local charity.

At one of the fun days, City's best player of that era turned up, with Franny Lee's son Gary looking after him. Gio Kinkladze was a cult hero with the fans, and on his day he could be a world beater. Besides watching him play for the first team, many of us had watched him train at the Platt Lane training complex. One day stands out above all else. The training had just finished, and loads of kids including my two lads wanted his autograph and a photo with him. Even though it was pissing down, he wouldn't leave until everyone was happy and got all the photographs and autographs they wanted. That was in stark contrast to what happened ten minutes later, when the team captain, Keith Curle, was about to enter the building where the players were having their meals. I remember a father asking Keith for an autograph for his kid as Keith was walking past. Keith said he would be back in a minute. Like hell he would, the tosser had no intention of coming back, and he never did. What harm would it have done to sign an autograph for the kid? Some people at City simply did not give a shit about the fans, and needless to say Keith was one of the few players in that era who never came to one of our meetings or events.

Another time I wanted an autograph for my lads was when I was in the player's lounge. I asked Gio for his autograph for my lads who, were with me. Like a prick, though, I didn't have a pen or any paper. That didn't faze Gio. He went hunting for a pen and some paper, came back, and duly signed. The lad had a heart of gold. It was a big blow for the club but was hardly surprising when he left for Ajax after we got relegated to the old third division.

It wasn't long though till we organised a trip to Amsterdam to watch Gio play, and we invited him to meet us. I was a bit apprehensive because a couple of years earlier, I had organised a coach trip to Amsterdam that did not go exactly as planned. When we'd arrived in Holland, we'd found out that the hotel was actually in Rotterdam, which was many miles away. Plus, we'd left someone behind.

I thought it best if I kept that information to myself as I set about organizing what was to be an epic trip.

I decided to plan this trip with military precision, and as I was also going to Amsterdam to visit my brother, who lived there, a few weeks before our planned trip to meet Gio, I thought I would suss out a bar in which to meet Gio. After spending many delightful hours researching a suitable bar, I organised for us to go in a large bar opposite the Blarney Stone on the Korte Nieuwendijk, near Centraal Train Station. The name of it escapes me because it changes its name regularly, and the last time I visited, it was a steak restaurant. I arranged everything with the bar owner, and we agreed on a discount price of lager because I assured him there would be seventy of us coming over, and we would be supping loads over the course of the evening. Well, that was easy enough to sort out. Next was to organise the transport and the hotel. I thought the best way was to get a travel company to take over the arrangements at this stage. It was going very easy, I thought. What could possible go wrong?

While I was organizing the trip, a reporter from the *Guardian* heard about it and wanted to travel with us so he could do an article for his paper. I thought *'Bollocks to that'*. I did not know him or what his agenda was, and he could quite easily portray us in a negative light. We politely declined his offer. Plus, at this stage we did not have a clue whether Gio would actually meet us, and if he did not, I was sure the reporter would have made us look like a right load of dickheads.

I was finding it hard to get seventy tickets for the Ajax game, so I told everyone who was going on the trip that if they wanted to watch the game, it was best they organise their own tickets direct with Ajax. I wrote a couple of times to Gio, telling him of our plans, but I received no reply. I also got in touch with Ajax direct. They didn't reply about him meeting us the night after the game, but they said we could watch him train and meet him in the morning after the game.

At last we were headed for the Dam. Due to bad weather, we couldn't go our original route via the Hook of Holland; we had to go to Dover to Calais and take a big trek over Europe. We were a bit knackered when we got to the hotel, and because no one could be arsed going to the game, we went straight into Amsterdam to sample the famous Amsterdam nightlife.

We all met up with Keith and Lesley, who had made their own way to Amsterdam and had done the sensible thing by flying over. We also met our old mate Johnny Waters, who still lives in Haarlem, and Simon Curtis, who writes for

King of the Kippax. He was living in Amsterdam at the time, and we had a belting night – except for Gaynor, one of the girls with us. She hadn't been in Amsterdam long when she had her handbag nicked from McDonald's while she was having something to eat and drink. She lost quite a bit of money, but we all chipped in to help her out. Everyone had a cracking night in Amsterdam because there is so much to do to keep everyone entertained. Johnny ended up gate-crashing the hotel kipping in Aide's and Noel's room. At the time, Noel was the editor of a City fanzine called *Bert Trautmann's Helmet*.

In the morning, only about half who came on the trip decided they wanted to go on a tour of the Ajax stadium, watch the players train, and get a chance to meet Gio. The rest of us went back out in Amsterdam for another session. Before I left, I gave Greg and Gaynor a letter to give Gio, explaining where we would be in the evening. I will be honest: at that stage, I had little hope that he would turn up.

We later met up with the others who had been to the ground. They had a great time on the tour, watching the players train and had also met Gio so they were chuffed to bits, but he didn't commit to meeting us in the evening. We were having a great time anyway and we all met up in the bar I had arranged for us a few weeks earlier. Some of the others who were with us did not think Gio would turn up to meet us, but meet us he did. When he came in the bar, it was like a conquering hero had returned. He got a reception like he'd probably never had before and would never get again. He spent nearly three hours with us signing everything from passports to clogs, even Tommy's sheepskin coat, and even one or two body parts. He spent ages just talking and having a laugh with us all. He was an absolute diamond with us.

Gio meeting us turned a great weekend into a fantastic one, and no one who was on that trip would ever forget it. Back at the hotel, Johnny had gate-crashed Aide's and Noel's room again. In the morning, Derbo realized he had lost his false teeth. I phoned the owner of the bar, who pissed himself laughing because he said he had found two phones, a credit card, three lighters, a packet of fags, and an empty wallet – but no teeth.

As we were setting off early in the morning, loads decided to stay a few hours longer and get a flight home. It was a memorable weekend. We set off in high spirits, and this time the only ones left behind this time were the ones staying of their own accord.

Gio was never really settled at Ajax. He then went onto play for Derby County, amongst other clubs, but he never ever regained the form he had at City.

When Franny finally stepped down as chairman of Manchester City, he was replaced by David Bernstein, who was the vice chairman of the club at the time. Most of us did not really know too much about David, but seeing he had already been at the club for a few years, we hoped he would bring with him a level of stability that the club desperately needed – and that the fans had not witnessed for many years. David went about his business in a quiet, calm, dignified way, which was a very refreshing change considering how the club had previously been run. He was also a successful businessman in his own right, and he soon became highly respected by virtually all who came into contact with him, both inside and outside the footballing world.

Our branch was the first supporters club event he attended, and the room was filling up as soon as the doors opened. My mate Botty was always on door duty for us, and Mario, Keith, and Aide were on hand to make sure everything ran smoothly and everyone was on their best behaviour. The meeting was a breath of fresh air. David spelt out the road we had to go down to get the club back on an even keel. He was completely honest about how big a job it was going to be, and he never gave us any false hope that it was going to be a quick fix. None of us were under any illusions; we all knew the club was in deep shit. We simply were not sure how deep the shit was. It also did not take a genius to work out that we had many obstacles to overcome, and there was no easy solution. The one assurance he did give us was that he would work tirelessly to turn round the fortunes of the club. We left the meeting feeling that at last we had a chairman with class who had the confidence to take the club forward. Under David's stewardship, it was not long before the club started to regain its self-respect.

We were massively disappointed when David eventually left the club. No one was 100 per cent sure why we parted company with him, but rumours were doing the rounds that he was at odds with other board members over the spending policy on which the club was embarking.

The fans were disappointed that he'd left. For all intents and purposes, he had done a brilliant job in turning the fortunes of the club round, and we were certainly in a vastly healthier position both off and on the pitch. If he had not come in at that time, it is anyone's guess how the club would have fared.

One of his legacies was that he carried on the negotiations that saw City eventually move from Maine Road to our new stadium at Eastland's. The stadium was originally built for the Commonwealth games in Manchester. It has gone through a few name changes; it was originally called City of Manchester Stadium, or COMS for short because it was quite a mouthful. The fans also called it Eastland's, but after a record sponsorship deal, it is now named the Etihad Stadium. While under David's chairmanship, the Manchester City Youth Academy was formed and quickly gained a reputation as one of the best in the country. He also oversaw the move to a much better training facility at Carrington, where the players trained till 2015, when they moved into a state-of-the-art training complex opposite Etihad Stadium. The facility rivals the best in the world. Arguably his proudest but most nerve-racking moment as chairman was when City went to Wembley in the 1999 play-off final against Gillingham. If we had not got out of the old third division when we did, it is doubtful that the success we are enjoying now would ever have happened.

David came to three of our meetings altogether, and everyone was greatly impressed by the way he conducted himself. He always spoke softly, but he had everyone's attention. When he left City, it was our loss and someone else's gain. He later became chairman of the Football Association and went on to become chairman of Wembley Stadium Ltd.

David was eventually followed as chairman by City fanatic John Wardle, who was another superb chairman. If John had a fault, it was letting his heart rule his head, but as with any fan who was a chairman of the club he supported, that was always going to be a danger. Later on in the book, you will read how much he and David Makin, his partner at JD Sports, did for City.

The play-offs against Gillingham in 1999 was a bittersweet pill to follow for us City fans. It is every football fan's dream to watch their team play at Wembley, but we were thinking more of an FA Cup final or a League Cup final, not the fucking play-offs from the old third division. We were glad we now had a chance to get out of this division. Not only City fans but most football fans in England must have been thinking, 'How the fuck could a club like City, with its history, tradition and fanatical support, ever get into that position?' It would take a book of its own to do justice to how we had sunk so fucking low. But recriminations were for another time. Now we were going to Wembley.

Our average crowd for the season was about thirty thousand, whereas Gillingham's average crowd was about nine thousand. Common sense would dictate City would get a bigger allocation of the tickets. Oh, there I am again daydreaming, thinking the people who run football have common sense. No fucking chance. In their wisdom, some bright spark decided we should get roughly the same allocation. We had to accept the decision, but now we were relying on City to allocate them fairly well. If a cup was won for cock-ups, the ticket office would have won hands down, but for the staff to shoulder the burden of blame for the farce that followed would be unfair because they only followed decisions made higher up. Other clubs that get to Wembley, including Gillingham, don't seem to have a problem distributing their allocation, but City fucked it up big style, with fans queuing up for hours and hours to get a ticket. Bernard Halford, the club's secretary, copped for an enormous amount of criticism. Luckily for our branch, Neil, our ticket organizer, managed to sort our tickets for the majority of our members, so only he got a headache or two. Many of our members were doing their own things for the weekend, so we only had to organise two coaches, one for the weekend staying for two nights, and one for just Saturday, going straight there and back. We were staying in Hemel Hempstead the night before and the night of the game. Once at Wembley, we went in a great bar that had City fans in one room and Gillingham fans in another. There was a great atmosphere. We did not stay long because it was the first time Cath, Steven, and Sean had been to

Wembley, so we wanted to get in early and enjoy the experience.

Although we were favourites to win, I had an awful feeling that we were going to blow our chance of getting out of the god-awful division. I was as nervous as fuck and was left a nervous wreck when Gillingham scored another goal to make it 2-0 with minutes to go. When their second goal went, in many City fans gave up and left the ground by the hundreds. I could not get my head round that, we had not been to Wembley for donkey's years. If we did get beat, we would probably not be going again for many years. I was certainly going to stay to the death, to savour the moment. Then in the ninetieth minute, Kevin Horlock scored for City. *Too little, too late,* I thought, but Cath was a lot more positive.

The steward nearest to me came over and said, 'Don't worry, mate. You will score another.'

At the time I wondered what drugs he was on, and I said to him, 'If we score another, I will give you a big smacker on the lips, because there is no fucking chance of us scoring another or so I thought. This is Manchester City we are watching. Then the board went up showing five minutes of extra time. Loads of City fans who had left turned round and started legging it back to get in the ground again. I would not have let them back in myself; they had abandoned City when they needed their support the most, so tough shit as far as I was concerned. Once the board showing five minutes extra went up, the mood in the ground changed, with City fans and the team getting a second wind. At the same time, Gillingham and their fans started to get nervous.

With seconds to spare, Paul Dickov did the unthinkable. Against the odds, he smashed in the equalizer, sending City fans into raptures and the Gillingham fans into despair the steward next to me shit himself in case I carried out my promise to give him a kiss. He need not have worried because I was bouncing round the place like a man possessed. There was no more score, and City went on to win the penalty shootouts. The rest as they is history.

As it happens, the ref for the game, Mark Hasley, and his partner were staying in the same hotel as a load of City fans. His partner happened to be a City fan as well. Paul Hince from the *Manchester Evening News* ran a story mentioning those facts. Notwithstanding, it was the FA who'd put Mark in that hotel. Anyway, there were all sorts of conspiracy theories doing the rounds. After it spread on to the national papers, to put it mildly, Mark did not welcome the uncalled-for attention; after all, he was only doing his job. But we all know what the national press is like, and if the truth gets in the way of a story, the reporters don't care who they hurt.

A few months later, Mark attended one of our meetings because he was based in Bolton and lived only about ten miles away from Prestwich. Paul Hince, the reporter who'd written the article, also attended. Let's just say there was a one-way, heated discussion and leave it at that.

Mark was also our guest when we had a sportsmen's dinner with Kevin Keegan, and he got nearly as big a round of applause as Kevin when his name was read out. A few months later, he came to my fiftieth birthday celebration, and he gave me a signed Premier League referee's shirt, which I thought was great. I used to have his mobile phone number, but my wife deleted it because I kept phoning him up when I was pissed up after the games if I did not agree with the ref's decision. Well, it seemed a good idea at the time. I'm not too sure whether Mark also thought it was a good idea, and I bet he has not missed my calls, especially the ones in the early hours of the morning.

He is an inspirational person because he fought back from cancer to carry on his career. He has now retired from refereeing, and it was fitting that his last match was against City. Mark received a magnificent reception even though City lost. Mark still regularly appears on TV as a pundit, giving his opinion on refereeing decisions.

Over the years, Man City have had some fantastic goalkeepers who have played at the club for many years and ended up being heroes with the fans. One of the most famous was Frank Swift, who played long before my time and died tragically in the Munich Air disaster. He was on the plane as a reporter for the *Manchester Evening News* when the disaster happened, claiming the lives of many Manchester United players and leaving many of them seriously injured.

A whole host of City goalkeepers and ex-goalkeepers have been to our meetings over the years. Andy Dibble, Martyn Margetson, and Nicky Weaver came while they were still at the club, and former goalies Big Joe Corrigan, Tony Coton, Eric Nixon, Alex Williams, and the late Bert Trautmann attended and got a brilliant reception when they too attended the meetings.

The goalkeeper who stands out for me is the late Bert Trautmann. Although I never remember seeing him play except on the telly and a brief appearance in Johnny Hart's testimonial, I have met him a few times at various events. His life and career is extraordinary, to say the least.

Bert was born in Germany and served as a paratrooper in the Second World War. For three years he served on the Eastern Front, earning five medals including the highest honour for German soldiers, the Iron Cross. God knows what hardship he and the other soldiers went through during the war, and what horrors they witnessed whichever side they were on.

Near the end of the war, Bert had been transferred to the Western Front and was captured by the British troops just before the war finally finished. Bert was then transferred to a British prison of war camp in Lancashire. When he was released three years after the war finished, he could have been sent back to Germany, but he decided to stay in England and settled in Lancashire, where he worked on a farm and started playing football for his local club, St Helens Town.

He must have been playing well because it was not long before he gained a decent reputation, and scouts from many football clubs came to watch him play. Fortunately for the Blues, he signed for City in 1949. It was not a popular decision with a lot of people in England; the horrors of the war were still fresh in people's memories. It was certainly not welcomed by everyone in the local area, and there were mass protests and demonstrations. Many in the local Jewish communities joined in a demonstration, which was attended by roughly twenty thousand people. Many people had lost loved ones in the war, and the Jewish population had suffered terribly, so their reaction was probably not too surprising. However, Bert eventually won over most fans with some fantastic goalkeeping displays. Then club captain Eric Westwood, who had himself been in the British army and had served in Normandy during the war, made a public display of welcoming Bert to the club by saying, 'There are no wars in the dressing room.'

Bert really shot to fame in the 1956 FA Cup final, when City played against Birmingham and won 3-1. Bert was in a collision with a Birmingham player, Peter Murphy. Bert was dazed and unsteady on his feet. There were over fifteen minutes left, and in those days there were no subs allowed. Bert played on. The pain didn't get any better, and the next day he went to the hospital, where he was told it was a sore neck and it would go away. A couple of days later, he got a second opinion at Manchester Royal Infirmary, who realised Bert had broken his neck. Is that unbelievable, or what?

Bert was in Manchester to attend a sportsmen's dinner at City's ground, and that was where I first met him and realised what an incredible person he was. He had an aura around him that is hard to describe. When he spoke, you could hear a penny drop because people were silent so they could hear what the great man was saying. I don't say this about many people, but it was a privilege for me to be at that event. It is not often an opportunity comes round to meet someone like him, and we were so grateful he accepted our invitation to attend one of our meetings.

When he attended our meeting at Heaton Park Social Club, he was followed round by a camera crew from Germany that was doing a documentary on his life. He remained friends and stayed in contact with many ex-City players, and the reason he came to our meeting was to present Roy Clarke, another ex-City player, with a trophy on behalf of our branch in recognition of the service Roy had done for City. Another mate of his, ex-City player Paddy Fagan, also attended. It just shows the presence of the man: after all these years, Bert was still highly in demand, and he is honoured at City by being in the hall of fame. Many of the older fans at the meeting remembered his playing days, and it was great to listen to them speak so highly of him. It is hard to imagine now the hardship, pain, and suffering so many people went through during the Second World War, and yet then something as simple as football can help heal those differences.

Chapter 13

Pre-season Tour

Unlike the exotic places we go to now, back in the day we could end up playing Halifax, Scarborough, Radcliffe Borough, and Exeter. We also did a couple of mini tours to Scotland and Ireland. On the Scottish trip, we played four games in the pre-season friendlies, but the main one was at Kilmarnock. The day before the game, my family and I went to the players' hotel and had a chat with Kit and a few other players. We stayed for about an hour and had a brew and some butties with them, and of course we got a couple of photographs. They were all relaxed and chilled out, and they made us very welcome. There were thousands of City fans up for the game, and we met up with loads of people we knew. In one bar, we met up with two very special fans, Chris Greencare's mum and dad, who were also up for the trip. Chris was a young

A Football Fan's Story

player who was also our branch president, and he was hoping to make a big push for a regular first team place. He suffered an injury a couple of days before the team set off for the tour. Needless to say, we were all gutted for him as he was unable to play in any of the games in Scotland.

In Scotland we stayed with Cath's relatives, James and Maureen, because they lived just down the road in Irvine. That was dead handy for us. Unbelievably, City won 4-0, with Uwe and Kit both scoring twice. The Scottish people were great with us went out of their way to be nice to us. Well, except for one or two of the hotel staff.

After the game, we went back to the hotel, where many City fans we knew were staying; it was the same one we were in before the game. We were having a quiet drink and something to eat, and then at 7.00 p.m. two of the ladies went to the bar to order some more drinks. To everyone's surprise, the bar staff told them that they could not be served because they had on their City shirts. No shit, Sherlock! It was hardly surprising because we all had them on when we'd been in the hotel before the game, and now we had been in the bar for a good hour after the game. Instead of having a row, the ladies took off their shirts. Luckily, they both had their bras on. Then they said, 'Well, you can serve us now, can't you?' What pissed everyone off was it was no big deal to us if the policy was 'No football shirts after 7.00 p.m.'; all they had to do was tell us, and we could have got changed at any time. It remains a mystery why they did not inform us till the deadline. I wish I'd had a camera when the ladies whipped off their shirts, because the staff's faces were one of surprise and shock. We pissed ourselves laughing. That will teach the staff for being a jobsworth. While in England, it is the norm to go out in football shirts, especially on a match day. It is not something that happens much in Scotland, but a little courtesy warning would not hurt anyone. Cath's cousin wrote a letter of complaint to the hotel manager but did not get a satisfactory reply, which was not surprising. Still, a little incident like that could not spoil the evening. Irvine is a smashing place with plenty of bars, and like most place in Scotland, the people were very friendly and the fish and chips were bloody lovely.

Another year we were playing pre-season in Athlone and Cork, in Ireland. Yours truly organised another trip. We were going by coach and had ordered two coaches because there was a big demand, with nearly a hundred from the branch going. We were getting picked up by the coaches from Heaton Park, and then we'd get the Hollyhead Ferry to Ireland, where we'd take coaches again to the venues. Everything was organised quite smoothly, or we thought it was. As we patiently waited at Heaton Park Metro Station in Prestwich, which was the pickup point, there was no sign of the coaches. A bit of a panic started to seep in, but three-quarters of an hour late (and much to my relief) they showed up. The reason they were late was because they were subject to a 'random' police spot check when they left the depot. I don't believe in coincidences. Of all the coaches out on the road that morning, they decided to stop the ones taking City fans on a tour to Ireland? You could not make it up. The drivers were as good as gold and were chilled out about the stop check. They reassured us that we would get to the ferry on time. We did, but only just…Bill Black who was chairman of the Levenshulme branch was also panicking a bit as he helped me organise the trip but all's well that ends well. The thing with organising anything, whether it's tickets, coaches, hotel rooms, or inviting guests to the meetings, is that there is only so much an organizer can do once you have made and confirmed the arrangements, but you have a massive responsibility. If anything does not go according to plan, you are the one in the firing line. It is like if you book a flight, and when you get to the airport, the plane is delayed. It is the poor staff who give you the boarding pass that get the flak, not the pilot or the owner of the company. I have learnt over the years to grin and bear it, and to follow Murphy's Law. Fortunately the majority of people who come on the trips and attend the meetings know me very well and realize even the best-laid plans can go out the window.

We stayed in Dublin for the Athlone game. We were not far from our hotel when we came to a stop. The coach couldn't get down a street because a car was blocking the road, so Flynny rounded up four or five of the biggest lads. They got off the coach and lifted the car out of the way so our coach could carry on with our journey. Job done, no problem, and we had a great time in Dublin. It was the first time many of the people on the trip (myself included) had been to Dublin. It is such a great place, and the welcome we received from the people was second to none. Everyone we met was very friendly and accommodating, and the match was not bad either. As a bonus, we won 3-1. After a good drink, a decent kip, and a lovely Irish breakfast, it was time to say goodbye to the lovely people of Dublin and set off for Cork.

It was a fair trek from Dublin to Cork, but we had a great laugh on the coaches, spending most of the time singing different songs. That was where *The Invisible Man* song got its first real introduction in its full version:

'If you drink, you will die. If you don't drink, you will die. So it is better to be drunk than be sober when you die. Just like the fan of the invisible man, we're not really here...'

Another plus was we had a couple of stops to wet the whistle. The locals must have thought we were bonkers because we would stop in a little village with just a couple of bars. The City flags and banners would be put up, and once everyone had a drink, and there would be non-stop singing. The bar owners loved us wherever we stopped because their takings for the day suddenly went up tenfold. If there is one drink I am not keen on, it is Guinness, but the lads on the trip who drank the black stuff said that on that trip, it was the best Guinness they had ever had. One of the reasons I might not be too keen on it is that it takes fucking ages to pour the stuff. I never understood why it takes so frigging long! The lads I knew could drink it quicker than the staff could pour it.

There were a couple of thousand Blues at the game, soaking up the sun and having a drink. We were close to the pitch and were having great banter with the players. Paul Hince, the reporter, was there, and he likes his Guinness as well. Another great surprise was we won that one as well, 3-1. The great thing about going to a friendly is everyone is so fucking friendly! No one really gives a shit if the team plays well or is shit. By half-time many are so pissed they don't know or care what the score is, and they usually don't find it out till the next day. Contrast that to an important league or cup game, and the same fans who are chilled out and relaxed turn into nervous wrecks. Recently we were on holiday with Julie and Sue, two of our mates. City were getting beat, and Julie was having kittens and stressing out. And this was just watching it on the box! Fuck knows what she would have been like if she had been at the game. In the end, she could watch no more and went to the bar next door, where the Galatasary game was on. If you get football fever, that is how it can grip you. Over the years, I have seen a lot worse than that. Once the game had finished, she was dead calm even though we got beat. We can all handle getting beat; it is in the manner we get beat, that can sends us crackers.

The day after we beat Cork, the Cork branch of the City Supporters Club was having an afternoon party. We went to that, and it was a great afternoon. They had a singer and a buffet laid on, and I was invited to give a speech on behalf of the City fans who were guests of the Cork branch. To be honest, I could hardly stand, never mind put two sentences together, so I just stood up and let rip with the Invisible Man song. The whole place was rocking as everyone joined in.

Back at the hotel, in the evening it was getting a bit to lively for the bar staff so they shut the bar early, but we could still get room service. I had had a little kip on the coach, so I soon got my second wind and was raring to go again. I went to my room, phoned room service, and ordered four pints. The porter brought them up on a tray. I took them off him and followed him down in the lift back to the bar. His face was a picture; it could only happen in Ireland. Loads of others saw what I had done and then followed suit.

In the morning we were ready to set off, but Mike and Tommy were missing, we rang their room and got no answer. Cath and I checked the nearby bars just in case they were having a swift one before we went, and Paul went looking for them, banging on their room door. We also got the staff to check the room, and Cath went up with the staff and went in the room. It was empty, we were wondering where the fuck they could be. Time was dragging on, and we had a long drive to get to the ferry. One coach went ahead, and I stayed to try to figure out what was what. I knew they were staying in a room with a lad who was flying back to England, so speculation was they must have left early and flew back. I didn't know what to think. Most people didn't have mobiles in those days so we could not phone them or send them a text. I asked the staff if they had checked the right room, and Paul went up again to double check there was no one there. There was nothing else we could do, so we set off without them; otherwise there was a big danger of us all missing the ferry. They were good mates of mine, and I was sure if they were going to fly, they would have let us know, but we couldn't wait any longer and did not have a clue what else we could do. It put a bit of a damper on the long drive back, because not knowing what had happened to them was a bit of a worry. In the past I have had had the misfortune of leaving people behind, but I was always too pissed to know about it. This was different. We simply did not have a clue where they were.

What transpired was the night staff had got them to change rooms but hadn't told anyone, so they were still in bed when we left, in a different room. Luckily there was a minibus of Blues still in the hotel, and they got a lift to the ferry with them. Our mate Steve Theale drove down from Manchester to Hollyhead to pick them up. All's well that ends well.

City then went on to China to continue their pre-season training, but they only played one game because the weather was too bad. Aide went to watch them in China, but I waited till they came

A Football Fan's Story

back. They played Scarborough away, and Steven, Sean, and I went to Yorkshire to watch it.

Looking back at those times, supporting City seemed quite bizarre. City were terrible, but the fans still got behind the team. New supporters branches were springing up. Fanzines were very popular; the main two were *King of the Kippax*, which is still going, and *Bert Trautmann's Helmet*, which finished a few years ago. There were others that were also well read, like *Chips and Gravy* and *This Charming Fan*.

We were getting full houses at every home game and were selling all our allocation for away games. Unlike nowadays, the fans stayed till the end of the games no matter what the score was. Even if we got beat, fans would stay to the end stay to applaud the players off the pitch. That is one thing I can't get my head round. Now, match tickets cost anything between forty and sixty pounds for a normal seat ticket, but thousands leave the games ten or fifteen minutes before the end! It also happens in most Premier League grounds, not just at the Etihad Stadium. I don't see the point of leaving early, especially now that there are so many world-class players on show, and quite often we end up scoring in the last few minutes. Leaving early seems so at odds with what being a fan is all about, but to each to his own. I suppose if you pay sixty pounds for a ticket, you have the right to do what you want.

As the years progressed, we eventually started having better pre-season games, one of which was in Hamburg, Germany. To us, it was like a proper European game because we hadn't played in Europe for years. Loads of City fans travelled. It was a family affair for us. We flew from Manchester to Amsterdam, changed planes, and then flew from Amsterdam to Hamburg. I swear to God I have never in my life laughed as much as I did on that flight. First of all, the first person we saw on the plane was Bobby Charlton a former United and England player. He was on our flight because United were on a tour in Amsterdam. The plane was full of City fans, so he got a bit of stick. Derbo, the creep, went up to him, shook his hand, and congratulated him for his services for England. Derbo was the next to get some stick, but it was all in good fun. There were two lads across from me, and one was taking the piss out of everyone and everything. He was so funny that I thought I was going to wet myself. One of the stewards tried to make an announcement telling him to shut up; otherwise the plane would not take off. But the steward was laughing so much he could not make the announcement. We took off, and for the next hour the lad had us all in stitches. The fucker should have been on stage.

After a quick couple of pints at Schiphol Airport, we got the plane to Hamburg without any hiccups. Once we landed, things got off to a bad start because our luggage didn't turn up. We were promised it would be delivered to the hotel the next day. After a good night's kip, I was ready for a few beers before the game. It was red hot, so many of us were all in T-shirts, shorts, and flip-flops. We got a cab to a big square in the centre of Hamburg. Our lads went to Burger King for a scran, and Cath and I went for a drink. Derbo saw me as I was walking up to meet him at the square. There was an almighty roar, and loads of glasses were getting thrown and smashed near us. People started running in all directions then towards us. Fuck me, it was only just after 10.00 a.m. I hadn't even had a pint, and it was kicking off big style. Fuck this for a game of soldiers. Time to get out of here! I had to pick up Cath and get her over a barrier that was separating the square and the pavement, and then we beat a tactical retreat. I laughed later, but not at the time. It was a funny as fuck, watching Derbo and the others trying to run with their flip-flops on. Derbo and the other lads went one way, and we went the other way to meet our lads in Burger King.

As we were telling our lads what had happened, saying we thought we were lucky to get away with not being hit, two big, daft, grinning -twats started banging on the window and pointing at me. Fuck me – Dumb and Dumber had spotted us. I was a dead giveaway because I was wearing a City T-shirt. Then their mates turned up as well, but I thought they would only take the piss. No self-respecting gang of hooligans was going to attack a fifty-year-old bloke and his family in a Burger King, were they? I was dead wrong on that score. One fucking arsehole came in and gave me a big 'I am fucking hard' look and hit me a couple of times in the face, much to the delight of the grinning morons he was with. I had been hit harder while having a play fight when the kids were nippers. He was well off his tits on drinks or drugs, or both. I would have loved to retaliate and give the dickhead a good hiding, but I wanted to calm the situation down, not make matters worse. I had Cath and the lads with me, and some of the grinning morons were now in the doorway and making their way towards me. Thankfully, one of the staff, a huge bloke, came from the back and ushered the halfwits outside and then locked the door. They weren't even Hamburg fans but local rivals, St Pauli. What the fuck was that all about? Once again, wrong place and wrong time. After a short while, the staff member got us a cab, and we shot back to the hotel to chill out, relax for a bit, and let everything in the square calm down.

Good job we did, because the hotel was getting ready to welcome a couple of hundred City fans who were arriving around noon for the game. The staff had written on a big white board in red, 'Welcome, Manchester United Supporters.' 'Excuse me,' I said 'you better sort that out.' Our luggage by then had turned up, and the rest of the trip went well. There was no more hassle with any of those dickheads, the Hamburg fans were great, and we got on well with them. The Hamburg night life had something for everyone, and we enjoyed the game and the whole experience. Tommy, Arnie, Cath, and I even went on a boat trip the morning after the game, so apart from a minor setback or two, we had a belting three days in Hamburg.

When I found out City were off to Thailand for a pre-season competition, I thought to myself, *I will have a bit of that.* I had never been to Thailand before but had heard it was a great place. The competition we were invited to play in was the grand-sounding title of the FA Premier League Trophy. I did not give a fuck what it was called; it could have been called the Dog's Bollocks Trophy for all I cared. That was one trip I did not want to miss. Quite a few Prestwich and Whitefield branch members were going, and a group of sixteen of us would travel together.

The first leg of the journey was to Dubai. The plane was fantastic – nothing like the cheap and nasty ones you get on short-haul flights. There was loads of leg room, free drinks, very nice food, TV and radio, and even a telephone. The staff were pleasant. It did not seem to take long to arrive at Dubai, but that might have been due to the drinks freely flowing. Once at Dubai, we had to wait a couple of hours till the onward flight to Bangkok. What better place to wait than a very nice Irish bar slap bang in the middle of the airport? How very thoughtful of them. Tommy was nearly stopped from boarding because he had misplaced his boarding card, but we soon managed to sort it out and get him on the plane. This part of the journey was just as good as the first leg with the same sort of standard and facilities, so we arrived in Bangkok in a nice, relaxed mood.

Our journey was not yet quite over because we were staying in the beach area of Pattaya, which was a couple of hours away. Some of the lads were staying at a hotel round the corner from mine, but they ended up staying at ours during the day because we had a great swimming pool and patio area, and the staff were not bothered because they were buying food and drink. We lost Tommy and Steven the first night for an hour or two as Tommy had a bright idea of getting a tattoo, the things you do when you are pissed.

Anything and everything goes in Thailand, and it is a bit of an eye-opener for anyone who is not broad-minded. There are lady boys and naked go-go dancers competing with hostesses to relieve you of your money. There is a large area called Walking Street where you can buy literally anything; it was even featured in a television documentary. We went to watch Thai boxing when we were there, and of course we cheered for the Blue team. I love the street food in these sorts of places, and even though I was not sure what I was eating, it was delicious and very cheap.

After a great night, we were set to get the minibus to Bangkok for the game. It was an evening kick off, and so we were going to stay the night in a hotel in Bangkok. Derbo, Kev, and a couple of others decided to stay by the pool, give the game a miss, and just watch it on the telly in the pub. Fuck me. Halfway round the world to watch City, and they watch it in the pub? Unbelievable! The traffic was very bad, and getting to the hotel to check in took much longer than anticipated, so it put us a bit behind schedule. Once we checked in the hotel and had a couple of beers, we realized we were going to be a bit late for the kick off. Good thing James H. Reeve was not with us, because he would have gone bonkers at me. We made it to the ground just before half-time because the traffic was mental. At least those fuckers back in Pattaya would have watched the first half in a pub. Once at the ground, we did not have a clue where our entrance was, so we approached a policeman who very kindly escorted us to our seats. We were playing against Bolton Wanderers and drew 1-1, but we lost 5-4 in the penalty shootout. After the game, we went back to the hotel, and I could not be arsed going out because I was a bit knackered. I had a couple of drinks and had an early night.

Bangkok is another place where a broad mind is required, and there are many different areas where various needs can be met. I must say Pattaya is much more relaxed by comparison. A couple of days later, we played Everton back in Bangkok, but this time Cath and I joined the other lads by staying by the pool and going to watch the game in a bar. If you can't beat them, join them. I did not want to face all the barmy traffic again. We drew with Everton, but this time we won the penalty shootout. There were only four teams in the competition: City, Everton, Bolton, and the Thailand national team. Bolton won it. That was the only time I have been to Thailand, but the place, the people, the food, and the hotels are superb, and there is something to suit everyone's budget. Fuck me, I sound like someone from the tourist office! But it is a great place, and a brilliant trip beats going to Halifax any day.

We could not go all that way without acting like tourists and doing a trip, so we got a boat trip. First we went to an island where there was a firing range, and every gun known to mankind was for hire. Tommy and Steven thought they were Rambo with their bandanas on. Health and Safety would have had a heart attack if they had visited that place. After shooting everything there was to shoot and blasting everything there was to blast, we jumped back on the boat. Our guide took us to a nice, quiet beach. The first person we saw when we got off the boat was a Thai worker with a City shirt on, so we chilled out for a couple of hours, having a beer and kicking a football about. We would have stayed a bit longer, but I noticed the captain of the boat and his mate were drinking a bottle of some strong-looking stuff, and I did not fancy a pissed-up captain driving us back. Ricky Hatton, the boxer, was staying near us, but we did not meet up with him. I realize where the term Thai bride comes from, because at the hotel in the mornings, Cath was the about the only non-Thai woman in the place, and the women all sat with their Western husbands. I think the word 'husband' might be a loose term, because the brides seemed to get changed every other morning.

CHAPTER 14

Charity Fundraising

One of the things that the branch excelled at was raising money for charity and good causes. We assisted members, ex-players, and local and national charities. Each Christmas we would donate five hundred pounds to the Henshaw's for the Blind Christmas party. We also got involved with a local charity called MedEquip4Kids, which raised money for the local children's hospital services.

Over the years, we organised many sportsmen's dinners, and we even did a couple in the afternoon besides the usual evening ones. They were a great way to raise money for the good causes and charities in which we were involved. We held some at the Village Hotel in Prestwich, and one we helped organise was for Paul Lake's testimonial. The great thing about that one was there were fans from other clubs attending, as they appreciated what a truly gifted player he was and how good he could have become. We had one on a Sunday afternoon that Franny Lee and Mike Summerbee attended. Mick McCarthy, the Irish manger, and United player Norman Whiteside were also guest speakers at one. The late Malcolm Allison – who, along with manager Joe Mercer who swept all before them in the late sixties and early seventies was also a guest speaker. We had one for Ian Brightwell's testimonial, and ex-Everton star Duncan McKenzie was also a guest speaker; Duncan was a brilliant footballer in his day and entertained us brilliantly with some of his stories. When Stuart Pearce became our manager, he was our top table guest at a charity function we held in Manchester and Mike Summerbee and James H Reeve also attended

The most ambitious one we attempted was with ex-England manager and (at that time) City manager Kevin Keegan. Although Kevin has been a guest at many dinners and functions over the years, he had never been to one as the main speaker, so we were immensely proud when he agreed to attend. It took quite a bit of negotiations behind the scenes to get the OK and have a date sorted. It wasn't as simple as simply phoning up Kevin and him agreeing to come; it did not work like that. The seeds were sown many months before. John

Wardle who was a director at City and a co-founder of the giant sports company JD Sports Ltd, was a great advocate for our branch. John saw the work we put in for our members and appreciated the passion we had for our club. He had been to our meetings and was impressed with the professional way the meetings were run. When Kevin joined the club, we started straight away inviting him to a meeting. He actually phoned my house to talk to me and make arrangements for attending the branch meeting. I wasn't in, and Sean spoke to him but didn't catch who he was at first. When he said he was Kevin Keegan, Sean thought it was a wind-up and nearly put the phone down. Thank fuck he didn't – I don't think Kevin would have been too impressed. Kevin came to the supporters meeting at the Working Men's Club, and the event went brilliantly. Kevin was superb with the fans, especially the younger ones, and he made sure they got autographs and photographs. By that time, we had held around a hundred meetings and events. That one ranked as the best one we had put on.

A few weeks later, I was at the ground at an afternoon dinner with Sean and Cath. Kevin was a guest, and he was to do a question-and-answer session. When he saw me, he came over to our table for a chat. I introduced Sean to him, and he had a laugh about the phone call. I told him of my intention to have a sportsmen's dinner and added we would like him to be a guest. He said he would have a think about it but couldn't promise anything. By this time, he had been at our table for fifteen minutes, and the organisers were desperate to get him back to the top table so they could start their question-and-answer session.

After many more phone calls, a date was finally set. Getting a date turned out to be the easy part because so much work had to be done to prepare for the event. Thankfully we had loads of help and support to make sure everything went smoothly. The demand for the tickets was very high, and it was held at Lancashire Cricket Club. It was a great honour for the branch that Kevin attended the sportsmen's dinner, and altogether there was 650 people there. We could have sold four times the tickets and charged twice as much, such was the demand. However, we were raising money for charity, and we wanted ordinary fans and members of supporters clubs to attend; we didn't want to price them out. In hindsight, I should have charged the ones nearer the top table a bit extra because they got a much better view than the ones at the back. We also had TV screens transmitting the event at the middle and back of the hall, so no one missed anything. City director and ex-player Denis Tueart attended, as did many ex-City players.

Former referee Mark Hasley was also a guest, and our very own James H. Reeves was the compare. At that time, Sean was into magic tricks, so he went from table to table performing some great tricks. Everyone agreed it was a special night, and I have never even tried to surpass it. I've met Kevin a couple of times since then, and once he came uninvited to one of our branch meetings, where he heaped praise on how well we organised the dinner, saying how much he'd enjoyed it.

He told us he was a bit nervous. He had never spoken for so long before at an event like that, and he had spent ages practicing and rehearsing his speech because he didn't want to let us down. You would not think someone like Kevin would be nervous, but he was doing something out of his normal comfort zone. It is one thing answering questions at an event; it is another talking non-stop for the better part of an hour. He was superb, and the organizing that went on for that event was on a different level than what was I was used to, but thanks to all the help I received from the other committee members, it went off without any hiccups.

I don't think people realize how much work goes on behind the scenes to plan and organise these events. I used to be nervous as fuck till all the guests arrived and the event was under way.

I used to breathe a sigh of relief if James H. was comparing, because he could handle any situation. I and others were disappointed when Kevin left the club. He was a breath of fresh air for the club and, his style of football was a joy to watch.

I don't honestly know how I get myself involved in some of my predicaments, but I should imagine being drunk and volunteering usually plays a part in it. That was the issue I pondered as I found myself standing on top of the massive roof of the Kippax Street stand as I was preparing to abseil down it. I am no adrenalin junkie, so fuck knows what possessed me to volunteer to undertake this bit of madness on a bright, sunny Sunday morning when I could have sat in my house watching the TV and having a cup of tea. I have been in the Kippax stand on hundreds of occasions, and from the ground to the top of the roof, it looks massive. Standing on the fucking roof makes the ground seems miles away. In fact, if the clouds had come a bit lower, I am sure I would have been able to touch them. Then I remembered I was doing this to raise money for the Marie Curie Cancer Charity, and many people sponsored me to complete this bit of insanity plus my mate Bill Black was also doing it so I could not bottle out otherwise I would never had lived it down. Cath's mum and dad and our niece Toni were there. Derbo, Kev, and Ken had come to give me moral support – well, that is what they said they came for. I think they really came in the hope I'd make a right tit out of myself so they could take the piss. Getting over the top to start lowering yourself down is the worst bit, but the instructors were there to inspire confidence in me. I must say they earned their fucking money with me that morning, because I needed a lot of inspiring. Once I was over the top and after the initial shock of dangling in the air while holding a bit of rope hundreds of feet in the air, it was not too bad. As I was getting lower, I started to enjoy it a bit, but I was chuffed as fuck when my feet touched the ground. If there was ever a time I thought I deserved a drink, it was that day, so tally-ho and away to the pub we went.

MedEquip4Kids is a local charity and they asked me if I would help out on a charity event they were organising. Of course I said yes but I did not have a clue at what I had let myself in for. I did not even know what the event was oh silly me.

I still cannot fathom to this day out how I ended up volunteering to do a sponsored climb up a frigging' mountain. And not just any mountain, but Mount Toubkal, which is in the Atlas Mountains and is the highest mountain in North Africa. There was a group of about twenty of us, and we had to trek for three days through the area till we reached the base camp at the bottom of Mount Toubkal. A major difficulty was the high altitude. It was a very big problem and was something we had to acclimatize to. I have a car, so the farthest I ever walked was to my local paper shop at the end of my street. It was the challenge of a lifetime, and I put in a bit of training and ended up trekking up Mount Snowdon with my niece Zoe. I also did a lot of walking up the hills round Ramsbottom, which is just on the other side of Bury.

We could not have done the trek if it was not for the help and knowledge of the local people, called Berbers. They carried and set up the tents, and they cooked all the food. After a hard day's trekking, it was great to see the campfire and the tents in the distance, knowing we did not have too far to go till we would be welcomed with the traditional sweet tea and something to eat. We usually camped near a stream, and that was where we would wash. If we walked near an orchard, the farmer would come round with fresh apples for us. If we walked by a village, all the locals would come out to wish us well. These people had it hard, but they were so friendly and helpful. It made me feel humble while we were trekking. I did not have a care in the world as I lapped up the experience, thinking how glad I was that I had decided to do the trek. The scenery was breathtaking, and sitting round the fire at night watching the sunset was one of those once-in-a-lifetime moments. It was a phenomenal experience, and somehow or other I made it to the top of the mountain. It was not easy, and we set off early in the morning when it was still dark. That was the only time I doubted whether I could do it, but then I thought about all the wonderful people who had donated to the charity, and I thought positively and focused on the task at hand. It took a lot of willpower as much as stamina to keep going. The closer to the top we got, the colder it was, and it was harder to breathe. It was very slow going, but that was when I had to muster all the positive vibes I possessed till I got to the summit.

I was chuffed to bits to have made it, but I was just as chuffed when it was time to start going back down, which was easier but not by much. It was all too easy to slip and slide down the mountain, so there was no room for complacency. One slip would be bad news. I got there and back in one piece, and I raised nearly three thousand pounds for the chosen charity, MedEquip4Kids, which was based in Prestwich and raised the money for youngsters in the local hospitals.

One of our member's cousins suffered a serious brain injury whilst following City in Europe, and he ended up in a German hospital in a coma, then in intensive care for weeks. A special plane had to be hired to fly him back home because his insurance did not cover him. We undertook the biggest fundraising exercise we'd ever attempted. We needed to help finance his family members who'd visited and stayed with him in Germany. Two of City's biggest websites, Blue Moon and Blue Watch, helped support the campaign, as well as the fanzine *King of the Kippax*. The Football Supporters Federation also offered their help, support, and advice. There were bucket collections outside the ground and at the pubs near the ground. My mate John Reid took a bucket to the Townley pub near the ground and raised a couple of hundred pounds in an hour. The fans in a pub called Mary D's were also brilliant. Ian, Debs, Cath and myself and few others went to Blackburn when City were playing there and collected over six hundred pounds in about an hour and a half from the City fans. Our mate Tommy Booth was there, and he put in a generous donation. Liverpool fans also helped as well because a good mate of Carl's was a Scouser, and he did some fundraising with his local supporters club.

We also held a charity night at Blackley British Legion, where first team player Michael Johnson attended. Then chief executive Gary Cook and press officer Vicky Kloss also attended the evening. Although City get inundated with requests for charities and good causes, they really pulled out all the stops to support us, and they donated many great prizes for us to raffle and auction. To his credit, Gary Cook also made a substantial private donation, which was very kind of him.

Manchester City FC gave us tremendous help and support, and so did dozens of individuals and City supporters branches. It really makes you humble when so many people who have never met Carl rallied round. Months later, when Carl was back in England and was feeling up to it, City donated a private box for him and his family to watch a game. Gary Cooke came to visit him, and so did the boxer Ricky Hatton. What a fantastic gesture! Carl was extremely grateful for all the support and help he'd received from everyone.

The strangest fundraiser night I got involved in was when one of our members, Chris, got attacked after a City and United game. He got hit over the head with a metal bar and was very lucky to survive. Initially it was thought he could suffer brain damage but slowly his condition improved. At the minimum he was to be off work for several weeks so we decided to raise money for his family by doing a race night at the local church hall.

We have organised dozens of race nights and can do them with our eyes shut now, so we expected another run-of-the-mill event. I should have known better. A couple of hours before it was due to start, the police phoned me because some loony had told them there was going to be trouble at the event. I reassured him it was going to be a family event in a church hall, and there would be no problems. We picked the church hall on purpose, because the same day Chelsea were playing United in the Cup Final, and we wanted a place where there would be no chance of any problems. Only people who were invited would attend. When I arrived with my nieces Toni and Zoe and their friends, my wife and sister-in-law were setting up the place. A policewoman turned up to have a word about what was going on. I told her it was a family event and not to worry, but with her attitude she would have done well with the Gestapo. She left, and I thought that was the end of the police.

The bar was not due to open till 7.00 pm and we were the only ones in the hall. Thirty minutes later we were a bit surprised when two policemen came running in, truncheons drawn. 'What the fuck is happening?' All the parishioners going to the church next door were gobsmacked. It was surreal because the church bells were ringing, people were going to church, and the old bill were running round the church with their truncheons out! The police had received a phone call that it was kicking off.

'No problems here,' I told them. There was only me and the Dolly Dealers in the place. I thought the situation was very strange, but then I could hear police sirens, so I thought there must be a problem somewhere nearby. As long as it was fuck all to do with me, I didn't have anything to worry about.

It was only later on, when everyone came in, that I found out what had happened. While waiting for the hall to open, many of the lads met in the Nat's, one of the pubs in the village. A bit of a clash started with the United and City fans in there, so the City fans moved off to a pub and restaurant nearer to the hall called the Orange Tree. Next thing the United fans came into the Orange Tree, and it kicked off big style. Even though there were families enjoying an evening meal, apparently it ended up like something out of a war zone. The place was wrecked, tables and chairs were used as weapons, and dozens of glasses and bottles were smashed. A couple of people had to go to hospital, but thankfully no one was seriously injured. I remember telling John Reid to go into the Orange Tree because it was a nice, quiet place. I won't tell you what he called me later on when he saw me. Well, how the hell was I to know it was going to be mental in there and kick off good style? Fuck me, nothing else could possible go wrong – could it?

The police visited us again later on but went away reassured. The race night was in full swing, and there were plenty of women and kids in there, plus the priest had popped in to have a look, place a bet, and have a swift dram. Not for the first time, I thought, *'How does shit like this happen to me?'* All I was trying to do was raise a bit of money for a mate. Things might have got off to a bad start, but now everything was on track and running smoothly. Surely nothing else could happen.

Everything was going great when, a short while later, the police came again. I thought it was another look-and-see routine visit. No chance. They said there had been a bomb warning. Yes, you got it: a fucking bomb warning in a church hall. You couldn't dream that one up! I said, 'Get real. Do you really think we are going to blow ourselves up?' I think even the Gestapo lady realised I had a point. Apparently there are three types of category warnings, and this was a green warning, which was the lowest. They didn't think it was a credible warning, but they had to act on it. We had to reassure her that we could account for everyone in the room. I had to make an announcement, but everyone thought I was taking the piss and started laughing. They took no notice of me, but they soon realised how serious it was, and we all had to check under our tables and chairs for anything suspicious. My wife had booked the room, so she had to sign a declaration that we were responsible for the search and were happy with the outcome of how the police handled it. Then once again normal service resumed. At least it gave everyone something to talk about for the next few days. The bottom line was we all had a great night and raised lot of money, plus Chelsea had beaten United in the Cup Final.

I found out a few days later that the culprit who started the bomb scare was some halfwit who didn't like Chris. He was the one who also kept phoning the police, and he also turned up at the church hall that night gobbing off. Botty politely persuaded him to leave, Botty did not tell me on the night because he knew I had enough shit on my plate, and he did not think I needed another dose. How right he was. I was glad not all the events we organised were as topsy-turvy as that fucker was. At least we can laugh about it now, but I didn't at the time.

As the branch got more of a high profile especially as we raised a lot of money for charity, for some strange reason I was getting more and more demand from the local media to have a say about this and that in connection to City, and I was quite often heard on the radio. I thought it only fair to agree to their requests as they had given us a lot of support in our charity work. This resulted in a unique event taking place after yet another City promotion to the Premier League. Greater Manchester Radio broadcasted their *Breakfast Show* from my house. A couple of hours before the show started, the outside broadcasting team arrived and started doing their stuff with cables, microphones, and other bits and pieces they needed. Heather Stott was the presenter and was brilliant with us all. I had arranged for loads of my mates to pop round because we had beaten Blackburn, as City had been promoted, everyone was in a great mood. My niece Zoe, who at the time was in primary school, came in. Heather asked her why I had let her in the house with a red jumper on, and her reply knocked Heather for six. She replied, 'It's my school uniform. I don't want to wear red today, and I would rather wear my City shirt, but my teacher won't let me.' I didn't brainwash her from an early age – honest. Because it was a breakfast show, Cath had to keep frying loads of bacon, so the sizzling could be heard on the radio. At least everyone had loads of bacon butties. They were in the house for about three hours doing the show. Heather was busy interviewing all the people who turned up at the house, and I was busy brewing up for everyone. It was a fantastic experience and a great morning. That year the radio station won the outside broadcasting team of the year award, and the live broadcast from my house featured in the acceptance speech.

As a branch, we also got filmed for a Coca-Cola advert, but for reasons outside of our control, it was never broadcasted, even though I watched a copy and it was a classic. Well, I wouldn't say anything else, would I?

We only got invited to do the advert as somehow or other they had heard about our fundraising events so we thought it was an offer we could not refuse.

Coca-Cola had sponsored the League Cup and were doing a series of adverts featuring football fans from different clubs up and down the country. They were going to film us going to an away game at Wolves. The night before the shoot (Well, I have to use their jargon.) I met with the crew in a hotel in Manchester and got wasted. I was rough as a butcher's dog when we met them at the social club the next morning. The production company had organised the tickets and the transport, a double-decker bus. All we had to do was turn up. There was a good mix of all ages, including men, women, and kids. Even though we met at the social club, I don't think the crew expected us to start drinking so early in the morning. They agreed to let us take a carry-out on the bus as long as we drank the beer out of Coca-Cola cups. Before we set off, everyone had to sign a form saying we didn't have any criminal convictions. Fuck me. If everyone who had a conviction had signed yes, there would have only been about two blokes and the women and kids on the bus. Everyone including the kids got twenty-five pounds and all the Coke they could drink, plus loads of butties. The kids got giddy after a bit, and while still on the motorway, they started launching the empty Coke cups onto the production team's vehicle following behind, much to their shock and horror. On the way there, we stopped for a piss stop, and I threw up behind a tree. Fuck knows what the crew thought of that.

When we arrived at the Wolves' ground, the police boarded to check us out. I realised we had not got rid of the empty cans and bottles. I wondered, *'How the heck do I get out of this one?'* The director of the film crew unwittingly came to our aid. He just told the police he wanted to film us coming off the bus and politely asked the police to get off. The director was a Yank, so they let him get on with it. As everyone was getting off, the lads managed to get the empties off as well. After the game, we were all back on the coach, except the crew. The police would not let us wait for them because we had to go with the police escort. They had left loads of stuff and equipment on the bus, but there was not a lot we could do about it. Mobile phones were still not all that common back then, so I could not get in touch with them. It was no big deal, and I took all the stuff back to my house. Later on, they arranged for someone to come pick it up. Once the filming had been cut and put on a tape, one of the team members came to the house to show it me. It was in black-and-white, and I was not on it, but you could hear my voice. Oh, well. My five minutes of fame would have to wait. In fact, everyone's five minutes had to wait. Even though it was another great day out and a once-in-a-lifetime experience, it was never shown on TV. We believe it was because round that time, City were changing sponsors, and the new ones didn't want the name of the old sponsor to been shown. It just goes to show though how much time, effort, and expense goes into shooting an advert that will be on the TV for only a minute or so. Some of the team had flown in from America, and everyone was gutted. It wasn't to be shown, but at least we had a great day out – free coach, free tickets, free beer, free Coke, and twenty-five pounds each, plus free butties. I wish we could do that every week!

As I have said the local media were great. You knew they would not try to stitch you up, especially on live radio, because it wasn't edited, and exactly what you said went on air. They were also great for publicising our monthly meetings and the charity events we were organising, but the national media were never as helpful.

After one City and Millwall game, there was loads of trouble, and a few windows on Oxford Road got smashed. A reporter from the national press whom I did not know phoned me up and said three City fans had been arrested for smashing a jeweller's window and robbing it. He asked if I would condemn them for bringing City fans and the club's reputation into disrepute. When I asked him how he knows they are City fans, he said, 'Because they are.' I thought straight away he was an arrogant little shit, and I wasn't going to feed his agenda. I said I would not condemn anyone under any circumstances until I knew the facts, and even then I probably wouldn't. I doubt any one would give a flying fuck about my opinions any way. I said if they went to court and were found guilty, we could have this discussion again. Needless to say, I never heard a thing from him. I also never saw any report in the paper or media saying City fans – or any anyone else, for that matter – had been arrested for robbing a jeweller's after the game. I think he just wanted to shit stir and get cheap headlines.

Most of the lads were up for an early drink before the home games, and so we decided to combine an early drink with a bit of extra entertainment and a bit of fundraising. These gentlemen's mornings have been going strong for twenty years and are as popular as ever. We used to do two per season. I am no longer involved organizing them, but Ian is doing a cracking job by keeping the mornings going and raising loads of money for charities and good causes. We got a bit ambitious and even held them twice before away games, both at Oldham, which is not too far away. The problem was both times the double-decker buses did not wait for us and pissed off shortly after everyone was dropped off at the game. The reason given was that everyone was a bit too lively and giddy for the drivers. The second time they left early. I could see them leaving from where I was in the ground and thought, *Oh, no. Not again.* We were slowly running out of coach companies and decided to stick to organizing the gentlemen's mornings before home games.

The events were ticket only and always sold outs weeks before the event. The format was pretty straightforward. We would have Little Oz the DJ doing his stuff, as well as three exotic dancers … well, you know what I mean. If not, just use your imagination a little. We always had a top-class comedian, and on several occasions Manchester City fan, the late Bernard Manning, was the star turn. We used to do raffles and auctions, as well as drinking competitions and a good old sing song. These events might not be everyone's cup of tea in the political correctness climate, but live and let live was our motto. Even though there were over three hundred City fans drinking as early as 9.00 a.m. there was never one spot of trouble, which is a credit to everyone involved, especially the door staff: Botty, John, and Leon. Another comedian who goes down well is a Middlesbrough fan, Chris McClade. He may be barking mad, but he is a great bloke.

Over the years, we always got a good turnout from the Feyenoord and Antwerp lads. Those lads really know how to have a great time. They usually come over for three or four days, and they usually go to another local game as well as watching the Blues. All the events we organise would never run smoothly if so many people did not help out behind the scenes and do mundane tasks, such as selling raffle tickets, buying the guests drinks, and handling anything else that needs doing. There is usually no shortage of volunteers to look after the girls on the gentlemen's mornings. The helpers show them where to get changed, get them their drinks and snacks, and let them know when they are needed on stage.

On one occasion, one of the dancers asked a lad if he could get her a bottle of Coke. The place was hammered, so it took him a bit to get served. When he knocked on the door, she shouted for him to come in. He nearly dropped the bottle of Coke on the floor because she was sat there, feet up on a chair and stark bollock naked, without a care in the world while doing her nails. The lad did not know where to look – well, that's what he told us, anyway. The dancer said to him, 'don't worry, love, you can tell everyone today you have seen the crack of Dawn.' We pissed ourselves laughing when he told us. There were always plenty of volunteers to assist the girls at these mornings, which was hardly surprising. Besides everyone having a fantastic time, it was also a great way to raise money for a good cause or one of the charities with which we were involved. The Blackley Blues attend these events in great numbers and a couple of the lads, Paul and Derek always helps out by selling loads of tickets. I met some great Blues from Blackley including, Carl Heald who organised the Blackley branch plus Hedley, Tranty and Dryer, all top lads. I bumped into Paul and Derek in Manchester before the home game against Leicester and had a good chat about the old days.

At the last gent's morning that was organised by Ian, a shitload of money was raised for charity, so it is fantastic to see a tradition started all those years ago is still going strong to this day. Football fans in general, and City fans in particular, have always had a great fundraising history, and their generosity never fails to amaze me.

CHAPTER 15

Feyenoord and Antwerp Blues

For many years, the branch has been in contact with some Dutch Blues, including Angelo, Patrick, Michele, and Denis, who are also fanatic Feyenoord fans. Many fans on the continent have a Premier League club as their second team. These lads have been coming over for donkey's years, and they come at least three to four times a year. They have been coming since back in the day when City were really shit. My brother Bob who now lives in Amsterdam, helped form the Dutch Blues Supporters Club, and that is how the connection with us began. I regularly meet up with them when they come over, and I have been to many games with them.

Angelo and Dennis wanted to come over for the first Derby at the new stadium, so I managed to get them tickets for the game. They asked if I could pick them up from the airport, which was no problem. But the night before they phoned to confirm everything, and I realised they meant Liverpool Airport. Ugh.

Bury were playing at Rochdale the day before the Derby, so they went to that game as well, and in the evening I met up with them for something to eat and drink. I had an early night because I wanted to be in fine form for the Derby. The morning of the game, we met at the Heaton Park Working Men's Club for a few drinks and something to eat. We also had comedian Chris McClade come down to entertain us. He was in good form, and all of us were in a great mood as we got on the coaches to go to the stadium, it was the first time Angelo and Dennis had been to the new stadium, and they were impressed with how it looked. The game was a cracker and was a great victory for the Blues, who easily won 4-1. The atmosphere in the ground was electric, and it is always that feeling when we beat the rags, but to do it so easily and to put four past them made it even better. We were in high spirits, talking about the game while waiting for the coaches to take us back to Prestwich.

Denis spotted them first but didn't think much of it when he saw a group of lads dressed in black approach our group, which consisted mainly of elderly blokes, women, and kids. There was a schoolteacher with us who was with his son, and he was suddenly attacked by this group of idiots for no reason other than we were City fans. I bet the pricks hadn't even been to the game. There was a lot of screaming and shouting, and when our group defended themselves and fought back, the scum ran off like the bullies and shithouses they were. The police were nearby and went after them, but they escaped down the backstreets of Miles Platting. We had seen it all before and didn't let it spoil our day, and we carried on celebrating well into the night. It's been said many times that so-called hooligans have a fictional code of honour, where they won't fight or attack ordinary fans and only fight with like-minded people. What a load of bollocks. Scum like the ones we came across that day would not have attacked our group if they'd known we would fight back. As soon as we did, the bastards could not run fast enough. Yeah they must be dead hard, smacking a schoolteacher who was with his son. What a load of shitheads.

Not long after that game, a group of us were on a long weekend trip to Amsterdam and Angelo arranged to get eight tickets for the Feyenoord game. We arranged to meet them in Rotterdam before the match. The trouble was we were having a good drink in Amsterdam and lost all track of time.

The other slight problem was the kick off was two hours earlier than I'd thought. Oops. Anyone can make a small technical error, can't they? Plus, I still was not in possession of a mobile phone. They finally managed to contact us: Michele had phoned Cath in the UK to find out where we were. I eventually phoned home, and Cath told me the Dutch lads had been looking for us and were waiting for us outside the ground, so we had to move our arses. We realised we would not get to the game till about half-time, but that didn't deter us. We jumped in a minibus, and there was a further delay because we had to pull in at an off-licence; it would take a while to get to the ground, and we were still thirsty. When we got to the ground, good old Michele was still waiting outside with the tickets for us. What a nice guy. He did give me loads of friendly abuse, and probably some not-so-friendly abuse, but it was all in Dutch, so I could not understand. I did hear the word 'cunt' once or twice, but I am sure he was not referring to me. Yeah, right. It's not the first time I've dropped a clanger and been late for a game, and it certainly was not the last. It was a fantastic atmosphere in the ground, and Feyenoord won, so when we went for a drink after the game with the lads from Holland, everyone was in a great mood; even Michele had a smile on his face. I have always thought the Dutch were friendly, and this set of lads were no exception. Their knowledge of football and of the Premier League was second to none. We stayed a couple of hours after the match and then went back to Amsterdam to dance the night away – or in my case, go back to the hotel pissed up and fall asleep.

It was a great weekend, and it was even better by the fact that ex-City goalie Tony Coton was on our flight over. I had met him before, so he sat with me on the plane. He invited us for a drink at the bar in Schiphol Airport. It would have been disrespectful to refuse, so we didn't. We had a couple of beers in Tony's company, and he told us about his time at City and what was going on behind the scenes. It was utter barmy. He loved his time at the club but was disappointed that he did not figure in the manager's plans; he realised he had to move on. The reason he was in Holland was because at the time, he was goalkeeping coach for United. He was over in Holland to do some scouting at a youth tournament that was taking place over the weekend.

Some City fans felt bitter towards Tony because of his connections with United. As Tony said to us, he would have loved to have stayed till the end of his career at City, but they did not want him. He would have jumped at the chance of being goalkeeping coach at City, but again he was not asked. He had to earn a living like everyone else, so when United offered him a job, he would have been a mug to refuse. Tony was and still is a big Birmingham City fan, and he told us some great stories about his time in the midlands. It was a very pleasant couple of hours.

When it was time to get going, I got lost after going to the toilet. I could not remember where the lads were, so I jumped on a train, but after a couple of stops I realised I was going the wrong way, so I had to get off and double back, leaving the rest of the lads and my bags at the airport bar wondering where the fuck I was. We all met up later on in a bar near the hotel at which we were staying.

Through the Feyenoord lads, we met the Blues from Antwerp. Loads of us have been over to watch them play, and we have had great weekends with them. At least two times a year, Gorba, Bart, Wacko, and the other lads come over here to see City. Antwerp is a great city and is full of history and culture, which is usually lost on us when we are there. Usually we have drank too much to notice anything but the bars.

One match sticks out for all the wrong reasons. Eight of us went over for their last game of the season. It wasn't a great game, and afterwards we went back to a famous pub near the ground called the Great Old. We noticed before and after the game that there were lots of riot police about in their vans, plus the police water cannons were knocking around. I thought it rather strange because there wasn't many away fans, it isn't a massive ground, and the Antwerp fans were in a great mood. We were in the back of the pub playing pool, and all the Antwerp fans were singing and enjoying themselves. When I went to the toilet, I noticed the police had positioned themselves opposite the pub and had on their riot gear. When I asked the lads why this was, they said, 'No problem, Don. This is normal with the police here.' It might be normal to them, but it didn't seem very normal to me.

We were in the back of the pub and so didn't see much or feel the tension rising, but we heard a lot of singing. As the evening wore on, the fans outside started letting off flares and hurling abuse at the police. The tension and the police provocation mounted, and it wasn't long before the water cannons were used on the fans. I was pretty oblivious to most of this because by now I was drunk and kept nodding off in the back room. There were clashes with the police, and the police started wading in with their truncheons. All the lads who were involved in the clashes were chased down the road by the police. Some of the police were also on horseback. That left us lot in the back of the pub, but we didn't know much that was going on and weren't involved in anything except drinking, playing pool, and falling asleep. Regardless, whoever was left in the back of the pub was arrested. They had to wake me and a few others up to arrest us. Eighty-four fans were arrested and taken to the police station. At 5.00 am. They released all the English lads and most of the Belgians without charge, thank fuck.

I thought I had bad luck, but one of the Belgian lads, Tom, was arrested by his own fucking brother, who was one of the riot police. How crackers is that? Tom said because there was such a big police presence and no away fans, the police had to justify their presence by doing something. Also Gorba got bit by a police dog. You would not think shit like that would still be happening in this day and age. There were headlines in the Belgian and Dutch papers saying there were eighty-four arrests. There was fuck all said that most were released without charge. I have been involved in some barmy things in my time watching football, but that has to rank as about one of the barmiest.

The Belgium fans who were arrested brought a joint civil action out against the police and the mayor of Antwerp. It dragged on through the courts before it fizzled out due to the fans not being able to carry on funding the legal action. I would definitely go and watch Antwerp again, but I would stay clear of going back to the Great

Old. Antwerp's ground is a bit rundown and they don't get big crowds, so they don't have any money for improvements. The people who do attend the games certainly know how to enjoy themselves, and the atmosphere was really good. Like the Dutch, the Belgians know their football, and they were very friendly and helpful.

When City played away at Lokeren, which is another Belgium football club, loads of us went over and met up with Angelo, Michele, Denis, Patrick, and other Dutch and Belgium City fans. The bonus of that trip was that City won 1-0. Lokeren, like the Antwerp ground, was in dire need of improvement, but they also don't get big crowds and don't have much money so I can't see it happening anytime soon.

Chapter 16

Footballing Heroes

Calling a footballer a hero for getting paid to kick a football about can be seen as a bit over the top, considering what members of the armed forces and emergency services have to do on a daily basis. But many kids have pop stars as heroes, and most football fans either hero-worship a player or players, or the whole football team. A footballer can turn from hero to villain or vice versa overnight, depending what they do or don't do. The great thing about being a football fan that is over the years, you have the opportunity to watch some great players play at the highest level, and fans' opinions of players vary from week to week. I have seen and met some great players who, for various reasons, have been hero-worshipped by some fans and slagged off by others. This chapter highlights some of the fan favourites and the not-so-favourites.

In 1981 there were some new signings for City that not only helped get us out of the relegation area but also got us to Wembley. We also got to a two-legged semi-final, but the three new signings were cup tied and could not play. The semi was against Liverpool, and in the first leg at Maine Road, a perfectly good goal was disallowed, much to the disgust of the City fans. Liverpool went on to win the game, but we were in a confident mood as we headed to Liverpool for second leg. There were thousands of City fans at Anfield, and there were no signs of any scroats after my jacket this time. I was wearing a scruffy old donkey jacket, so I doubt even a Scouser would have gone to the trouble of robbing me for that fucker. We were in a pub packed full of City fans before the game. The police with their dogs came in to clear the pub. There was no warning or fuck all. I think because there was so many City fans in Liverpool, they wanted to get us all in the ground so there would be less chance of kicking off with the Liverpool fans. But that was the norm in those days. Football fans were treated like scum, and there was no please or thank you. It was just 'Do as I say', and if you answered back, you were looking to get hit with a truncheon or get arrested. In those situations it was best to keep your gob shut and fuck off. But at times, even that simple task was too much for me to achieve if I'd had a drink, so now and again I ended up with a smack or two, or I was put in the back of a police van after being confronted by the police. We went to the ground and only managed a draw, so it was Liverpool who went on to the final of the League Cup. We had to wait a long time for our revenge but it was very sweet when we beat Liverpool in the final of the League Cup in February 2016.

I don't think we helped endear ourselves to the locals or the police by singing at full belt,

'In your Liverpool slums, in your Liverpool slums, you look in the dustbin for something to eat. You find a dead cat, you think it is a treat. You are the dirtiest bastards we ever did meet, in your Liverpool slums!'

Don't feel too sorry for the Scouser's, though, because they had plenty of insulting songs about us. Never mind, hey? The season was not over, and we had plenty of more excitement to look forward to, plus a couple of visits to Wembley.

As it turned out, 9th May 1981 was a great day for us. We were back at Wembley for the first time since we'd won the cup five years previously against Newcastle United, in 1976. In 1981 it was known as the Centenary Cup Final because it was the hundredth final. It was against Tottenham Hotspur, who had some fantastic players at the time, including two Argentineans, Ossie Ardiles and Ricardo Villa. Tottenham also had a stupid song recorded for the final, sang by the players and pop duo Chas and Dave. The less said about that, the better, because 'cheesy as fuck' is the only way to describe the song.

There were three relatively new signings that helped us get to Wembley, because the team had been struggling under the Malcolm Allison regime, and John Bond had come in and turned the tide. Tommy Hutchinson, an ex-Scotland player, was John Bond's first signing for the Blues. Tommy played a huge role in getting City out of the relegation area and to Wembley for the FA Cup final. Even though Tommy was skilful with the ball at his feet, it was with his head that he scored the opening goal against Spurs. But with only about eleven minutes left, Spurs had a free kick. Tommy was in the wall, and unfortunately the ball hit Tommy as he moved. The ball flew past the unfortunate Joe Corrigan and into the goal. There were no more goals in the next ten minutes or in the extra time, so it was to be the first ever cup final replay at Wembley five days later.

Bobby McDonald was also signed from Coventry City. He was a solid defender and could score the odd goal or two as well. In fact, on the way to Wembley, he scored one in the 6-0 thrashing of John Bond's old club, Norwich, as well as two goals in the quarter-final replay against Everton. Bobby will probably be more fondly remembered for one game when we played Watford. There were only three minutes gone in the game played when Joe Corrigan, the goalie, had to go off with a dislocated shoulder. In those days, there was only one substitute on the bench, but it was never a goalkeeper, so Joe went off and Bobby went in the nets. He pulled off loads of saves, and with Denis Tueart scoring for City, Bobby's heroics saw City go to the top of the first division (now the Premier League). It was an inspiring day in goal for Bobby, and his brilliant achievement kept a clean sheet and helped the team win.

Gerry Gow was the third of John Bond's signings. Even though Gerry only played about thirty-six games for City, his influence cannot be underestimated. His tough, no-holds-barred tackling, along with his help in the scoring department, soon won him an army of fans from the Blue faithful. We signed Gerry from Bristol City, where he is still hero-worshiped. In 2012 Bristol granted Gerry a retrospective testimonial for his previous service to the club, and they played against a Manchester City legends side. Many fans from Manchester travelled to Bristol for the game.

The FA Cup replay was on a Thursday night, and it was like the lord mayor's show for us City fans, for the first game, many like me had gone for the weekend, and even in those days, it wasn't cheap in London, so it was a big ask for City fans to dig deep again, take the time off work, and go back down to London for the replay. Even though we didn't completely sell our allocation, we took many more than I'd expected, and just under half of the ninety-two-thousand-person crowd were City fans. There were fewer fans at the replay because the capacity was reduced as it was an evening game. Many City fans who were unable to get tickets for the first game were able to get them for the replay. For some bizarre reason, when clubs reach the FA Cup final, the fans of the teams in the final only get a small proportion of the tickets; the rest are allocated by the FA. In the replay, both sets of fans received a bigger allocation, and the atmosphere for the replay was electric, with both sets of fans in fine voice.

Most Tottenham fans were great, but there were some dickheads in both games who, instead of enjoying the whole Wembley experience, decided to attack small groups of City fans. But like shithouses do, the Spurs fans soon disappeared when closer to kick off, and the City fans arrived in their thousands. The dickheads did not fancy their chances when the odds were not in their favour.

A Football Fan's Story

In the replay, there were hundreds of Spurs fans in our end, and when Spurs scored they started celebrating and goading the City fans, it was the last straw for the City fans. Some crowd trouble broke out, and the Spurs fans got chased out of the City end, with many Spurs fans getting pushed over the side of the tunnel leading to the concourse. Many others jumped over to get away, and others ran to the bottom of the stands to get away from the trouble. I didn't have any sympathy for them because I remembered what they were like outside the ground, especially in the first game when many unsuspecting City fans got attacked. But that is what bullies are like the world over: they can give it out, but they cannot take it.

Unfortunately for City fans, Ricardo Villas's second goal goes down as one of the all-time Wembley greats. To our annoyance, it is shown every year around cup final day. City went on to get beat 3-2 by the Spurs, but on the plus side, it was a classic game. It was disappointing for all the City fans, especially the ones who had made the journey again for the replay. The players did us proud and earned the club a bit of self-respect. Although we never won, the players gave it their all, and as fans we can never ask for more than that.

Wembley's stadium is famous the world over, and it is where the England team play. All footballers want to play there, and all football fans want to go there to watch their teams play. Although the ground looks great on telly, in those days the inside of the ground was a shithouse and was in dire need of improvement. Nonetheless, it was a great experience to go there. The stadium has now been rebuilt, and although I have not been since it was modernised, by all accounts it is a world-class stadium with state-of-the-art facilities.

Many years after the cup final, I and a few of the committee lads sat in the pub talking about who we could invite to a future branch meeting. Someone came up with the idea of getting Bobby, Tommy, and Gerry to the same meeting. After a few beers, it seemed like a brilliant idea, and we agreed to get on with organising it. Upon waking up in the morning with a hangover, it seemed a crazy idea. We hadn't a clue where they lived, and we had no contact information for any of them. There was no Internet facilities available with up-to-date info at people's fingertips, and I certainly didn't know how to use a computer back then, anyway. But what the fuck – we liked a challenge. We set to work on our seemingly impossible mission.

After making an appeal in our monthly newsletter, someone came back with the name of the pub Gerry was working in at Portland, near Weymouth – my old stomping ground from my navy days. This made sense because later in his career, he went on to be player-manager for Weymouth. Soon we made contact with Gerry, and he was well up for it. Then shortly afterwards we tracked down Tommy in Swansea; he was coaching youngsters in South Wales. Bobby was working for the electric board in the Midlands. The hardest part was getting a weekend sorted which all three could make and that City were playing at home. It took dozens of phone calls, many letters, and a few sleepless nights on my behalf, but it slowly came together.

We organised the branch meeting for the Friday before the Bradford game which was on the Saturday. We had been in touch with the club, and they were great in terms of lounge passes and tickets for the game for the trio. Our branch had organised to go in the lounge as well, so we were all together. Leading up to any event, I was always on edge in case something happened and the guests could not attend, or some other shit happened. I am never fully comfortable till all the guests have arrived. We had arranged to pick up both Gerry and Bobby from Manchester's Piccadilly train station and take them straight to their hotel, where Tommy would be meeting us because he was driving from South Wales.

The Friday night meeting was a great success. Tommy Booth turned up as well to see his old team mates. We did the usual question-and-answer stuff, but we also got the lads to tell us more about their time at City, and especially the cup final. Many fans had brought pictures and copies of the cup final programme for them to sign. One thing I noticed was all three could certainly drink and were putting away the pints. I was dreading seeing the bar bill at the end of the night, but they were really enjoying themselves and mixing well with the fans, so we could not ask for any more than that. We had put all three up in the Village Hotel in Prestwich, and after the meeting, it was back there for a late drink.

In the morning, we headed off to the ground for the game against Bradford. When we got there, all three were invited onto the pitch to be presented to the fans, and they got a terrific reception. Everyone was mobbing them for photographs and autographs. All three of them lapped it up because they had not been sure what sort of reception they would get from the fans.

Tommy had to go back to Wales after the game because he had commitments, but not before all three went over to the player's area to meet up with the some of the backroom staff who they knew. I thought it was great for all three of them to make the effort and come up for the event, especially for Tommy because it was a right trek for him and a bit of a rush; it was more or less straight there and back for him. The trip brought back so many happy memories for all three of them.

I always remember Bobby looking round the ground. Between two of the stands, there were a load of seats that was nicknamed the Gene Kelly Stand. It had no cover, and with the Manchester weather, you were usually singing in the rain anyway. Bobby looked at it and called it a fucking monstrosity, and he wasn't wrong. We won the game 1-0, so it was a great weekend all round. Before we headed back to Prestwich, we had a couple of drinks near the ground, where again the two remaining players had a great time with the fans.

Then it was back to the hotel, but I could not keep up with them because they drank like fish. I only had more drink and went home early to my bed. The players loved the fact that even sixteen years after they had left City, the fans held them in the highest respect. I met up with Bobby and Gerry in the morning, and after a full English, I went to the train station with them. I had a farewell drink with them and could not thank them enough for coming. In return, they thanked me and asked me to thank all the others for the hospitality they had received. Apparently Gerry is now working for Tesco's, and Bobby has his own soccer school, coaching youngsters. Last I heard, Tommy worked for the Welsh FA.

Ian Brightwell was one of the fastest and fittest players at City, and it is hardly surprising. His mum is Ann Packer, the Olympic gold medal winner and 800 meter runner. His father is Robbie Brightwell, a former track and field athlete who was captain of the men's British Olympic team at the Tokyo Olympics. They were both awarded the MBE in 1965.

Ian is another player who is a lifelong Blue, and he signed for City when he was still at school. He was part of the 1986 FA youth cup–winning team. Ian didn't score a great many goals in his career, but the stand out one was at Old Trafford in 1990. City were playing well but were still losing the game. The ball came out to Ian just outside the area, and he let fly. The ball went sweet as a nut into the top corner. City fans went mental. Although the official allocation of City fans was behind the goals, there were also hundreds of City fans, including me in the Stretford paddock. When Ian was later interviewed, he said, I just wellied It. and just hoped for the best. Whatever terms you want to use, it was a cracker and thrust Ian into the spotlight of media attention.

A Football Fan's Story

I first met Ian in the unusual surroundings of the gent's toilets at the ground. Before you jump to the wrong conclusions, it was after a game, and I was in the toilets of the Maine Stand when Ian came in. It's not every day you are in the toilet with a famous player, and once I got over the shock, I asked him how come he was having a piss with the riff-raff. He laughed and explained he was in the player's lounge with his family, and there was no toilet there. Can you believe it? A top football club that didn't even have a toilet in the player's lounge? Well, it's easy to believe if you know anything about City.

Our branch got involved in Ian's testimonial year just before he left the club. We attended a sportsmen's dinner in Prestwich, and we also organised a couple of events at the Heaton Park Social Club. One of them was an absolute classic. The night we held the meeting it coincided with the *Manchester Evening News* awards evening, at which the majority of the first team players attended. Once it had finished, Kit Symons, the captain, organised a minibus and brought all the players to the social club. What a result for us! They were all in good spirits, and it showed how much our branch and Ian were respected by the club, for all those players to come down.

Before the first team squad turned up, we were having a normal question-and-answer session with Ian. Somehow the topic got on to a drinking competition, so before I knew it, Ian and I were on the stage ready to go toe to toe in a drinking competition. It soon went a bit barmier. The women in the room were shouting and cheering, 'Get your tops off!' I don't think anyone was remotely interested in seeing me bare-chested for one second, but Ian swiftly whipped his top off, so I felt obliged to do the same. Before I go any further, let us picture the scene. We have over three hundred City fans attending a meeting, and I and one of City's stars are on stage semi-naked and about to have a drinking competition, and we're being roared on by the crowd. After a count of three, it was down our necks. Well, to be precise, it was down Ian's neck. I had hardly made a dent in mine before he'd finished his, so we had a rematch. I should not have bothered because the result was exactly the same: Ian's drink was finished in seconds. What he conveniently forgot to mention was that he was a champion in this drinking game lark; he had won many challenges in the past, and his missus also told me when he was in Miami, he was crowned champion after one competition. He'd so impressed the locals that he was paraded round the pub on someone's shoulders. Apparently he has an unusual gullet, so it goes down very quick. I learned the hard way yet again.

Soon after that little episode, Kit and the players turned up, and I got them all up on stage. They received a fantastic standing ovation, and I got Kit to address the audience on behalf of the players. At this stage I thought to myself, *'What the hell do I do now?'* Time was getting on the members were having a brilliant time. The players were in fine spirits, and I thought I needed to do something else instead of another question-and-answer session. While I was rattling my brains what to do next, I asked ex-City goalie Eric Nixon, who was with Stockport County at the time, how he had enjoyed his time at City and what was it like at Stockport County. He just took hold of the microphone and starting singing the Elvis Pressley classic 'Living Doll'. Well fuck me, he was brilliant. The whole room was up rocking, and then he sang a couple of more songs, with everyone joining in. When he gave me the mike back, I led a rendition of City songs, and the players joined in. Obviously we couldn't resist singing anti-United songs, and the players enthusiastically joined in for those too. One player fell off the stage, and thank god he wasn't injured. Another one wasn't sure where the toilet was, and our goalie at the time, Tommy Wright, had to point him in the right direction before there was a mess on the floor. That meeting went down in branch history. I am glad there were no mobile phones with cameras in those days, or loads of players would have been in the doghouse, sacked, or both, and I don't think the club would have been too keen on sending players again. Oh, well. Another belting night was had by all.

'Feed the goat, and he will score' – that was the iconic chant that went round the ground on match days.

Shaun Goater, a great goal scoring centre forward, was born in Bermuda and played for a number of clubs in the lower leagues before he graced the hallow turf of Maine Road. He was also in the Bermuda National Team, and he played thirty-six games for his country and scored thirty-two times. That is some record, but we won't probe too deeply about the standard of the opposition; we will simply rejoice at his record. Shaun went onto become City's leading scorer for four years on the trot, and was hero-worshipped by the fans, but that hero worship was hard won, and it was not always an easy ride for Shaun, especially at the start of his career at City.

He made his debut at Bradford away on 28 March 1998. I do not possess a photographic memory, but I remember it well as it was my youngest lad's birthday, and Steven, Sean, and I went with other lads from the branch in a sixteen-seater minibus. As usual the day was ruined by the score because City went down 2-1. None of us were that impressed with Shaun Goater's first game, with some of the verdicts ranging from 'He is shit' to 'He never is a fucking centre forward'. I am sure I was less restrained in my opinion, and although I can't remember my comments precisely, I am sure I tipped him for the top. (Yeah, like fuck I did.)

We bought him that year to save us from the drop to the old third division, and although he eventually found his goal scoring boots, it was not enough to keep us up. Unfortunately for Shaun, he was also tainted because at one stage of his career he was at the swamp, which is one of the nicer names we give to United's ground Old Trafford. But we are glad for a number of reasons that he never made it there, and after playing for Rotherham and Bristol, he joined us. We got glimpses though over his next few weeks at the club of how good Shaun would be. He scored three goals in the last few games, but the jury was still out, and the fans were split on their opinions.

Over the next few seasons, the City fans saw the real Shaun Goater, and he was City's top scorer for the next four years on the bounce. Plus, he was the first City player since Franny Lee to score more than thirty goals in one season.

Back in Bermuda, Shaun was granted freedom from Bermuda, and 21 June 2013 was declared Shaun Goater Day. That in itself tells you how much the bloke was thought of.

With Shaun banging in the goals left, right, and centre for City, he soon won over all the fans, even the ones who'd doubted his abilities when he'd first joined. He cemented himself in City folklore in his last season for the Blues when City played United at Maine Road, with the game 1-1 against the rags (a polite name we call United fans). United had the better of the game, and United player Gary Neville was watching the ball go out for what he thought would be a goal kick, but Shaun pounced. He took the ball from Neville's feet and smashed the ball into the back of the net to make it 2-1, and that was his ninety-ninth goal for City. All the City fans went metal. Neville's face was a picture, and we took the piss out of him something wicked. Could things get any better? Damn right, they could. Shaun scored another goal to make it a 3-1 City victory, it was Shaun's hundredth goal in a City shirt, and it was against the rags at Maine Road. What a victory it was! It was a day to never forget. I was supposed to go home straight after the match, but I stayed out celebrating well into the night

Also in that season, he made Premier League history by scoring the fastest goal by a substitute ever. What makes it all the more spectacular was it was at the swamp against the rags, and it ended up a 1-1 draw, he had only been on the pitch nine seconds the rags were sick to the back teeth of Shaun that season.

The final season at Maine Road was also Shaun's final season at City, and for the last game he was made club captain for the day. A week later, he was a guest at our family fun day. Hundreds of people turned up, and we had a private room where Shaun could sign autographs and have photos with the fans. Mario, Paul, and Keith helped organise it; otherwise, it would have been chaos. The lads from the P&W football team were also there in their special T-shirts, and the Goat signed them all. I also got a T-shirt signed by Shaun, but in all the rush and not a little bit of confusion, he signed it to John, not to Don. Oh, well. Not to worry – there are a few other words that spring to mind that he could have called me instead of John.

After signing autographs, Shaun then came on stage to a tremendous ovation. James H. Reeve did a fantastic interview with him, what made the event with Shaun so special was that it was Shaun's wedding anniversary, and he should have been in London with his wife, but because he had agreed to come to our event, he honoured his commitment. What a guy! Shaun has also been awarded the MBE for services to sport and young people in Bermuda and went on to play for a number of other clubs before hanging up his boots, and a few years ago he made another appearance at the Prestwich and Whitefield branch, where he got another great reception. Another fantastic night was had by everyone who attended. Shaun really enjoys going to the supporters events, and he is still in big demand even though it's been many years since he left the club. The fans still love to meet him, and he is also very popular when he makes appearances on TV and radio.

Over the years, City have dropped some bollocks in the transfer market, and they never seemed to learn their lesson. One of the biggest mistakes City ever made was when they signed Steve Daly from Wolverhampton Wanderers in 1979 for nearly one and a half million pounds. To be fair, he was a pretty decent player when he was with Wolves, and it is hard to fathom out why he was so shit at City. He came up through the youth ranks at Wolves. He was with Wolves when they beat City in the 1974 League Cup at Wembley, but he was not picked for the team on the day of the final. We got beat, and that is enough said about that final. The signing of Steve caused a raising of the eyebrows back then, because at that time not many players had been sold for one million pounds, and certainly not a midfielder. Rumour had it Malcolm Allison, the manager of City at the time, had agreed to a deal with Wolves. Meanwhile, Chairman Peter Swailes had also been in contact with Wolves, and fingers were pointed at Peter for paying the higher price for the player. Peter loved the headlines and publicity, and that is one reason why many laid the blame at his door.

His debut for City was OK, but we got beat by 1-0 against Southampton. It was a sign of things to come. His next game was away at West Bromwich Albion. Five of us went down together, and we got near the ground just in time for the pubs to open and have a couple of pints. Someone suggested having a drink in West Brom's Social Club, which is next to the ground. On the way round, one of the lads spotted someone familiar walking past the ground and said, 'Fuck me, that's Steve Daly.' I had to have a double take because it seemed so unreal: one of the dearest player in England walking towards the player's entrance on his own. While talking about it afterwards, we thought this was very odd because he wasn't with the rest of the team or a mate, or anyone at all. It can be risky for away fans to be walking around a ground. If some nutters (apart from us) had spotted him, there could have been some big problems. Anyway, not to look a gift horse in the mouth, I greeted Steve like a long-lost mate and told him how pleased we were he had signed for us. Then the punchline came: 'Have you any spare tickets?' To our surprise, he said he would leave us some at the ticket office collection point. We shook hands, wished him well, and went on our way.

After a few pints and a laugh with the West Brom fans, we set off for the City end. Pete reminded me about the free tickets, and I didn't think there was a chance in hell he had left us any, but we went round to the ticket office on the off chance he had kept his promise. Fuck me, he had left us three in the main stand! In those days, at least half of the grounds were standing, and you thought you were dead posh if you were in the seats. Well, we had a right result, but because there were five of us, we flogged them outside the ground. That gave us enough money to get us all in the standing area, amongst the City fans. That's where all the good news ends because City went onto get beat 4-0.

I think the price tag had a big impact on his form. He did not get off to a great start, and the media soon got on his back. This was quickly followed by a load of abuse from the opposing fans, and this really got to Steve. There were only glimpses of the player who had done so well at Wolves. He didn't last long with us and went to America a couple of years after signing for us, for a fraction of what we had paid for him.

He now does after-dinner speaking, and by all accounts he is a better speaker than he was a footballer. One of the lads from the branch was at a dinner where Steve was a guest, and he had a great chat with him at the end of the evening and invited him to a branch meeting. Steve readily agreed, and we were looking forward to his attendance. We arranged for him to stay at the Village Hotel in Prestwich and advertised on the local radio and in the *Manchester Evening News,* the match day programme, and our newsletter that he was coming. A couple of days before the meeting, he reaffirmed his commitment to attend, so we were all looking forward to meeting him.

The morning of the meeting, we phoned to check all was OK, and to ask what time he would be arriving. He never answered his phone or returned the call. That was when I got the feeling something was up. My fears proved to be spot on, because the fucker never turned up and never had the decency to let us know. Maybe he was taking it out of us because he'd had a shit time in Manchester. Because of his no-show, I decided we would never invite him to be a speaker at one of our sportsmen's dinners. Sod him. It might not affect his bank balance or ruin his after dinner speaking career, but at least it made us feel better. We still had a great night because we had Gary Owen and Peter Barnes, two ex-City players, as well as James H. Reeve in attendance. The problem when organising meetings is we are relying on the goodwill of the person attending, and if they say they are definitely attending, who are we to not believe them? Quite often we had guests cancelling at short notice because something cropped up, but we can accept that, and as long as they let us know, it is not the end of the world. But to lead us up the garden path like Steve did is a bit of a shithouse trick, so he was certainly no hero to City fans.

When fans talk about their favourite players who have done well for the club, they usually refer to them as legends as well as heroes. I am not too keen on the terms because they are thrown about far too easily and can dilute the meaning of the words. Many City fans refer to Andy Morrison, who was City's captain when we won the playoffs against Gillingham, as a legend. I would prefer to call him inspirational, but if he asked me to call him a legend, I would call him whatever he fucking wanted. You would as well if you ever saw him close up. His arms are bigger than my thighs, and he is a giant of a man. His biggest quality is that he is a born leader. It was only after reading his book that

I realised what an absolute nutter he used to be. I thought I got into some mad scrapes and found myself in the shit more times than I would like. My problems are not worth mentioning compared to Andy's.

Andy was born in Scotland but moved to Plymouth when he was a nipper. He played for a number of clubs, including Plymouth and Huddersfield, before coming to City in time for the 1998–99 season. The first time I had the pleasure of meeting Andy was when we were doing a cheque presentation to Henshaw's for the Blind Children's Christmas party. Gary Lewis, who worked for the Junior Blues at the time, asked Andy if he wanted to come to the meeting, and he jumped at the chance. Andy had not been at the club too long, so we were chuffed as fuck that he turned up. When I first saw him, I thought that with his build, he would be more suited as a rugby player or a boxer, but it did not seem prudent of me to mention my thoughts to him at the time. At the meeting, Andy was brilliant. There were some partially sighted youngsters in the audience, and he mingled and chatted with them like he had known them for years.

When some guests came to the meetings, they came because it was expected of them, and so they did what they had to do and then fucked off as quickly as they could without appearing rude. Not Andy. We had a great question-and-answer session with him, and after it finished, he stayed late, chatting and having photos and signing autographs. Andy later had a reputation as a bit of a drinker, and if you have read his book, you will realize it became a serious problem, but with us he was a true professional and stuck to soft drinks.

When Andy joined City, we could not have been in any more shit if we had tried. It was through Andy's leadership that he took the club kicking and screaming to the play off finals, where we eventually beat Gillingham. We can never underestimate the influence Andy had at the club. He was a born leader, but it does not seem credible that he only played less than fifty times for the club because injuries hampered his progress.

I met Andy a few times over the years at various functions and events, and I always thought he was a great bloke. Looking back at one event, I dropped a big bollock, and thank fuck he did not take offence. One of the members of the City website, Blue Watch, donated a special twenty-year-old whisky for all the guests. Yours truly duly gave them to each guest, including Andy. I did not at that time realize the extent of his drinking problem. It was only a couple of years later, after reading his book that I fully understood how serious his situation was and the shit that he'd gone through. I am sure he would have given the whisky to someone deserving. I am simply glad he did not get the hump with me, but at that time how was I supposed to know he had given up the demon booze? I am so pleased that he seems to have got on top of his problems, and his life is back on track. He always loved the passion of the City fans, and he told me he remembered when he was playing for Huddersfield against City at Maine Road, and Huddersfield went on to beat City. Andy and the players were getting ready to leave, when a steward came and told them they would not be able to leave for a while because about three thousand City fans were rioting outside. Once again the City fans had been let down by the players and were demanding answers from Francis Lee, who was the chairman at the time.

The last time I met Andy was not too long ago, at the Prestwich and Whitefield branch twentieth-year celebrations. I had a great chat with him, and he even gave me his phone number, but Cath deleted it because she knows what I'm like when I am pissed. I sometimes think it's a good idea to give people a ring at two in the morning.

I believe that it was because of Andy's upbringing, and because he started his career in the lower leagues, that he had a great rapport with the fans no matter what club he played for. He is not like some of the snotty fuckers I have come across who won't give fans the time of day. He is in the same mould as Kit Symons, Uwe Rossler, and Chris Greenacre, to name a few who are brilliant with the fans. One thing that really pissed off Andy at the time, but he can laugh about it now, is that when he finished playing for City, the then Manager Kevin Keegan allowed Andy to go on to the pitch against Crystal Palace so he could say goodbye to the fans and also give them a chance to show their appreciation and to wish him all the best for the future. He decided to take two of his kids, Arron and Brooke, on to the pitch. He felt so proud as he made his way onto the pitch with all the fans singing his name and giving him a standing ovation. He told me he was genuinely moved by the affection shown by the fans, and the hairs on the back of his neck stood up, such was the emotion of the event. The City TV camera team were given the brief of filming Morrison, and he would receive the DVD later, so he was really chuffed. As he was walking onto the pitch, the Crystal Palace players were out on the pitch warming up, so it added to the occasion for his special moment. When he sat down with his family to watch the DVD, he told me he could not understand at first why it was mainly focused on the Crystal Palace players who were on the pitch, and not him. Then it slowly dawned on him there was a

Crystal Palace player called Clinton Morrison, and the dozy fuckers doing the DVD had spent the five minutes filming Clinton Morrison from Crystal Palace and not the person in the middle of the pitch getting all the applause, our very own Andy Morrison from City. He was gutted when he first saw it, but he soon shrugged it off as one of those things. Joking aside, how could anyone working for City cock that up? Oh, well. It is not the first time someone at City has cocked something up, and it certainly won't be the last.

Andy is now a Manchester City Football Club ambassador. Once Andy was asked what that involved, and he said, 'Anything the club wants me to do, I will do it.' That is Andy all over: whatever he does, he does it 100 per cent. He loves the club and the fans, and they love him. More important, they will never forget his determination and leadership that he brought to the club.

Chris Greenacre was our branch president for many years. He was a young lad when we first met him, but he was a great credit to himself, his club, and his family. Originally from Leeds, he was a big Leeds United fan. He came to City as a youth player, and he came from a very close family. We met his mum and dad often. Unfortunately, his dad, also called Chris, has now passed away. It was a great shock and a big loss for the family.

Chris came to my house a few times for tea or a brew, and he brought his granny round one day while he was dropping off a couple signed balls for raffle prizes. He also came to many meetings and was our guest at a couple of sportsmen's dinners we organised. Through him I met many players and was also invited to the reserve team's end-of-season party. Well, it was not so much a party as a piss-up and pub crawl in town, but I really enjoyed it. I knew lots of the reserve players because many had been to the branch meetings, plus I had bumped into a few of them at the training ground. Most of them were down-to-earth lads who were hoping to break into the first team. Most of them were sensible about how they behaved and how much they were drinking. I thought that would soon change if they played regularly in the first team.

Over the years we knew Chris, it was great to see how he developed into such a nice bloke, and how much he grew in confidence. His mum and dad told us Chris has told them he was so proud to be our branch president at such a young age. His parents thought it helped with his confidence because he was a bit of a shy lad when he was younger.

Chris used to share digs with some other juniors, including the first team's goalkeeper, Nicky

Weaver. I first met Nicky the first day he joined the club. We were down at the training ground getting something to eat, and we called him over and had a brew with him. Well, he had a brew. Aide and I had a pint. I got to know Nicky quite well, and he was another smashing young lad who came to a few meetings and always had plenty of time for the fans. I remember after one game at home, I was walking up Claremont Road near the ground when a car horn beeped behind me, then a Mercedes pulled up next to me. Fuck me, it was Nicky, and he asked if I wanted a lift. I was meeting up with some other lads and so declined, but it was a bit of a rough area, so I advised Nick not to hang about. Still, what a great gesture. I thought later on I should have got in and met the others – their faces would have been a fucking picture as I got out of Nicky's Mercedes! Nick was another nice lad who loved the club and the fans. He did really well at City, but he never reached his full potential. He was certainly an England goal-keeper in the making but like other players before him, he probably enjoyed the bright lights and the late nights a little too much. Who am I to blame him? He made a great living out of the game, and he went on to play for a few more clubs after leaving City.

Nicky is now at Sheffield Wednesday as a goalkeeping coach. It is fitting he is back there because he has been a Sheffield Wednesday fan all his life, and he had a couple of spells at Wednesday in his playing career. You will find it hard to meet a nicer lad.

Chris had a bit of bad luck at City. He got injured just before the pre-season when he was being tipped to break into the first team. He only played a handful of first team games for City, although he was leading goal scorer in the reserves. He was at the club for many years but realised it was not meant to be at City. He reluctantly left because he was desperate for first team football.

After leaving City, he joined Mansfield Town, where he scored just under sixty goals in three seasons. When Mansfield played at Macclesfield, Aide, Sean, and I went to watch him play. He got us passes to go in the players' lounge, so we could meet up after the game. Chris also signed for Stoke before joining Tranmere Rovers, where he started banging the goals in again. I was really chuffed when he invited me and my family to his wedding. It was a fantastic summer's day, and it was nice to meet his wife, Lyndsey, and his parents again. I have not been in touch with Chris for a while, so that is another New Year resolution I will sort out, but we still send and receive Christmas cards with his mum.

Chris and his wife now live in New Zealand, where he is the manager of Wellington Phoenix football team. It is great that two nice lads like Nicky and Chris have made good careers for themselves.

Frank Sidebottom was an original cult hero and was the alter ego of the late singer and comedian Chris Sievey. Frank appeared on many radio and TV shows, and he had his own slot on Radio Piccadilly. He produced many songs, and loads were about City. One classic was about Franny Lee: *'The Bog Roll Man'*. It was not hard to spot Frank because he had a big papier mâché head and a dapper suit, unless it was a City event, and then it was always a pair of shorts and the old black and red striped City shirt. The first meeting he came to was when Ireland Manager Mick McCarthy was also a guest. I am not sure what Mick thought, because as you can imagine, chatting to a bloke sat next to you in a pair of shorts and a papier mâché head takes a bit get of getting used to.

So it does not get too confusing, I will refer to Frank when he has got his head on, and I'll refer to Chris when he has not. Are you still with me? Good, I knew it was not too confusing. At the meetings, we used to get all the guests complimentary drinks, and fuck me, could Chris drink. I did a double take at the amount he was putting away – and that was before he even got on stage. I thought at this rate he wasn't going to make the fucking stage, so Derbo had to tell him to slow it down. Over the years I have been in the company of some big drinkers, but Chris bless him was up there with the best of them. Chris used to be with a band called the Freshies, and in the 1970s and 1980s they did some tours around the country.

Chris had a whole persona for Frank. He had him living in Timperley, and he did a stint as a roving reporter for *Granada Reports*. Frank came to many of our gentleman's mornings, and the punters loved him. I could not see what the great attraction of seeing a grown man wandering about the stage wearing a papier Mache head and wearing a pair of shorts, but what the fuck do I know? After a while, Frank got a makeover and got his head upgraded to a fibreglass one. Only a City-mad fan like Chris could come up with a creation like Frank. At the gents morning he wandered about on the dance floor, dancing with the lads with City songs in the background. It was a mad sight, but Frank was clearly adored by the fans. Besides the gent's mornings, Frank came to many of our other events. I always piss myself laughing when I look back at the time he came up to Stalybridge, where our branch was playing the Stalybridge lads at a charity football game. Frank was pissed up in the middle of the road, directing traffic. The car drivers and pedestrians must have wondered what the fuck was going on. After one gents morning in Blackly, Botty and I dropped Chris off at Heaton Park Metro Station so he could get the tram home. What a sight! Frank staggering towards his tram with his big daft head on. What the passengers thought was anyone's guess.

Chris was the original Moonchester, Manchester City's mascot. I could hazard a guess at why he did not last too long in that role. When Chris sadly passed away in 2010, money was raised amongst the fans for his funeral because Chris was skint when he passed away. Fans chipped in so he could have a decent send-off. There are now a couple of documentaries doing the rounds:' *Being Frank* and *The Chris Sievey Story*'. There is also a statue of Frank, which was funded by the public in his home town of Timperley. It is a fitting tribute to both Chris and Frank.

John Wardle and David Makin have both had a very long association with City. They are two people who the fans in general, and Manchester City Football Club in particular, have got an awful lot to thank them for. Both are from ordinary working-class backgrounds, and they built up their brand, JD Sports, from one shop in Bury. The pair have been lifelong City fans.

Nowadays, the club is awash with money thanks to the backing of the Abu Dhabi Ruling Family and their massive investment. Many fans are still pinching themselves now that it was Manchester City which Sheik Mansour and the ADUG group decided to invest in, and not any other club in England. The players and facilities we now have are second to none, much money has been invested in the youth academy, and the training facilities are amongst the best in the world. It is a far cry from not too many years ago, when money was not invested in either players or the facilities, and on a couple of occasions it was rumoured the club was on the brink because the finances were not in a good state. On more than one occasion, John and David are rumoured to have bailed out the club. Now is the first time in decades that the club is being run on sound financial footing, and the professionalism of everyone at the club is a very refreshing change to what has gone on in the past. We have had many false dawns at the club, but at long last the Club is now on the right track, and all the fans have something positive to look forward to.

During the Peter Swailes and Franny Lee eras, it was a case of what shit we were going to wake up to the next day. The club was in turmoil for what seemed a never-ending period and staggered from one crisis to another. The only saving grace was the fans. Two fans who will forever be revered are John and David

When the club was going through another bad spell under Franny Lee, David went on the GMR phone-in, and live on radio he laid into the leadership styles of Franny Lee. What made the attack more extraordinary was that by that time, David and John were big shareholders in the club. It was a moment that stunned the City fans because never before had a major shareholder spoke out in such a passionate way about the way the club was run. After that moment, the writing was on the wall for Franny, and it was only a matter of time before he left.

David also came unannounced to one of our meetings, and GMR Presenter Jimmy Wagg, who was also at the meeting, interviewed him on stage about how deep the problems were at the club. David laid the route of the problems at Franny Lee's door. That was another extraordinary moment in the history of our branch, and it gave us a first-hand insight into exactly how bad a state City were actually in. We thought the club was badly run, but when a senior shareholder went public about it, we were certainly given food for thought.

Stuff like that could only happen at City. The first time I met John Wardle was at Maine Road, where a presentation was taking place about the proposed move to the new stadium at Eastland's. John was then a director of the club, and I think he wanted to keep an eye on things, considering that he and David were now investors. He came over and had a chat, and he asked me what I thought about the proposals. Over the years, I met him many times, and he still has genuine enthusiasm for the club and, just as important, the fans. Even though he was a major shareholder and director, he liked a low profile and still sat in his seat with David, amongst the ordinary fans.

John came to many of our meetings and was always well received. After one game against the rags at Old Trafford, I was walking away from the ground when I spotted John, who was with his grandson. It is not often you see a director of a football club mingling with the fans after an away game, especially an away game against your local bitter rivals. It is rumoured that on a couple of occasions, he had to pay the staff and players out of his own money, such was the shit they were going through in those days.

John reluctantly became chairman when David Bernstein stood down. It was a position John never craved for, but he embraced the job well and won the respect of City fans for guiding City through yet another difficult time. John never lost his appreciation for the fans; he realised how much the club and the fans meant to each other, and after a period of time, he stood down for Thaksin Shinawatra to take over. They realised it was a massive investment that was needed, so that City could become serious challengers in the Premier League. There were reports that between John and David Makin, they'd lost about ten million pounds. How much is truth, rumour, or myth, I don't think people will ever find out. The same goes for a lot of stuff that went on at City for the last few decades.

One thing is certain: all Manchester City fans owe a huge debt of gratitude to David and John. Without them, and without their investment and their willingness to bail out City, we will never know how things might have turned out, but I am sure they made things a lot smoother. Unfortunately Thaksin Shinawatra was not the knight in shining armour many fans hoped he would be and it was not long before he to left the club and the rest as they say is history.

Some of the people mentioned will be heroes to some fans and villains to others. I would love it to be true that every footballer who played for City was a hero to the fans, but unfortunately that is not the case. Alan Kernaghan used to get booed as soon as his name was announced over the tannoy. Mike Summerbee's son, Nicky, got some dreadful stick, and so did Richard Edghill, even when he was club captain. Nowadays, big-money signings can get a dreadful time from the fans. At the moment, Aleksandar Kolarov and Eliaquim Mangala are getting a rough time. Even fan favourites like Kun Aguero and David Silva are not immune from getting stick from some fans at times.

There are some things in football that will never change. Football players can be fan favourites one minute and villains the next. Football fans can be a fickle lot at the best of times, but they pay their money and are entitled to their opinions. In this day and age, fan forums are one way they express it. Two of City's most popular forums are Bluemoon and Bluewatch, and they have helped out the branch with fundraisers and charity events. They're also a great way of finding out what is going on and of expressing your views.

Chapter 17

Drinking Culture

By now you will have probably figured out there is a massive drinking culture in both the Royal Navy and in the world of football. The history of drinking in the Royal Navy goes back centuries. Apparently sailors were first given half a gallon of beer daily, and then it was increased to a gallon. This tradition was probably given because the water was rank and due to the harsh conditions the sailors endured. Also, many of the sailors were press ganged, which in layman's terms means they were kidnapped and forced to join up, so keeping them half pissed probably seemed a good idea.

The legal term for press gang was impressment, and believe it or not, it was perfectly legal. At one time, the navy had tens of thousands of sailors who were impressment men. Many were taken from merchant ships, and many were prisoners who were given a choice of joining up or staying in prison. When counties had to send men to the navy as part of a quotation system, they would send petty criminals. Many men were also taken from taverns in seafaring ports.

The Royal Navy also used impressment in British North America, and this often led to resistance and rioting. In fact people resisted in the village of Eastern, near my old stomping ground of Portland, near Weymouth. Four people were shot and killed by the press gang, and one of them was a lady who had joined in the protest. The practice carried on till around 1835, when legislation was passed to stop it. It is hardly surprising there was a big drinking culture in those days.

Beer was originally the drink of choice in the navy, but the farther out they sailed, the more different drinks they would take on board. Spirits were easier to preserve, so drinks like brandy, arrack, and other concoctions from around the world became popular. Then in the mid-1660s, when Jamaica was captured by the British, rum became more available and popular. It was officially issued from 1730, and half a pint was deemed to equal a gallon of beer, so beer was phased out and rum became the drink of choice for the Royal Navy.

A heavy part of a ship's rigging back in the day was called the main brace, and sailors were normally given a double tot if they had to repair it. The term 'splice the main brace' was an order given aboard naval vessels, and it became the common term for any issue of extra drink. Double rations were often issued before they went into battle; again, the thinking must have been if they were pissed, they would not give a shit about what they were doing.

In 1880 the Navy Grog Committee unsurprisingly found the rum ration was linked to discipline problems, and they decreased the ration to one-eighth of a pint till it was finally abolished in 1970. You can get a bit of an idea of how the culture began, and with the amount of drink consumed, it seems back in the days the sailors were semi-permanently pissed. It is a surprise that they managed to do any work at all, never mind set sail and fight battles.

In 2009 a report commissioned by the defence chiefs showed that alcohol abuse is a much bigger problem amongst navy personnel than it is amongst the people on Civvy Street. No shit, Sherlock. I could have told them that and saved them the survey money. One in five who took part in the survey admitted to drinking fifty units of alcohol a week, which is roughly twenty-five pints I should imagine most would be drinking that in a weekend. The researchers concluded that many sailors were drinking to hazardous levels, and it had a direct impact on their health. The results conclude alcohol misuse is common within the navy.

When I left the navy in 1977, the problem was just as bad if not worse. In all that time, sweet fuck all has been done to address the issue. We never had any alcohol education, and if we were ever on a charge for drinking-related offences, nothing was done to change our habits. There were no alcohol awareness programs. I think there are many reasons why the problem was so relevant when I was in. With me, it was having money, having not care in the world, dealing with boredom in navy barracks, being one of the lads, and also releasing stress and pressure from work. Plus, I was simply young and daft.

Whenever I was at sea on either HMS *Achilles* or HMS *Devonshire,* I very rarely drank because I was so immersed in the navy life and the routine on the ship. Once on shore with the rest of the lads, we went bang at it, and we always had to try the local beers and spirits. Drinking to excess was just part of life in the navy, and getting drunk when going ashore seemed the natural thing to do.

In 2013 a coroner wrote to the Ministry of Defence about the culture of excess drinking in the navy after a lieutenant commander was shot dead on a nuclear submarine while docked in

Southampton in 2011. The able seaman who killed him was said to be extremely intoxicated the night before his shift, and he was in charge of a rifle when he shot the officer and injured two others. The hearing had heard, in the forty-eight hours leading up to the shooting, the able seaman had drank twenty pints of cider and lager, plus double vodkas and cocktails before he was put on guard duty with the SA80 rifle. Witnesses said binge drinking was endemic amongst the crew, and many would get drunk out of their minds. Bearing in mind these people are on a nuclear submarine, it seems crackers that the drinking culture has never been properly addressed. Does the problem have to get any worse before something is done? Since that dreadful incident, the navy is supposed to be taking steps to tackle binge drinking and replace the culture with moderate alcohol consumption. *'Good luck with that then'.*

Once leaving the navy, the ex-sailors can find it very hard to adapt to life on Civvy Street, I know I did, and there was no help or advice or guidance to assist in the readjustment, leading many to drink to excess, become homeless, turn to drugs, and have mental health problems.

I don't know whether I would have been classed as a problem drinker. I can go for days, weeks, or months without a drink, and that was the same when I was in the navy. I could get pissed as a rat for three days solid and then not touch a drop for a month, especially if we were at sea.

The similarities between the navy and football is frighteningly similar. One of the things about following your favourite team is the social aspect of it. It's not like leaving your house, going straight to the ground, and coming straight back, although a minority do that. The fun is meeting up with your mates in the pub to discuss how things are going, and if there is a game on the telly beforehand, that can also be a talking point. Inside the ground, there are plenty of bars, so if your thirst has not been quenched or if you get your second wind, you can have another drink or two before the game starts. The law as it stands does not allow you to take alcoholic drinks to your seat, so instead of having a nice, relaxing drink, people tend to neck it a lot faster than they would normally do. Most experts say that is exactly what you should not do.

At half-time, you only have about fifteen minutes to queue up and buy your drink, and if you don't want to miss any of the match, you have to drink it fast. After the game, it's back to the pub to discuss the game and what went wrong or right. Going to away matches is usually a full day of non-stop drinking. Whenever we went away by coach or minibus, we used to get a carry-out. We always tried to get to a pub near the ground by the time the pubs opened. For example, if we were playing Southampton away, we would set off at about six in the morning and have a few cans of beer on the way. Then we would get to a pub around opening time. If people are lucky or rich enough to go in the hospitality lounges or private boxes, then its non-stop drinking from the time you arrive at the ground till the time you leave. Again, as the law stands, you can't have a drink while within the sight line of the game. In other words, if you can see the game in play, you are not allowed to drink alcohol. Yeah, I'm sure that is rigorously enforced.

The rise of hooliganism in the 1970s and 1980s was at the time credited to fans drinking to excess, but as research over the years has discovered, there was much more to hooliganism than alcohol-induced violence. After saying that, alcohol plays a massive part in violent crimes, whether it is at football grounds, at the pub, on the street, or even in the house. It goes without saying that people do things under the influence of drink that they would not normally do when sober. Drink is so far entrenched in the culture of football that many drinks companies have sponsored various football clubs and cups, and they have a long relationship with football clubs both in England and abroad.

Football and alcohol are billion-pound industries and are interlinked to each other.

If football fans have a problem with alcohol, the same can be said of football players. Going back through the decades, players have either had their careers cut short, have been jailed for alcohol-related offences, or have been banned from training or sent home in disgrace. Many high-profile footballers have hit rock bottom because of their drinking habits. One young City player who was tipped for great things was recently 'retired' from the game when he was in his early twenties because of his problems with the drink. Even I am surprised at times when you read about former footballers who are in the paper as a result of drinking problem. Many times I thought, *'Fucking hell, I didn't expect that of him'*. It goes to show drink has no favourites, and no one is immune from the problems that alcohol abuse can cause. Thankfully for the players, there are now organisations that are set up to help, and the Professional Football Association is involved in helping current and former players. Many clubs are now involved in alcohol prevention courses with their youth academy players, which can only be a good thing.

Many players who have come to our meetings over the years have told us about their drunken exploits, and many ex-players have written books detailing their problems. Some of the stories are funny as fuck, some I can relate to, and some are just sad. Over the years, I have had a drink with many of the players and ex-players, and some of the stuff I've been told and seen, and what they come out with at the meetings, you cannot make up.

One problem which is the same as in the navy is when players finish playing at, say, thirty-five years of age. They are at a loss what to do with themselves, especially the players from the 1970s and 1980s, because they were not on the fortunes the players are on now. While they were playing, the clubs sorted everything out for them, like in the navy. When they leave it's like 'Oh, shit. What do I do now?' Some players like Franny Lee planed well ahead, but unfortunately a lot did not and hit rock bottom. Nowadays many of the football stars come from abroad and don't have the same attitude about alcohol as the British players, so there appears to be less of a problem with the top players compared to years ago.

The standard of football in the Premier League is of such a high standard that players have to keep their fitness levels up. If they don't give 100 per cent, they will soon find themselves out of the squad. Football clubs also look carefully at the lifestyle of the players before they buy; if they are paying top money for a new player, they don't want someone who is going to give them problems. Most players from Europe and beyond have never seen the need to drink to excess or go on drinking sessions, and I believe they are having a positive influence on the drinking practices of the players, especially the top players in the Premier League. I remember Kit telling me that after we played Sheffield United away, when they were on the way back to Manchester, Alan Ball got the driver to stop the coach at a pub where there were a load of City having a drink. Alan got all the players to go in and have a drink with them. He put it down to having a bonding session with the fans. Can you imagine that happening nowadays? Not a chance.

Chapter 18

More Away Day Blues

We were busy organizing an away trip after beating Nott's County and Villa in the FA Cup. We drew Newcastle away. Ever the optimists even though it was an early kick off, we quickly had enough people to fill a coach as we were convinced we would win. My old mate George from the navy lived up in that neck of the woods, so he was going to sort a pub out that we could get in early. Everything was going smoothly till I received a phone call from Newcastle police: a new policy had been implemented where coach companies had to give the organiser's name and phone number to the police. The policeman was friendly enough and wanted to know what my plans where. Well, I was a little economical with the truth on that one, but he made it clear we had to be at the rendezvous for the police escort on time – no beer on the coach, and no one pissed;

otherwise, we would be going back to Manchester. I said no problem but was not confident I would be able to respond positively to any of his requests, never mind all three of them.

We got to the pub to meet George, and most of the lads were already half pissed by then, because they'd had a good drink on the coach. George had not at that time turned up because we arrived a bit early, so we banged on the door. The landlord seemed a bit surprised to see us but let us in anyway. 'A bit surprised' might been a bit of an understatement – he had on only a pair of boxer shorts and a string vest, but his eyes lit up when he saw how many of us there were, so he quickly got his act together, and he got the cleaner and his missus to help serve us. By now I was wondering where George was and was a bit puzzled why the landlord seemed surprised at our arrival. It was only when George came into the place that we found out we were in the wrong pub. Where we should have been was the pub across the road, and the landlord and staff were waiting for us. Oops! Oh, well; anyone can make a mistake. We did not want to disappoint anyone, so we managed to have a couple of drinks in both pubs. We were very thoughtful like that. When it was time to leave for the game, we bid our farewells and said we would be back after the game, and we would make sure we got in the right pub.

As it happened, we got to the rendezvous on time with no hassle. We had no beer on the coach but failed miserably on the last request. We were the last coach to arrive for the escort, but someone had to be last, so it might as well have been us. As part of the escort, a policeman sat on the coach with us, but he was friendly enough; it is great having a police escort to and from the game because the police motorbike outriders stop the traffic at junctions and traffic lights, and we sail through. They just want to get us in and out of the ground as quickly as possible with the minimum of fuss, and that was certainly ok with us.

The game didn't start well for us. Our mate Andy 'Dibbs' dropped a couple of bollocks, and we were soon getting beat, things did not get any better and we lost the game 3-1. We had arranged to go back to the pub (the right one this time), where there was a spread laid on for us, and we hoped the police escort didn't stay too long with us, otherwise we would have to double back and it would take us longer to get back to the pub. We need not have worried. As soon as the coaches had cleared the city centre, the police left us, so it was back to the pub to drown our sorrows. The landlord John was an ex-marine and a great mate of George's. We had a good time and were all well bladdered. We wanted to give John some money for the food because it was a brilliant spread and must have cost him a few bob, but he wouldn't take anything. What a top bloke. There were many lads in the pub who supported Newcastle and Sunderland, as well as a couple of Middlesbrough fans, but everyone got on great apart from two Newcastle fans who went outside and had a fight with each other over a daft disagreement. Well, 'fight' was not a proper description because they were both pissed and rolled about on the floor. When it was over, they shook hands and went back into the pub for a pint. George told me they were best mates and that was a bit of a regular occurrence.

When it was time to go, we said our goodbyes, thanked everyone for their hospitality, and then set off back to Manchester. George lived a mile or so from the pub, so on the way we dropped off George. He got off the coach near his house, and as we drove away, he gave us a wave. Then he slipped and fell down the fucking hill, he got a few cuts and bruises, and was covered in shit. What a day! We hoped it would not be too long till we returned to the pub because even though we'd lost the game, we had a terrific time, and everyone had made us most welcome.

As is so happened, it was only a few months later that we went back to Newcastle, but the outcome was a bit different in a couple of ways. Not so many were going this time, so we arranged two sixteen-seater minibuses, and I took my eldest lad Steven with us. Because we did not book a coach, we did not bother telling the police about the trip. This time we met George at the right pub, and the landlord had made a load of sausage butties, which was a nice gesture from him. When we set off to the game, we gave one of the Newcastle fans in the pub a lift to the ground. The match did not go well for us, and it came as no surprise that we got beat again, but we were used to getting beat and were not too down about it because we had the pub after the game to look forward to, where we could drown our sorrows yet again.

After a few drinks and a bit of banter with the locals, we said our goodbyes and went to get on the minibuses. It turned out there was just one minibus. Some scroat had nicked one of them from the car park, *'unbelievable'*. The two drivers had gone for a walk and something to eat so some sneaky bastard seized their opportunity. The landlord was furious and promised revenge. That was fine for later, but how the fuck did we all get back to Manchester? It was decided that the driver would do two trips. There were plenty of volunteers to stay in the pub – surprise, surprise. Steven and I were on the first bus with half the other lads. After he dropped us off, we thanked him and wished the driver good luck. At least nothing else could go wrong – could it?

After the second lot got picked up and set off for home, they stopped for a piss stop at the side of the road near Scotch Corner. The driver asked if everyone was back on the bus, and Barry shouted, 'Yep, were all on.' The driver duly set off – leaving Barry's brother behind. What a dozy bastard! You can't make it up. Barry didn't realise till they got off the coach back in Prestwich that his own brother was missing. I would have loved to be a fly on the wall in their house when he eventually got back.

As highlighted in the Newcastle trip, things often didn't go according to plan. We were going to Aston Villa for the last game of the season one year, and I had booked a coach no problem. When going to away games, we usually stop about half an hour before the ground and would book in a pub, because the West Midlands police are not the most football friendly lot. We didn't let them know we were coming, but it didn't take them long to find out. After about an hour of being in the pub, the police turned up and told us to get on the coach. Obviously there was a bit of a discussion between us and them. The bottom line was if we didn't get on the coach, we were all going to get arrested and charged; I didn't ask what they would charge us with because they would have made one up. This stuff still goes on now, and the Football Supporters Federation offers great advice and support to fans caught up in these situations. They have even helped fans take legal action against the police. There was no point arguing because we were on a loser to nothing. The landlord was gutted because apart from us, the place was nearly empty, and he saw a nice little earner going out of his pub door.

We got back on the coach and had a police escort. After about fifteen minutes, the penny dropped. The bastards weren't taking us to the ground – they put us on the motorway back to Manchester! Fortunately the police soon left us, so we came off at the next junction and made our way back to the ground. I bet the coppers pissed themselves laughing. After that bit of nonsense from the police, we got to the ground without any further hassle. Believe it or not, we won the game, so were chuffed to bits. After the game we were not going to hang around the West Midlands in case there was any more funny business from the police; we got a lot closer to home before we stopped for something to eat and drink. It is hard to believe that some police forces still behave as they do, but the West Midlands police have always had a bad reputation amongst football fans

DON PRICE

There is a big Blue pub in Whitefield called the Bee Hive, and we often met there before we set off to a game. On one occasion it was a night game at Leeds. Although I had booked the coach a couple of weeks previous, I had confirmed it all in the morning of the game as I always did, to make sure there were no mix-ups. I was reassured there were no problems. However, warning bells started to kick in when the coach did not turn up on time. As time dragged on towards kick off, it became obvious that the coach wasn't coming, and there was no answer from the firm's contact number. Oh, shit. This was not good. Some of the lads had cars and weren't too pissed, so they drove. I managed to phone a firm I knew, and they sent two sixteen-seater minibuses for the rest of us, so all was not lost, we would miss kick off, but at least we would get there. I was getting wound up and thought I would get some vodka and orange to take with me. Zoe, my young niece, was coming with us as well, and they wouldn't search her going into the ground. '*Happy days*', the joys of being a football fan. When I contacted the coach company the next morning they were very apologetic and came up with some lame excuse but as we had used them quite often in the past with no problems we gave them the benefit of the doubt, plus they gave us a discount of our next trip.

Norwich was always a great place to visit even though it was a pain in the arse to get to from Manchester. I had first been to the ground when I was in the Royal Navy, and I'd been a few times since. I have always liked their style of football, and unlike other grounds, you knew there was not going to be any hassle or mither from the Norwich fans and more important, none from the police either. We used to take a big following, there was always a great atmosphere, and usually we got a decent result. Most times I went there, I stayed overnight because it was a right trek. A big pub where all City fans met was called the Complete Angler, which was not too far from the ground to walk.

When I was working at Prestwich Hospital, I had the weekend off when we were playing Norwich away one season, so I thought I would go. None of the lads fancied it except Derbo. Because it cost a lot of money on the train, and it was too long a trip to be stuck on a coach, I thought '*bollocks to it I'll drive*'. The slight problem I had was that I had an old Lada, and although it wasn't guaranteed to get us there and back, it would keep us warm if we broke down because the heaters in Lada's were shit hot.

Also working in the hospital at the time was the father of two City players, Jason and Darren Beckford. I decided to overcome my shyness, and went over to the laundry to where he worked, and asked if he could get me a couple of tickets from his sons. I thought it was a long shot, but if you don't ask, you don't get, true to form though I did not any tickets.

On the morning of the game, we set off at about 5:30am. Just in case the car broke down and I had to get the AA out, I was in the relay scheme so if the worst came to worst and we broke down, we would still get to the ground in time to watch the game. I need not have worried because the engine was purring like a cat, and we got down to the hotel where we were staying without a problem. After checking in, we went to the pub, and it quickly filled up with City fans. I soon recognized fans whom I had met over the years on my travels or from Maine Road.

The atmosphere was always great at Norwich, and this day was no exception. As the game finished a draw, both sets of fans went home happy. After having a good drink in the pubs round Norwich, we got our heads down at the hotel. In the morning we had a bit of breakfast before setting off back to Manchester.

We had been driving about thirty minutes when I saw a couple of police cars in my mirrors. They were behind me for a bit, and then one overtook me with lights flashing and siren blaring. I said to

Derbo, 'They are going to stop some fucker in a minute.' I didn't realise straight away, but I was the fucker they were going to stop.

We must have looked a strange sight: my Lada with two City scarves hanging out of the windows, sandwiched between two police cars. They said they had stopped me because someone had reported me for drink driving. I thought, *'Thank fuck for that'*. I might have committed a few offences over the years, but drink driving was never one of them. Whether they were bored because it was a Sunday and they had sod all else to do, I am not sure, but I don't think for one minute they thought I was over the limit. They didn't seem that surprised when my breathalyser test was negative. Shit happens, no harm was done and we were soon on our way. Next stop Manchester. Norwich is still one of my favourite grounds.

If I could help it, I would not drive to away games unless I was staying overnight, like I did at Norwich. At most away games, there were usually a few people going from the branch, so most of the time we got minibuses or a coach. If the train companies were doing special offers, we would also let the train take the strain, so to speak. The good thing about the trains was they had toilets, so we did not have to worry about piss stops like we had to with minibuses.

Don Price

Kev gave me a ring a couple of days before we played Spurs away. He said he had some tickets, and Julie, his missus, was going to drive. He wanted to know if I fancied it. Do bears shit in the woods? I had the weekend off from work, so with an offer of a match ticket and a lift to the match, it was a no-brainer. On the day of the match, Julie and Kev picked up me and Derbo. It was straight to the off license, and then London here we come.

After about the third piss stop, it probably occurred to Julie that offering to drive us was not such a great idea after all. London is not an easy place to drive through, so we parked up and got the tube into London. We met up with City fans we knew and had a good drink and a laugh before the game. Julie was glad when we got into the ground because we were getting a bit noisy on the way to the stadium. The game ended in a draw, so we left the ground in a good mood.

After the game, we went for a drink near the ground and had a good chat with the Spurs fans. Fifteen minutes later, the atmosphere in the pub changed for the worse. A dozen Spurs fans came in and started looking round the pub. It quickly became obvious they were looking for City fans with whom to cause trouble. It was a bit pathetic because they were all grown men, with most having beer guts. It was as though they were left in a time warp. If they wanted a proper fight, they could have gone to the pubs near Euston Station, where there would have been many more City fans to fight, but they would have been outnumbered, so they thought they would be dead hard and try to pick off some stragglers. Fortunately for us, they never spotted we were City fans, otherwise I am sure they would have caused problems with us. It was a bit of a relief when they left. A Spurs fan I was talking to said he had seen them before; they just want to cause trouble with away fans. Every club has their dickheads, but the rest of the Spurs fans were great. After a couple more drinks, we made our way to the tube station so we could get back to the car. It was probably while we were on the tube that Julie decided the next time we had tickets for a game in London, we would get the train. We were a bit boisterous, to say the least. She was certainly glad when we were safely in the car and back on the road to Manchester, and she was very happy when we fell asleep so she could have a bit of peace and quiet.

Chapter 19

'Celebrities'

Manchester City have always had celebrity fans, with many jumping on the bandwagon when we started being successful. One famous City fan who has been going even when we were in the lower divisions is former Oasis star Noel Gallagher. I met him at a couple of away matches, and what struck me about him was that he was just one of the lads. He had no airs or graces about him, and he wasn't trying to be someone he was not. He was sat in front of me at Arsenal's ground, and I got his autograph. He told me he loved living in London because it was dead easy for him to get to the games. I knew the feeling from my navy days. He said he would rather sit with the lads than go in the private suites, and the fans were great with him as well. They were not all over him like a rash, mithering him. They were nice and friendly, and he in turn was chilled out and relaxed. It wasn't long till I met him again. This time it was at Leicester away, and again he was sat in front of me. My niece Zoe was with us, so I asked for his autograph again, this time it was for Zoe. He spotted the midget gems Zoe was eating, so she gave him some. His mates wanted some as well, so I gave him the packet to dish out between them. I still get stick to this day from Zoe for giving away her midget gems, but she lived off the story at school for a very long time.

Another long-term Blue with no airs or graces is the former boxer Ricky Hatton. I first met him when he was a guest speaker at a sportsmen's dinner, and he was down to earth and funny as fuck. In the early part of his boxing career, when he had a fight coming up, he used to keep an allocation of tickets at his house. We had previously been in touch with Ricky's dad about some tickets, and also about trying to get him to a branch meeting. When Ricky was fighting in the Manchester Arena, I wanted six tickets. Sean and I went round to pay and collect them at his house. Debbie Derbyshire, who is the alter ego of City's female mascot Moonbeam, came with us because she wanted a few tickets as well. It seemed unreal. I had never met him before, and here I was in his house, talking like best mates and getting my tickets and autographs. His brother was in the house, and he seemed a nice lad as well.

After a fight, he used to have drinks with his mates in the local boozer, and they would wear daft shirts or jumpers for a laugh. Ricky did a lot of work for local charities, and though we never managed to get him to a meeting, we arranged for him to meet the lad who had the serious accident in Germany at the Etihad Stadium, which was great of him. It was a gesture that everyone involved appreciated.

Micky Gomez is another local boxer who is also a City fan. He is a smashing lad, and when he came to our meeting, he brought his title belts with him. He had a big cult following during his boxing career, and his followers used to wear big Mexican hats. It looked a barmy sight, but they made a great noise to make the atmosphere quite electric.

Kevin Kennedy and Bruce Jones, who played Curley Watts and Les Battersby, respectively, on the long-running soap *Coronation Street*, are also big City fans. They have attended our meetings and went down a storm with the members. Besides them coming to the meetings, I have met the pair of them at the ground on a few occasions. One thing I liked about the pair of them, same as many others, was they are down-to-earth fans who are not up their own arses, and they have time for the City fans. At times it must have been a pain for them because people would request autographs and photographs, but they had time for everyone. Even though the pair have not been on the show for a few years, they are still well received by the fans.

The award-winning film *Jimmy Grimble* was about a young Man City fan who was bullied at school. It was filmed in and around Manchester and Oldham and at City's old ground, Maine Road. Jimmy's life turned round for the better when an old lady gave him a pair of old football boots that were supposed to have belonged to an old ex City player, and they also had magical powers.

Ray Winston and Robert Carlisle starred in the film, and because they were staying in Manchester, I wasted no time in inviting them to a supporters meeting. I didn't know which team Robert supported, but I knew Ray was a passionate West Ham fan. Unfortunately, I never got a reply from my letters, but it had been a long shot and I was not really surprised. Dozens of letters I sent to players and staff at City also went unanswered, but it is always worth a try.

The movie was being filmed at Maine Road as well as other places around the Manchester area. While filming was taking place at the ground, City fans were asked to take part in crowd scenes and to turn up at Maine Road at nine o'clock in the morning. It was an opportunity I couldn't miss. When I arrived, it was organised chaos, but that was nothing new where City were concerned.

Outside caterers were busy making all the extra's bacon and eggs, sausages, barm's, and anything else we wanted for breakfast. There were unlimited brews of tea and coffee going. I was hoping to bump into the actors and use my charms to persuade them to come to a meeting, but they were nowhere to be seen. After a couple of hours of hanging about, no one had a clue what we would be doing and when we would be doing it. I decided to give my chance of film stardom a miss that day and headed home, but at least I had a belting breakfast and a few brews, plus it was an enjoyable morning chatting with the other City fans.

Not to be deterred and remembering how good the breakfast was, I decided I would go back to the ground the next day and try again to showcase my talents, but again it was not meant to be. After another glorious breakfast and a couple of brews, I thought, *Sod it. Ray and Robert have blown their chances of starring alongside me.* Again, no one had a clue when anyone would be doing what, so I shot off home, leaving my chance for five minutes of fame behind me.

I must admit I still have not seen the film, but by all accounts it was very good. Well, it *must* have been because it was about the boys in blue. I keep meaning to get a DVD of it, so I will make that my New Year resolution.

The original 'Rogue Trader' was Manchester City fanatic Nick Leeson. The press gave him that name because of his unauthorised trading, which caused the collapse of Barings Bank, England's oldest merchant bank. His bank's downfall was due to his trading on the futures markets, on the Singapore International Monitory Exchange.

It is mind-boggling how the chain of events happened, and it's even barmier that it was allowed to happen. Losses totalled round about £208 million. Nick finally knew his game was up and fled Singapore, leaving a note saying he was sorry. I bet he wasn't half as sorry as his bosses were when they realised what had happened. Eventually Nick was sentenced to six and a half years in Changi Prison, Singapore. I would dread going to prison in any country, and the thought of spending years in a foreign jail sends shivers down my spine. I think it must have something to do with watching all those banged up abroad programmes on TV.

After his release from prison, Nick was a guest for the fanzine *King of the Kippax*, who was hosting a fundraising event at the Platt Lane Complex. Some of our members were there and had a chat with him about attending one of our meetings. They got his phone number for me, and after a couple of phone calls, he agreed to attend one of our meetings.

DON PRICE

I arranged to meet Nick at Piccadilly train station in Manchester before a game, so we could arrange for him to attend a Prestwich and Whitefield event. We went for a pint in the city centre, and I found him chilled out and relaxed. He came across as a decent sort of bloke, but I doubt his former bosses would have thought the same. The pub was full of City fans, and they had to take a double take when he saw him sat there having a pint with us. We met up with him after the match and went to a few pubs near the ground with him, where he got a great reception by City fans. Then we went to the train station with him to see him off, and he was well up for coming to the meeting.

We arranged the meeting for a Tuesday night. Robert Taylor, a first team player plus a director from the club, and Mark Lillis, an ex-City player, attended. The meeting was packed out very early, and Botty, the doorman, had his work cut out that night. In fact, he had words with the director as he came to the front of the queue, wanting to be let in straight away. Needless to say, Botty was not impressed. Anyway, the meeting was brilliant and packed to the rafters. One of the lads had printed some mock cheques, and Nick signed them for souvenirs for everyone in the room. His arm must have been falling off by the end of the night, with all the signing that he did. Nick was a brilliant speaker, and everyone was in stitches from some of the stuff he was coming out with. Mark Lillis was also very funny and everyone was laughing their heads off. The night was a terrific success, all the guests had a belting night, and Nick enjoyed himself so much that he agreed to come again. He was in good spirits the next morning when I dropped him off at the train station, and it wasn't long before his next visit.

Nick was true to his word and returned for a race night we were hosting, and Gary Owen, an ex-City player and a radio pundit, also attended. Nick and Gary got on really well together, and it was another belting night. We had the race night on a Friday, and we all went to the game on the Saturday and, just to be sociable, met up after the game for a quick drink.

A few weeks later, we were playing at Swindon and staying overnight in a hotel. Nick met up with us at the hotel and had a quick drink with us before getting on the coach for the short trip to the ground. After the game, it was back to the hotel for – guess what? You're right again: more drinks. Later on in the evening, we hadn't seen Nick for a while when the landlady came up to me and said, 'Don, can you help me with Nick? We have a problem.'

As I followed her, I thought to myself, *Oh, shit. What now? Why can't anything just run smoothly for me?* Anyway, there was nothing much to worry about, and it was not serious. He had fallen asleep in the toilet. It happens to the best of us from time to time, doesn't it? Good job no one had taken a photograph; the *News of the World* would have paid good money for it because Nick was still big news at the time. Anyway, a couple of the lads helped me get him up and take him back to his room. I saw him in the morning, not surprisingly he had a bit of a sore head.

Another time, after the Blackburn match and after GMR had done the radio programme from my house, we met up with Nick and City's finance director, Alistair McIntosh, in Weatherspoon's in Manchester city centre. A few of the branch members turned up, and we had a great laugh and a drink. The press came in a couple of times, wanting photos with me, Cath, Nick, and Alistair inside and outside the pub. Cath said she realised now how Posh Spice felt after all the photo's they took.

A couple of weeks later, our branch was playing Droylsden branch in a friendly football match in Heaton Park. Nick agreed to play for us. He'd had a few drinks the night before, so he wasn't in the best shape, but his heart was in the right place. After a few drinks back at the social club, we all went up to the Bee Hive Pub in Whitefield. Nick and I were a bit worse for wear so Cath got us a cab and took us home. It was dead funny talking to Nick because he was convinced he was in London and was trying to give the cab driver instructions on how to get to his home address. Good job Cath was with us and took charge, or God knows where we would have ended up.

There are some steps leading up to my house, and it was a big effort to get Nick up them. It wasn't plain sailing for me either. There was no way we could get him up any more stairs to the spare bedroom, so we put him on the couch in the front room and threw a blanket on top of him. Then at one point it looked like he was frothing at the mouth, so we stuck him in the recovery position to be on the safe side. I thought, *if he can survive Changi Prison, he can survive a night at mine.* We had a laugh about it the next morning, and Cath dropped him off at the train station as I was in no fit state to drive.

Nick can demand a large fee for the after-dinner circuit if he chooses. It was pleasing he didn't ask for a penny from us, so when he ran in the London Marathon, our branch made a donation of five hundred pounds for the charity he was running for.

After that, I met up with him a couple of times in London, when we played Crystal Palace and Spurs, as well as once or twice at Maine Road. I last heard he got married again and now lives in Ireland. It was an enjoyable experience to meet Nick, and I wish him all the best for the future. He seems to have turned his life around and got back on the right track. He has written a couple of books, and a film was made about him staring Ewan McGregor.

El Rincon is a hidden gem of a Spanish restaurant and tapas bar just off Deansgate, in the centre of Manchester. The first time I went there was with Gary Owen. At the time Gary was also doing the match report for City and giving the players marks for their performance on the pitch. I had been in the lounge called the Blue Room after a game at Maine Road, and Gary and Rafa, the owner of El Rincon, were in there as well. I blagged a lift back to the town centre and thought there was no point going home straight away, so I tagged along with Gary and his missus and went into El Rincon. It is down a set of stairs, and it's a proper independent traditional Spanish tapas bar – nothing like the big chains that serve pretend Spanish food. Over the years, I have been in many times, and it is a favourite hangout for many of the *Coronation Street* stars.

On one occasion I was sitting at the bar, and Johnny Briggs, who played Mike Baldwin in *Coronation Street,* sat down next to me. City and United players were also regulars there. Years ago

I was in there having a chat with Gerard Wiekens, who was a Dutch City player, and Sun Jihai, who was a Chinese International and also a City player. I nearly ruined Sun Jihai's posh silk shirt as I tried to stick a City pin badge onto his shirt.

I've met other ex-players in there a couple of times. Denis Law is a real, proper, down-to-earth bloke. Tommy Booth gets in there from time to time, and I was pleased to be in there when it was the last ever game at Maine Road, and City star Shaun Goater came in with his wife. It was a

Very special occasion, and Gary Owen was in fine voice on the microphone. I had a good chat with big Sam Allardyce once, who was in there having a drink after a Bolton Wanderers match. Big Sam was the Bolton manager at the time, and he was another bloke who was down to earth and had time for anyone who wanted a chat, a photograph, or an autograph. Many players, ex-players, and managers rely on their TV image. With many people I have seen on TV or heard on the radio, I have thought, *'He sounds a right wanker'*. Then when I actually met them in real life, I had a different view of them.

Rafa does a lot for charity and good causes, and he always supported our branch if we wanted a raffle prize or auction item. He was only too willing to donate a meal for two and a bottle of wine for any night at his restaurant.

Years ago we were having a drink in the Portland Thistle Hotel near Piccadilly Manchester, and we got talking to a Spanish couple who were with their two lads. They had on Barcelona shirts, we gave them some City pin badges. They were in Manchester for three days and then were going to the Lake District. When I asked them where they were going later on, to my surprise they said El Rincon. I was surprised only because it is never advertised and cannot be seen from any main road. They told me that friends of theirs in Spain had been in, and it had an excellent reputation. I had to give them my five pennies worth to let them know how much I liked it.

CHAPTER 20

Corporate Hospitality

When City built the new Platt Lane Stand and the new Kippax Stand, they also incorporated hospitality boxes and lounges for the more affluent supporters. Unfortunately, because of some of the dire football we were playing, and especially because we were not in the Premier League, fans were not banging on the doors to pay top prices for the privilege of a bit of luxury. At times we were able to get the lounge and boxes at a discount rate. One such time was around my birthday in March. It also coincided with another member's birthday, Sean Riley, now a bigger Blue than Sean and I have yet to meet. In the last twenty five years, he has never missed a City competitive match, home or away – except for one in Russia in the Champions League where all the fans were banned as a punishment for the Russians racist behaviour and the game had to be played behind closed doors. Their fans are racist, and our fans get punished and were not allowed to go. *'How do you work that one out?'* What really rubbed salt in the wound was about one thousand Russians managed to get into the game. Even when City were banned from Millwall because of previous ground trouble, and when United didn't give City an allocation because of modernisation work going on at the ground, Sean and his wife Jane still managed to get tickets.

I managed to get a box for eight people. Apart from Sean and Jane, Cath, and our two lads, Kev and Derbo came. What a fantastic view we had! It was brilliant. We had our own waiter – not that he had much to do. Fuck me, a plate of sarnies nearly cost as much as one place in the box. In the second half, Derbo couldn't resist and said, 'I've always wanted to do this,' and he tried to launch a couple of bog rolls onto the pitch. He made a valiant attempt but failed miserably and they landed short on some poor fan below. Thank God it was only a toilet roll. The box adjoining ours had ordered loads of food and had not eaten even half of it. They must have seen us sharing a couple of plates of sarnies and gawping through the window at their feast, so instead of slinging it out, the waiter brought it in our box. We got half of their scran, and it was very nice. Somehow it was my fault that Sean Riley got steaming and Jane had a hard time trying to get him home on the tram and back home. Yours truly got a bollocking the next time we met.

We had some surprise visitors who popped in to see us, so we got to meet John Wardle again and ex-players Tommy Booth and Colin Bell, called into the box for a chat, and we had photographs and autographs. What a great day out we had. We also managed to win the game as well. In those days, it was always pot luck if we would get a victory, even at home, so it was great to celebrate our birthdays in great surroundings with great company – and most important, three valuable points.

Over the years, I have been fortunate to have been invited to different lounges and private boxes, and the standard and service is truly first class. One lad I knew was called Mike Woods, and he had a table for four people in one of the lounges in the Kippax at Maine Road. Quite often he would invite me up there with him. He was friends with many of the City players and knew dozens of ex-players. Ex-Ireland manager Mick McCarthy was best man at his wedding, and it was Mike who brought Mick to the meeting at Heaton Park, when Mick attended with Frank Sidebottom. The branch holds a big debt of gratitude to Mike because through his contacts, we managed to get players and ex-players to the meetings with fewer problems than we would have done without him. He seemed to know everybody, and he was well liked and respected by everyone at the club. Ex-United player Norman Whiteside was a great mate of Mike's and was a regular guest at his table. I met Norman a few times, and again I hate to admit it: for a rag, he is a nice bloke. Through Mike we got both Norman and Mick to a sportsmen's dinner as our guests.

The standard of the hospitality lounges and private boxes at the Etihad are on par with any other stadium in the world. It is a far cry when years ago, the best a fan could ask for was a hot Bovril, a pint of flat lager, or a meat and potato pie. The toilets were normally awful, with the urinals usually overflowing and you having to wade through piss to get to one. They were usually very busy, so people ended up having a piss on the floor or on the wall outside. God help you if you wanted a dump – that would have been a nightmare. Fans well-being and comfort were not a high priority in those days. It was simply a matter of getting as many people into the ground as possible. We never complained because we saw it as the norm in those days. The only alternative was to not go to the ground, so as fans we would rather suffer a few discomforts as long as we could watch the game. I have only been in the boxes at the Etihad on a handful of occasions, but each time it was a fantastic experience.

On one occasion, Johnny, who was over from Holland, and I were the last ones left in one of the private boxes. The booze had already been paid for, so we stuck what was left in some carrier bags and went to meet James H, Cath, and Sean, who had left just before us. We got out of the lift and took a wrong turn, ending up near the pitch. We thought it a good idea to sit down and have a drink. By this time security guards had picked up on the fact that we were where we should not have been. One of them knew me, so he got Cath to come get me. I did not know what the problem was. Well, I wouldn't, would I? Someone had to be the last one out, so it might as well be me. That is the thing: when you have had a shitload to drink, your view of everything is a bit different. It seemed so natural at the time. Johnny and I were shit-faced and sat in an empty stadium, looking at the pitch and having a beer. Talk about watching the grass grow! Needless to say, Cath was not amused and dragged the pair of us out of the ground.

After one occasion, I had been in one of the lounges and was a bit the worse through drink. When I was back to Manchester city centre. I ended up falling on the tram tracks and got my suit covered in muck and grease. I fucked off near Piccadilly Gardens for a sit-down and a chill-out. The soup kitchen for the homeless turned up, so I ended getting a cup of soup from it. It was fucking brilliant, nice and hot with loads of spuds in it. As I sat there enjoying it, one of the volunteers asked me if I was all right and if I needed a change of clothing. Fuck me, I must have looked a right dosser, it could only happen to me, one minute I am having a five star meal in a private lounge next I am having soup and bread with the homeless in Manchester. I thought it was time to call it a day, jump in a cab, and go home. Needless to say, yet again Cath was not amused.

Chapter 21

City v. Southampton

The curtain actually came down on City's Maine Road Stadium against Southampton on 11th May 2003. After being the home of City for eighty years, it was a ground steeped in history. It was built on the land of former brick works, and there was an urban myth doing the rounds, especially during City's poor spell, that a gypsy put a curse on the club because officials had evicted a gypsy camp from the site. The curse was never mentioned whenever we were playing well and winning trophies.

The original layout of the ground meant that there was only one roof and had seating for ten thousand. The people in the rest of the ground had to stand and were at the mercy of the Manchester weather, till money was found to put roofs on the other parts of the ground. In 1934 City boasted the highest attendance in England, apart from the 1913 Cup Final. City had a crowd of 84,500 fans in the ground for the sixth-round cup victory against Stoke. Over the years, various changes and regulations limited the crowd to just over 35,000, and the crowd for the last game was 35,150 with hundreds locked out.

Over the years, City's ground was used for eighteen FA Cup semi-finals, a League Cup final, four Charity Shield matches, eleven Rugby League Championship Finals, and a host of other games, as well as numerous classic games involving City. The ground also hosted Manchester United for four years because their ground had been bombed during the war, and it was being redeveloped. The ground had served the club, the players, and the fans well, but it was time to move on to the new stadium over in East Manchester.

Before the last game, we had an end-of-season gentleman's morning. The demand for that one was huge. The ones before and since always sell out early, but this time many fans were disappointed because we could not squeeze any more people into the place. We had the usual fun and games and some fans turned up in fancy dress, and everyone was in a great mood. Loads of City songs were being sung, and 'Blue Moon' was blasted out a few times. Then it was time to leave for the ground. Because it was a special day, we left in style and had booked four stretch limousines to take us on a bit of a tour of Manchester before going on to the match.

Cath, Steven, and Sean came in the limo with me. We had not gone long when it was time for our first stop for a drink in Deansgate, in the city centre. We then went to Eastlands to take a look at the stadium we would be playing at the next season, and then it was off to a bar that at the time was run by Mike Summerbee and his son, Nicky. That was dead handy because it was just outside the new ground. The limo was fully stocked with drink: there were gin, brandy, whiskey, and plenty of lager. There was none of Cath's favourite tipple vodka, so she got stuck into the gin instead. It was a great experience to be chauffeured around town, relaxing in the back of a limo with a nice drink. It was something I could certainly get used to, and it was certainly much better than going in the back of a transit van, like I had many times in the past.

When we got to Maine Road, all the fans were in party mood, with many more fans being in fancy dress. There was a real buzz about the place: many were taking photographs of the ground and were reminiscing about their time spent watching City. Inside the ground, the place was rocking. Everyone was well up for the game, and the atmosphere was brilliant. Unfortunately for me, we had not been in the ground long when Cath decided the gin did not agree with her. She felt like shit and wanted to throw up, so we had to call time on the game, and I took her home early. The stewards thought I was joking when I asked them to let us out of the ground, and the hundreds of fans outside who could not get a ticket thought we were barmy. I managed to get a cab pretty quickly, and it did not take too long to get home and stick Cath in bed. At least we won't ever forget the last game by City at Maine Road. As luck would have it, we got beat 1-0, so I was not too arsed that I'd missed most of the game. But trust City they couldn't even give the fans something to shout about on the last day of the season and the last game at Maine Road. Typical City. Once Cath was tucked up in bed I went back out and ended up in El Rincon which was packed with City fans and the place went ballistic when fans Favourite Shaun Goater turned up.

How times have changed at the club. In those last few years at Maine Road, we were going from one crisis to another. The ground had certainly seen better days, because there was so little money for ground improvements. It was such a blessing to be moving grounds as the new ground had a bigger capacity and better facilities. Even though City have only been at the Etihad for thirteen years there have already been lots of improvements to the ground, and already there has been an extension to the ground to take the capacity to over fifty-five thousand.

Nowadays the club is awash with money, thanks to the backing of the Abu Dhabi ruling family and their massive investment. Many fans are still pinching themselves that it was Manchester City that Sheikh Mansour and the ADUG Group decided to invest in the players we have now. The facilities we now have are second to none, and much money has been invested in the youth academy and the training facilities, which are amongst the best in the world. It is a far cry from a few years ago, when money was not invested in either the players or facilities; on a couple of occasions, it was rumoured the club was on the brink because the club's finances were not in a good state of affairs.

Now is the first time in decades that the club is being run on sound financial footing, and the professionalism of everyone at the club is a refreshing change to what has gone on in the past. We have had many false people down at the club, but now at long last we can be assured the club is now on the right track. During the Peter Swailes and Franny Lee eras, it was a case of what shit we were going to wake up to the next day. The club was in turmoil for what seemed a never-ending period, and the only saving grace was the fans. The club has a bright future ahead and it is very unlikely we will ever return to the dark days like we went through for so many years.

Chapter 22

The Final ever game at Maine Road

Although the official records show the final game at Maine Road was against Southampton on the 11th of May 2003, it was actually a few weeks later that saw the last ever game on the hallowed turf at Maine Road. It was the Prestwich and Whitefield Branch against the Merseyside Branch. The game came about as a result of a competition the club was running in the final season at Maine Road. The club had four nominated charities and all the supporters clubs were invited to take part in a fundraising efforts for the charities. The two branches which raised the most money would have the honour and privilege of playing the final ever game at Maine Road.

Paul Astley gives the lowdown on the match.

Don mentioned in a branch meeting that we were going to take part in the last ever game to be played a Maine Road because our branch and the Merseyside branch had raised the most amount of money for charity during the year. We were thankful that all the hard work Don and the branch put in raising money for charities and causes were rewarded by City. We were playing at Maine Road, and we had to get into shape! We had already played some games against other branches and against City Old Boys at Heaton Park, so we had the basis of a team. We all could play, although with an average age of thirty-plus and being comprised of piss -heads and party animals, we were a bit rusty.

We began a training regime in Heaton Park to prepare for the big game. Training involved playing football, well we did not fancy doing all that keep fit malarkey. We'd play games against whoever was in the park at the time, and on one particular occasion we played a game against a team of teenagers, who gave us a lesson in how to run and play total football. They beat us with ease. We knew we had to improve and were determined not to embarrass ourselves at Maine Road. You could say we developed an inner strength and a desire to succeed. The following weeks were taken up with more training and more football, and we were beginning to feel like a team. Soon we were ready for the big day.

It was Thursday, 12 June 2003, and the lads had booked the day off to work together with family members and assorted supporters. I drove to Maine Road in my Ford Galaxy; a few of the lads got a minibus from Heaton Park Social Club. We met up on the forecourt in front of the main stand, and we were to enter the ground via the players' entrance, a little doorway next to the main entrance.

P&W were allocated the away dressing room and would play in

City's away kit – the white 'first advice' kit with diagonal red and black stripes. Upon walking into the dressing room, we were greeted with the sight of folded kits on benches with our names printed on the back, what a buzz that was. This was the real deal as far as we were concerned, and we felt like professionals. We couldn't fail now. We got changed into full kit and walked down the players' tunnel to have a pre-match kick about and soak up the atmosphere generated by the capacity crowd of about 120. The pitch was immaculate despite it being the end of the season, and easily it was the best pitch any of us had ever played on.

Back in the dressing room, Don gave us a Winston Churchill motivational speech. My memory of it is a bit sketchy, but it probably went along the lines of, 'Get stuck in lads!' We took to the field and got our first glimpse of the opposition. The Merseyside branch, it has to be said, were not the most athletic of people. Most were either a bit on the plump side or a bit on the elderly side. Some looked to be on day release from their local care home! But they gave their all and, like us, enjoyed the day enormously.

The game kicked off, and P&W began dominating. In the first five minutes, our branch enjoyed 110 per cent possession! The lads from Merseyside were hopeless but bless them they kept trying. We raced to a 10-0 lead before our goalie had even touched the ball. I scored my first goal in front of the Platt Lane, a delicate lob over the advancing keeper. For my second, I have no memory, but my third came from me collecting a short corner and taking on a defender before curling a sweet right footer into the top corner from the edge of the area. What a goal, what a player, what a hat trick! I instantly thought of my daughter watching in the crowd, which added to the joy I had at scoring a hat trick at Maine Road.

In the end we won 17-0. Merseyside did have a penalty at one point, but Alan Holdsworth saved it. It was to be their only attempt at goal. The last goal ever at Maine Road was scored by Mike Burkey, a left foot shot from twenty yards into the bottom left-hand corner of the North Stand net. Burkey instantly retired from football at that moment. You might as well quit at the top! The final whistle came and went, and we headed back to the dressing room for cheap fizzy plonk. We sang and danced around like we'd won the Champions League, and after a great day we showered and changed back into our civilian clothes. City allowed us to keep the kits, and I still have mine to this day. We headed back to the Bull's Head in Whitefield for the mother of all piss-ups. It was in there that Bonehead form Oasis and Mike Joyce from the Smiths turned up out of the blue and bought us loads of drinks, none of us involved will ever forget it. All the team were extremely grateful that Don had managed to organise so many fundraising events that our branch had raised enough to enable us to play the final ever game at Maine Road.

'Thanks for that Paul'.

What an occasion for all concerned. For a moment in time, they were the stars for the day. The result did not matter because everyone was a winner. The players had that once-in-a-lifetime moment, and the charities received a boost to their funds.

We organised a medal presentation at the Heaton Park Social Club a couple of weeks later, and we gave the players their due. The lads from Merseyside turned up in force. Bernard Manning was the comedian for the evening, and James H. Reeve was the compare. It was a fantastic experience for all who took part. Great credit to City for organising the event, and great credit to both sets of players. I am sure they all savoured the day for a very long time.

Chapter 23

Time to Call It a Day

In my last year of running the branch, it had started to become a bit of a chore, and if I'm honest, it was getting a bit boring. The excitement and the buzz I used to get wasn't there anymore; no longer did I have the energy the drive or the desire to keep organising the events. I think there were a number of factors involved. I was not getting any younger, it was getting more time consuming, and the joy and delight was fizzling out. Over the years, the guests we had at the meetings read like a who's who from the footballing world, and the members were getting more selective about which meetings they went too, so we were not always getting the turnout we were used to. Plus, it was harder than ever to communicate with the club, and it was getting extremely difficult to get the players to attend meetings. In all honesty, like in the navy, I think things had just run its course and for me, it was time to step down. It was with a heavy heart I decided to stand down because running the branch had been a huge part of my life for so long, and it had been such a fantastic experience. The supporters, branch meant so much too so many people.

We could never have dreamed the journey we went on when we first met up at the Welcome all those years ago. The people we have met, the friendships that have developed, the events that we had put on are things that will stay in people's memories for many years to come. The branch is something that everyone involved can be rightly proud of.

As daft as it seems, the worse City were playing, the more the fans supported the club and the better we as supporters branches were treated. It is a completely different mind-set now. Some people at the club, and many of the staff who have helped us over the years, are no longer at City or are no longer in a position to help us. For me, the last few months of being the chairman had become more hassle than it was worth.

The last meeting we had before I stepped down was with a true cult hero of the club, Sean Wright Phillips. The place was packed, so at least I went out on a high. When I stepped down, so did Aide, who had also worked hard behind the scenes to help make the branch the success it was. The lads who have taken over the reins are still doing a cracking job. Keith, Phil, and Paul are keeping the tradition of the branch going, but with an emphasis more on organising away travel and match tickets to the games, and having just three or four meetings per season.

In recognition for our services to the branch, the City Chairman John Wardle invited Aide and me as his guests to the chairman's lounge at the stadium and gave us an engraved gift, which was a tremendous gesture and showed that some at the club had appreciated our efforts.

Where we were sat and the view we had of the game was the dog's bollocks. The seats were all padded and dead comfy, plus it was a free bar. What a result! It was a day I will never forget. After saying that, there is not much of the day I do remember, so don't ask me who we played or what the score was. I was grateful to Dave Ratcliff, who looked after me after the game and got Sean to pick me up, to make sure I got home in one piece without getting filled in or arrested. I'd enjoyed the hospitality to the best of my ability and took advantage of the complimentary bar.

The year 2014 saw the twentieth anniversary of the branch, and the lads who now run the branch organised a gala dinner at the Village Hotel in Prestwich to celebrate the event. Even though I'd had no involvement with the branch for a number of years, they invited me and Cath to the dinner, which I thought was a nice touch. We were delighted at the gesture.

I was even more delighted when I met up with Tommy Booth, Tony Book, and Andy Morrison again as they were guests on the top table. It was great to catch up and have a chat with the three of them. It was also great to see the branch is still going strong thanks to the efforts of Keith, Phil, and Paul, amongst others. Long may it continue to prosper! Many who were at the dinner were members who had been with and supported the branch from the beginning. It goes to show how important supporters, organisations are for the fans.

Looking back over those years shows just what football clubs mean to the supporters. The game has evolved tremendously since I started going in the 1960s. The standard of football, the standard of the players, the pitches, and the stadiums have all changed for the better. Footballers earn mind-boggling amounts of money now, and it is hard for a home-grown player to break through and maintain a place in the first team. Long gone are the days when half the team would be made up of

City fans, or when the entire team was English or British.

Many new rules and laws at football grounds have been brought in over the years to improve the experience of the football fans, and fans are divided whether all the changes are for the best, or whether they're another way to get more money out of the fans, one thing is for sure: football is a lot more expensive to watch now, but it is as popular as ever with the working-class fan. Many more women and children go to the games now than they did back in the 1960s and 1970s, and that can only be for the good of the game. There is still a huge role for supporters clubs to play, and the men and women who organise supporters clubs across the country have my full admiration. Many supporters clubs have campaigned for cheaper match tickets for fans. City have listened to the fans and have frozen season ticket prices for the 2016 and 2017 season which is a step in the right direction.

I hope you enjoyed reading the book as much as I enjoyed writing it. It dragged so many great memories from deep down. Even after so long out of the Royal Navy, I am pleased that I am still in touch with a couple of the lads, and not long ago I went to Gibbo's wedding. I still see loads of the people from the supporters club, and we have a good laugh about the great times we had. That is the thing about memories: they can't be taken away. We had some unbelievable times over those years, and my hope is the Prestwich and Whitefield branch keeps getting the help and support from Manchester City that it deserves.

Lightning Source UK Ltd.
Milton Keynes UK
UKOW02f0635030616

275514UK00001B/4/P